# THE LATE GREAT
# MEXICAN BORDER

D0401413

# THE LATE GREAT MEXICAN BORDER

## Reports from a Disappearing Line

EDITED BY BOBBY BYRD
& SUSANNAH MISSISSIPPI BYRD

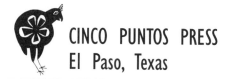

CINCO PUNTOS PRESS
El Paso, Texas

FIRST EDITION

Library of Congress Cataloging-in-Publication data

   The late great Mexican border : reports from a disappearing line/
      edited by Bobby Byrd and Susannah Mississippi Byrd.— 1st ed.
         p.   cm.
      Includes bibliographical references.
      ISBN 0-938317-24-5 (paper)
         1. Mexican-American Border Region. I. Byrd, Bobby. 1942-
   II. Byrd, Susannah Mississippi, 1971-
   F787.L38  1996
   972'.1—dc20                                             96-10507
                                                              CIP

Cover photograph copyright @ 1996 by Virgil Hancock.
Black and white photographs copyright @ 1995
      by Max Aguilera-Hellweg.

Cinco Puntos Press would like to thank Dr. Virgil Hancock
      for permission to use his photograph for the cover.

Book and cover design, and text composition,
      by Vicki Trego Hill of El Paso, Texas.

NATIONAL
ENDOWMENT
FOR THE
# ARTS

*This book is funded in part
by generous support from the
National Endowment for the Arts.*

# Contents

# Acknowledgments

Aguilera-Hellweg, Max. "La Frontera, Sin Sonrisa," and photographs "Cousins from Kansas Looking for Cheap Tequila" and "Profirio, Ice Cream Vendor." Copyright ©1995 by Max Aguilera-Hellweg. This piece was found by the editors at his photo exhibit, *La Frontera, Sin Sonrisa*, at the El Paso Museum of Art. Used by permission of the author.

Bowden, Charles. "Blue," from *Blue Desert*, University of Arizona Press. Copyright © 1986 by University of Arizona Press. Used by permission of the author and the University of Arizona Press.

Ferry, Barbara. "Following Jaime," Copyright © 1994 by Barbara Ferry. Published in *The Texas Observer* on August 5, 1994. Used by permission of the author.

Gómez-Peña, Guillermo. "Excerpts from *Warrior for Gringostroika*," excerpted from *Warrior for Gringostroika* ("Documented/Undocumented," "The Border Is...," A Manifesto" and "The Multicultural Paradigm"), Graywolf Press. Copyright © 1993 by Guillermo Gómez-Peña. Used by permission of Graywolf Press, Saint Paul, MN.

Leal, Teresa. "Recipe for a Radical," Copyright ©1988 by Teresa Leal. Published in *City Magazine* of Tucson, AZ, July 1988. Used by permission of the author.

Lynch, Linda. "Beauty and the Beast, Trashing the U.S./Mexico Border," Copyright © 1996 by Linda Lynch. Used by permission of the author.

Martínez, Rubén. "Prop. 187: Birth of a Movement?," Copyright © 1995 by the North American Congress on Latin America. Published in *NACLA Report on the Americas*; Vol. 29:3, Nov/Dec, pp. 29-34. Used by permission of the author and The North American Congress on Latin America, 475 Riverside Dr., #454, New York, NY 10115-0122.

Miller, Tom. "Discreets of Laredo," from *On the Border*, University of Arizona Press. Copyright © 1981 by Tom Miller. Used by permission of the author.

Nabhan, Gary Paul. "Cryptic Cacti on the Borderline," from *Desert Legends*, Henry, Holt & Co., Inc. Copyright © 1994 by Gary Paul Nabhan. Used by permission of Henry, Holt & Co., Inc.

Nathan, Debbie. "Love in the Time of Cholera: Waiting for Free Trade on the U.S./Mexico Border," Copyright © 1991 by Debbie Nathan. Versions also published in *Rio Grande Review*, Vol. 2, No. 1, Fall 1991 and *The Texas Observer*, January 15, 1993. Used by permission of the author.

Reavis, Dick J. "The Last of the Border Lords," Copyright ©1987 by Texas Monthly. Published in *Texas Monthly* in February 1987. Used by permission of the author and *Texas Monthly*.

Rodríguez, Luis J. "This Memory Begins With Flight," excerpted from *Always Running: La Vida Loca, Gang Days in L.A.*, Curbstone Press. Copyright © 1993 by Luis J. Rodríguez. Used by permission of the author and Curbstone Press. Distributed by Consortium.

Rodriguez, Richard. "Pocho Pioneer," Copyright © 1994 by Richard Rodriguez. Speech delivered in November 1994 at a White House Conference, "A New Moment in the Americas." Used by permission of the author.

Sáenz, Benjamin Alire. "Exile," from *Flowers for the Broken*, Broken Moon Press. Copyright © 1992 by Benjamin Alire Sáenz. Used by permission of the author.

Urrea, Luis Alberto. "None of Them Talk About Their Dreams," from *By the Lake of Sleeping Children: The Secret Life of the Mexican Border*, Anchor Books. Copyright © 1996 by Luis Alberto Urrea. Used by permission of the author.

Weisman, Alan. "The Deadly Harvest of the Sierra Madre," Copyright © 1994 by Alan Weisman. Published in *The Los Angeles Times Magazine* on January 4, 1994. Used by permission of the author.

# Introduction

*I've got to go home to the other side.*

—Novelist/journalist Willivaldo Delgadillo,
asking the editors for a ride to Juárez, 1996

THE UNITED STATES' BORDER with Mexico is more than 2000 miles long, stretching from Brownsville, Texas, to San Diego, California. That's a lot of geography, a lot of space. Most people in the U.S., when they think about the border, imagine places like El Paso, Tijuana, Nogales, Laredo and Brownsville. They don't think about the wild places of desert, stark canyon and semi-tropics where the border is nothing more than a line on a map that you carry in your back pocket.

For most of this century that political line between countries, whether it was passing through populations gathered on either side or through vast wild lands, occupied a very special niche in the popular mythos of the United States. It was the crossing to the underside of our consciousness, a passage from all things rational—law and order, regulated capitalistic democracy, Anglo-Saxon Protestantism—into a surreal cultural landscape where real Indians still wandered the streets, the Virgin Mary in the guise of a deified brown woman was the equal to Jesus Christ and seat-of-the pants economic improvisation was a way of life.

This is the border where Humphrey Bogart began his search for gold in *The Treasure of Sierra Madre*, where Wallace Beery starred as the crazed revolutionary in *Pancho Villa*, and from where the Beats, with Jack Kerouac and Allen Ginsberg in their vanguard, headed south in search of personal and psychedelic liberation. The border in this north-to-south scenario was a thin, porous membrane through which cultural explorers slipped into our collective unconscious. Manufactured goods, powerful political coercion and even the threat of military force also made the journey south, but these were not obvious ingredients in the common understanding of what occurred along the U.S./Mexico Border.

Passage north was a different issue altogether. Raw materials, cheap goods ("Hecho en México" was the stamp of inferior goods) and cheap labor were allowed to move north through the border, but the barons of U.S. culture resisted all elements of the Mexican culture. Politics, autocratic economics and ethnocentrism required that the border remain closed. But culture, because it is a vital organism, does not exist like that. It takes what it needs for its sustenance, even survival. So suddenly, at the tailend of the century, we turn around and discover that the U.S./Mexico Border has been breached and the invasion is already over. We are inundated with people, things and ideas mexicanas.

We shouldn't make the mistake, however, of assuming that the two countries and two cultures have become entwined in an embrace that bodes well for those of us who live on the border. If anything, we are learning that the U.S./Mexico Border is a region unto itself, one that supersedes the more abstract state boundaries on either side and which is considered by the powers that be—whether in Washington, DC; México, D.F.; Austin, TX; or Sacramento, CA—as irrelevant except as a place of passage for goods and people. We find we are living in a "de-constitutionalized" zone where the Bill of Rights can be ignored because of "sovereignty" issues (illegal immigration, drug smuggling, etc.) or just because the border region is poor and, in vast areas, sparsely populated. The region becomes disenfranchised, and the wishes and well-being of its citizens ignored. As a matter of habit and convenience, border residents get left holding the dirty end of the stick.

This isn't a difficult lesson to learn. In Texas all you need to do is walk the streets of places like Austin, Dallas or Houston, then spend the same amount of time wandering through Brownsville, Laredo or El Paso. Compare the institutions and public works that require state and federal funding—schools, highways and universities—and you'll witness first hand the difference between power and impotence.

But lack of equitable funding is not the only way that border communities suffer. Since the breakup of the Communist bloc during the Reagan and Bush administrations, those of us who live here have watched the slow but inevitable militarization of the border region. The reason we're given for the constant drone of helicopters flying over our heads and the buildup of weaponry along the border is that we're being protected from drug smuggling and illegal immigration. The reality is a "might makes right" policy that ignores the stupidity of U.S. drug laws and forces law enforcement organizations (the Immigration and Naturalization Service, the Treasury Department and the Border Patrol, as well as the local and state police) into a police state mentality. People of Mexican descent, be they U.S. citizens or not, have long been fair game for la migra (the Border Patrol). Many of us, especially since the 1994 passage of Proposition 187 in California and the recent jingoistic grumblings about the imperative of citizenship, expect that sooner or later the Constitution will be further ignored and federal troops will be called to patrol the border.

To further complicate and contaminate the cultural and geographic climate, new pressures from the state and federal levels of government are forcing their way to the border region. First, of course, is the passage of NAFTA. We have indeed heard that giant *sucking sound*, as Ross Perot called it. Thousands of jobs have fled the border for places deeper into the heart of Mexico where labor is even cheaper, the laborers even more forgiving and the power brokers more generous. Meanwhile, although we were promised infrastructure to support the onslaught of "free trade," none has been built; yet, the hordes of trucks keep crawling back and forth across the jammed bridges. They are packed with car parts, electronics, grain, tomatoes, mangos, pineapples, soccer balls, sugar, toys, computers, marijuana and other paraphernalia to bring joy to Mexican and U.S. citizens alike. In addition, the lack of political power along the border has spawned a new industry for the region—the dumping of radioactive and toxic wastes that nobody else wants. These substances come from places as far away as New York and Maine. There the people have deemed them dangerous and illegal, but on the border we are told that they are perfectly safe.

The purpose of *The Late Great Mexican Border* is to help refashion our collective understanding of the U.S./Mexico Border. Each essay documents some unique form of border experience, and in so doing, it illuminates fundamental changes that have been occurring in the region. The writers here write from the north side of the line, but that perspective is rooted in experience, by going back and forth across the border and by living within its influence. Their writing goes against the grain of commonly held views of life on the border. We hope that their work can provide some measure of understanding for folks who want to know more about our region.

THE EDITORS wish to give thanks for the support we received in collecting and producing this anthology. First of all, we wish to thank the National Endowment for the Arts for its financial support. Without those dollars, the publication of this book would not have been possible. We would also like to thank those persons—writers, publishers, and others—who sat on the peer panel that selected Cinco Puntos as a recipient of NEA funds. Cinco Puntos certainly does not reside in the power loop of contemporary literary affairs; yet, because of such open-minded funding decisions, we and other regional presses can bring our literature to a national audience.

We would also like to thank Debbie Nathan and Charles Bowden, both contributors here, for their support during the birthing of this book. Both recommended writers and/or pieces for inclusion, and they were glad to talk about the book during its evolution. Chuck, in fact, became so concerned about our working title for the anthology that he put his mind to finding a better one. Which indeed he did: *The Late Great Mexican Border*. Debbie, as her final gift, read and edited this introduction with a stern eye. Her maxim is: *Write like a mensch, not like a wonk*. That's a fitting entry in any writer's journal.

There are other persons whom we would like to thank: Tom Miller for opening up his rich files about the border to us; Virgil Hancock for permission to use his stark photograph as the cover image; Joe Hayes and Benjamin Alire Sáenz for always lending their good ears to our ideas and worries; Richard Baron, Becky Duvall Reese and Stephen Vollmer for directing us to Max Aguilera-Hellweg; Vicki Trego Hill for her remarkable skills as book designer and her unwavering friendship; and, of course, all of the contributors to this book, each of whom helps to make this a unique document de la frontera.

Finally, we would like to thank our respective spouses, Lee Merrill Byrd and Edward Holland. Each supported our efforts here with their hearts and minds.

And let us not forget Hannah Rebekah Hollandbyrd: she who functions beautifully as granddaughter and daughter.

# To the memory of
## *Ricardo Sánchez*
### (1942 – 1995)

POET RICARDO SÁNCHEZ was a true border person.

He could be cantankerous and fierce, he could be passionate and eloquent. Anger was both his weakness and his strength. His ear for border language, for cálo, was by far the most complex and musical of any of the Chicano poets.

He loved his family.

Everybody has their own apocryphal Ricardo Sánchez story.

I have several myself, but the stories that I like best are the ones of his growing up, before he went to prison for armed robbery, before he and all the Brown Beret vatos stirred up the streets with their poetry and oratory, before he earned his Ph.D. and entered the world of arts and letters where he learned that the written word can also slam doors shut—doors which should always be left open.

Once Ricardo and I were at the Adriana's Restaurant. He was decked out in at least a pound of turquoise and silver, a fresh guayabera shirt, his black eyes luminous. I had bought him a plate of enchiladas, I was having taquitos with a small bowl of caldo de res. He started talking about what it was like growing up in El Barrio del Diablo in El Paso across the Río Grande from Juárez. He and his friends would borrow somebody's horse, and they'd slip across the river to Mexico. The farmers over there grew gigantic watermelons and cantaloupes. The boys would steal a watermelon and maybe a couple of cantaloupes. Their mothers would scold them for stealing, but that night their families would feast on the juicy flesh of the melons. They were too poor to let anything go to waste.

I told him that I had a hard time imagining El Paso and Juárez with such pastoral roots. Now the río runs through a concrete trough, there are chainlink fences on both sides, the U.S. side feels like a military zone with green Border Patrol vans and helicopters. Everybody is armed. There are rumblings in the Congress about bringing in the Army "to protect our borders."

I said: "What do you think about that, Ricardo?"

He grumbled a string of exotic curses about the Border Patrol and U.S. Border policy in general. "Those assholes," he said, "have already lost the war." Then he went back to his enchiladas.

The waitress hovered around him like he was a king.

# Luis J. Rodríguez

# This Memory Begins with Flight

*"Cry, child, for those without tears
have a grief which never ends."*
—MEXICAN SAYING

T HIS MEMORY begins with flight. A 1950s bondo-spackled
Dodge surged through a driving rain, veering around the
potholes and upturned tracks of the abandoned Red Line
trains on Alameda Street. Mama was in the front seat. My father
was at the wheel. My brother Rano and I sat on one end of the
back seat; my sisters Pata and Cuca on the other. There was a
space between the boys and girls to keep us apart.

"Amá, mira a Rano," a voice said for the tenth time from the
back of the car. "He's hitting me again."

We fought all the time. My brother, especially, had it in for La
Pata—thinking of Frankenstein, he called her "Anastein." Her
real name was Ana, but most of the time we went by the animal
names Dad gave us at birth. I am Grillo, which means cricket.
Rano stands for "rana," the frog. La Pata is the duck and Cuca is
short for cucaracha: cockroach.

The car seats came apart in strands. I looked out at the passing cars which seemed like ghosts with headlights rushing past the streaks of water on the glass. I was nine years old. As the rain fell, my mother cursed in Spanish intermixed with pleas to saints and "la Santísima Madre de Dios." She argued with my father. Dad didn't curse or raise his voice. He just stated the way things were.

"I'll never go back to Mexico," he said. "I'd rather starve here. You want to stay with me, it has to be in Los Angeles. Otherwise, go."

This incited my mother to greater fits.

We were on the way to the Union train station in downtown L.A. We had our few belongings stuffed into the trunk and underneath our feet. I gently held on to one of the comic books Mama bought to keep us entertained. I had on my Sunday best clothes with chewed gum stuck in a coat pocket. It could have been Easter, but it was a weeping November. I don't remember for sure why we were leaving. I just knew it was a special day. There was no fear or concern on my part. We were always moving. I looked at the newness of the comic book and felt some exhilaration of its feel in my hand. Mama had never bought us comic books before. It had to be a special day.

FOR MONTHS we had been pushed from one house to another, just Mama and us children. Mom and Dad had split up prior to this. We stayed at the homes of women my mom called comadres, with streams of children of their own. Some nights we slept in a car or in the living room of people we didn't know. There were no shelters for homeless families. My mother tried to get us settled somewhere but all indications pointed to our going back to the land of her birth, to her red earth, her Mexico.

The family consisted of my father Alfonso, my mom María Estela, my older brother, José René, and my younger sisters, Ana Virginia and Gloria Estela. I recall my father with his wavy hair and clean-shaven face, his correct, upright and stubborn demeanor, in contrast to my mother who was heavy-set with Native features and thick straight hair, often laughing heartily, her eyes narrowed to slits, and sometimes crying from a deep tomb-like place with a sound like swallowing mud.

As we got closer to the Union station, Los Angeles loomed low and large, a city of odd construction, a good place to get lost in. I, however, would learn to hide in imaginative worlds— in books; in TV shows, where I picked up much of my English; in solitary play with mangled army men and crumpled toy trucks. I was so withdrawn it must have looked scary.

THIS IS WHAT I KNOW: When I was two years old, our family left Ciudad Juárez, Chihuahua, for Los Angeles. My father was an educated man, unusual for our border town, a hungry city filled to the hills with cardboard hovels of former peasants, Indians and dusk-faced children. In those days, an educated man had to be careful about certain things—questioning authority, for example. Although the principal of a local high school, my father failed to succumb to the local chieftains who were linked to the national party which ruled Mexico, as one famous Latin American writer would later say, with a "perfect dictatorship."

When Dad first became principal, there were no funds due to the massive bureaucratic maze he had to get through to get them. The woman he lived with then was an artist who helped raise money for the school by staging exhibitions. My father used his own money to pay for supplies and at one point had the iron fence around the school torn down and sold for scrap.

One year, Dad received an offer for a six-month study program for foreign teachers in Bloomington, Indiana. He liked it so much, he renewed it three times. By then, my father had married his secretary, my mother, after the artist left him. They had their first child, José René.

By the time my father returned, his enemies had mapped out

a means to remove him—being a high school principal is a powerful position in a place like Ciudad Juárez. My father faced a pile of criminal charges, including the alleged stealing of school funds. Police arrived at the small room in the vecindad where Mama and Dad lived and escorted him to the city jail.

For months my father fought the charges. While he was locked up, they fed him scraps of food in a rusted steel can. They denied him visitors—Mama had to climb a section of prison wall and pick up 2-year-old José René so he could see his father. Finally, after a lengthy trial, my father was found innocent—but he no longer had his position as principal.

Dad became determined to escape to the United States. My mother, on the other hand, never wanted to leave Mexico; she did it to be with Dad.

Mama was one of two daughters in a family run by a heavy-drinking, wife-beating railroad worker and musician. My mother was the only one in her family to complete high school. Her brothers, Kiko and Rodolfo, often crossed the border to find work and came back with stories of love and brawls on the other side.

Their grandmother was a Tarahumara Indian who once walked down from the mountainous area in the state of Chihuahua where her people lived in seclusion for centuries. The Spanish never conquered them. But their grandmother never returned to her people. She eventually gave birth to my grandmother, Ana Acosta.

Ana's first husband was a railroad worker during the Mexican Revolution; he lost his life when a tunnel exploded during a raid. They brought his remains in a shoebox. Ana was left alone with one son, while pregnant with a daughter. Lucita, the daughter, eventually died of convulsions at the age of four, and Manolo, the son, was later blinded after a bout with a deadly form of chicken pox which struck and killed many children in the area.

Later Ana married my grandfather, Mónico Jiménez, who like her first husband worked the railroads. At one point, Mónico quit the rails to play trumpet and sing for bands in various night clubs. Once he ended up in Los Angeles, but with another woman. In fact, Mónico had many other women. My grandmother often had to cross over to the railroad yards, crowded with prostitutes and where Mónico spent many nights singing, to bring him home.

WHEN MY PARENTS married, Mama was 27; Dad almost 40. She had never known any other man. He already had four or five children from three or four other women. She was an emotionally-charged border woman, full of fire, full of pain, full of giving love. He was a stoic, unfeeling, unmoved intellectual who did as he pleased as much as she did all she could to please him. This dichotomous couple, this sun and moon, this curandera and biologist, dreamer and realist, fire woman and water man, molded me; these two sides created a life-long conflict in my breast.

By the time Dad had to leave Ciudad Juárez, my mother had borne three of his children, including myself, all in El Paso, on the American side (Gloria was born later in East L.A.'s General Hospital). This was done to help ease the transition from alien status to legal residency. There are stories of women who wait up to the ninth month and run across the border to have their babies, sometimes squatting and dropping them on the pavement as they hug the closest lamppost.

OUR FIRST EXPOSURE in America stays with me like a foul odor. It seemed a strange world, most of it spiteful to us, spitting and stepping on us, coughing us up, us immigrants, as if we were phlegm stuck in the collective throat of this country. My father was mostly out of work. When he did have a job it was in construction, in factories such as Sinclair Paints or Standard Brands Dog Food, or pushing door-bells selling insurance, Bibles or pots and pans. My mother found work cleaning homes or in the garment industry. She knew the corner markets were ripping her off but she could only speak with her hands and in choppy English.

Once my mother gathered up the children and we walked to Will Rogers Park. There were people everywhere. Mama looked around for a place we could rest. She spotted an empty spot on a park bench. But as soon as she sat down an American woman, with three kids of her own, came by.

"Hey, get out of there—that's our seat."

My mother understood her but didn't know how to answer back in English. So she tried in Spanish.

"Look spic, you can't sit there!" the American woman yelled. "You don't belong here! Understand? This is not your country!"

Mama quietly got our things and walked away, but I knew frustration and anger bristled within her because she was unable to talk, and when she did, no one would listen.

We never stopped crossing borders. The Río Grande (or Río Bravo, which is what the Mexicans call it, giving the name a power "Río Grande" doesn't have) was only the first of countless barriers set in our path.

We kept jumping hurdles, kept breaking from the constraints, kept evading the border guards of every new trek. It was a metaphor to fill our lives—that river, that first crossing, was the mother of all crossings. The L.A. River, for example, became a new barrier, keeping the Mexicans in their neighborhoods over the vast east side of the city for years, except for forays downtown. Schools provided other restrictions: Don't speak Spanish, don't be Mexican—you don't belong. Railroad tracks divided us from communities where white people lived, such as South Gate and Lynwood across from Watts. We were invisible people in a city which thrived on glitter, big screens and big names, but this glamour contained none of our names, none of our faces.

The refrain "This is not your country" echoed for a lifetime.

W E PULL INTO a parking lot at the Union station. It's like a point of no return. My father is still making his stand. Mama looks exhausted. We continue to sit in our seats, quiet now as Dad maneuvers into an empty space. Then we work our way out of the car, straightening our coats, gathering up boxes and taped-over paper bags: our "luggage." Up to this juncture, it's been like being in a storm—so much instability, of dreams achieved and then shattered, of a silence within the walls of my body, of being turned on, beaten, belittled and pushed aside; forgotten and unimportant. I have no position on the issue before us. To stay in L.A. To go. What does it matter? I've been a red hot ball, bouncing around from here to there. Anyone can bounce me. Mama. Dad. Rano. Schools. Streets. I'm a ball. Whatever.

WE ARE INSIDE the vast cavern of the station. Pews of swirled wood are filled with people. We sit with our bags near us, and string tied from the bags to our wrists so nobody can take them without taking us too. My father turns to us, says a faint goodbye, then begins to walk away. No hugs. He doesn't even look at us.
    "Poncho."
    The name echoes through the waiting area.
    "Poncho."
    He turns. Stares at my mother. The wet of tears covers her face. Mama then says she can't go. She will stay with him. In L.A. I don't think she's happy about this. But what can a single mother of four children do in Mexico? A woman, sick all the time, with factory work for skills in a land where work is mainly with the soil. What good is it except to starve.
    "Está bien," Dad says as he nears my mother. "We will make it, mujer. I know it. But we have to be patient. We have to believe."
    Mama turns to us and announces we are not leaving. I'm just a ball. Bouncing outside. Bouncing inside. Whatever.

# Charles Bowden

# Blue

*They soon forgat his works; they waited*
*not for his counsel:*
*But lusted exceedingly in the*
*wilderness, and tempted God*
*in the desert.*
*And he gave them their request;*
*but sent leanness into their soul.*
—Psalms 106: 13–15

THEY PLAY A GAME HERE but nobody watches from a box seat. The players are called wets by those who hunt them.

They cross a hot desert, a dry desert, one of North America's benchmarks for thirst and they cross with one or two gallons of water. They walk thirty, forty, fifty, sixty miles in order to score. The goal line here means not six points but a job.

Here are the rules. Get caught and you go back to Mexico. Make it across and you get a job in the fields or backrooms. Don't make it and you die.

Each month during the summer about two hundred and fifty

people try the game in this particular section of western Arizona, a 3,600-square-mile stretch that runs from Yuma on the Colorado about a hundred miles eastward. Many get caught, mainly because the heat and thirst and miles grind them down. A bunch go down and wait to die.

Some die.

Nobody pays much attention to this summer sport. The players are nameless and constantly changing and so there is little identification with them or with their skills and their defeats. And the players are brown and this earns them a certain contempt and makes the attraction difficult to sell to spectators. The arena, a section of desert 100 miles long and 30 to 60 miles wide, is too unwieldy for easy viewing—no zoom shots here, no instant replay—and very uncomfortable with its heat, dryness, serpents, and thorns. A massive folk movement is pounding its way out of Mexico and Central America and this sector of the line and these deaths are but a small noise amid the clamor of the American border.

Those who play this desert game do pay attention. And they learn many things.

My education in these matters began months before. I was sitting at my desk in September when a news story caught my eye: seven Mexicans had died of thirst east of Yuma and several more had been snake bitten. It seemed like a high price for a job I would not take if offered. I began to train, walking around the city with my backpack stuffed with five or six gallons of water. The weight and feel of the load seemed impossible and then, before I fully appreciated this fact, my knee went out. A month later I was in the hospital looking up at two eyes staring over a surgical mask. The operation kept me a bit gimpy for two months and then it was too late to pursue my idea.

By then the desert had gone cold and there was little to learn in walking forty or fifty miles on the winter ground. I waited until June, until the solstice of June, thinking the longest day of the year surely would provide the heat and thirst required. The whole notion captivated me. I had separated from my wife and taken a studio apartment in a huge complex full of others in temporary flight from maimed marriages. On the wall I taped large topographic maps of the area where I would cross the line and march north. I sat there for hours sipping a drink and studying the vast expanses of sand and mountain, the delicate lines tracing the Cabeza Pieta National Wildlife Refuge, the warning announcements for the huge Air Force gunnery range. I would move slowly northward, leave the truckstop in Sonora where wets gather, slip through the legendary fence between the two nations, slide across the burning ground until finally, finally, I would come out at Interstate 8, the big road linking Phoenix and Tucson with San Diego, come out and be safe on this artery of commerce that followed the Gila River westward.

In the evenings I ran. In the mornings, I lifted weights. Always, I thought about the crossing and made the journey day after day in my mind. I told people I was angered by the news coverage of such events, by the way the deaths were ignored or entombed in tiny clippings. I would piously ask, "What do you think would happen if seven people from Minnesota died out there? Why, it would be on the network evening news!" as if such a result would make everything right again in the world. I half believed this rhetoric but it had little to do with my desire for crossing.

I get up at 4 A.M. and make coffee and sit in the small apartment and stare at the maps. The women I am seeing tell me, "Don't die out there. Don't get hurt." I smile and shrug. It is all false, all melodrama. I do not consider getting hurt; I do not consider not making it. That is not the threat or the attraction. I smell the aroma of the coffee and savor the bitterness on my tongue.

I have no interest in Central America and believe it a fact of life that the United States will meddle in the affairs of nearby countries that are small and weak. I feel little concern about Mexicans coming north. I don't care if they take jobs and I don't care if they are blocked by a wall of steel and weapons and forced to live with the nation they created, Mexico.

When I drift in my thoughts of the desert, then in those good moments, the desert is always blue. I am going to blue desert. Of course, this will not suffice for a newspaper so I focus on the Border Patrol, the tactics and problems of Mexicans coming north, the harshness of the land. But at 4 A.M. over that first cup of coffee, I warm myself in blue desert. I have no idea why the color attracts me. As a boy, I had a succession of hand-me-down blue suits and I hated them and have hated the color in clothing ever since. But I keep seeing this image and everything is blue and a great calm settles over me.

It is late at night and we are drinking wine in a club. The woman says, "Don't die out there on me. You come back."

I smile and shrug and hardly hear.

Everything is blue, luminously blue.

But of course there is a difference between my imaginings over morning coffee and the desert on a June night. The snake rattles by my boot at 2 A.M. and then moves off a foot into a brittle bush. The green-and-tan banded body is only about twelve inches long. We throw down our packs. Bill Broyles, my companion on this hike, slowly assembles the flash unit on his camera and then pokes the rattler to force a better display.

This is the moment I have been dreading and the key reason I could not face the walk alone. I have this nightmare of being bitten. It is very dark and I am alone and thirty or forty miles from roads, doctors and salvation. I go slowly berserk or perhaps I quickly die. The snake in my dream has an awful grin, a scaly Satan with fangs buried deep in the muscle of my calf. I can feel my flesh pulse as the reptile injects the poison in my blood.

So I have not come alone. In my backpack, I have a rope. Somewhere in the back of my head, I have this idea that if one of us is bitten, the other can tie up the victim to prevent him from wandering off into the desert in delirium and then the lucky one will walk out for help. That is how deep run my fears and fantasies of snakebite.

Now the moment has arrived, just an instant ago I felt the snake quiver under my boot and then the rattle and then nothing at all. The small reptile simply slithered off a foot, as shocked at our meeting as I was. And I hardly moved.

As Bill works his camera, I lie down on the ground four or five feet away from the snake and take a ten-minute nap. I am not afraid and I am not brave. I am absolutely indifferent.

We are twenty-odd miles into the passage. Around us are all the places I studied on the wall maps back at the apartment. If you have enough water, the names have a picturesque ring. If you do not have enough water, they sound like the lid opening on a crypt. The Lechugilla Desert is at our backs, the Tule Desert sprawls to the south, and the dunes of the Mohawk Valley yawn before us with the sand glowing under a full moon. We are stopped on the east flank of the Copper Mountains, just north of the Cabeza Prietas. Behind us, Big Pass opens with jaws seven miles wide. Fifteen miles to the southeast, the Tinajas Altas look near enough to touch. All these place are creosote, bare ground, dry washes, stunted trees. This earth is too dry for the deer, too dry for the javelina. This is the furnace room of the Sonoran Desert.

I cannot get the map out of my head with its names, tidy brown contour lines, blue strands hinting at drainages and babble of Spanish words and prospector lingo, all struggling to nail down the land. On my faithful map, this country appears as tidy and organized as a city park.

The photo session winds down, the thirty pound packs are shouldered and we move on. We do not talk much about the snake or about our reactions. We do not talk about thirst, hunger, or fatigue. There is no need. I sense we are starting to lose it and I do not even consider talking about this at all.

Of course, I suppose there are good tactical reasons for not launching a discussion on the fact that we have just treated a rattlesnake as an amusing toy and a media event. But I don't think like a line commander and my silence has nothing to do with careful judgment. We do not talk because there is no need or appetite for words. We have come at least twenty miles tonight and we have more than twenty to go before the sun takes the land back.

We are two specks on an ill-defined strand of migrant trails, faint footpaths that start at truckstops just over the line in Mexico and then lance north thirty to sixty miles, depending on the angle chosen, to Interstate 8. Yuma is more than forty miles to the west and Ajo eighty to the east and in between there is not much at all. There are no springs or streams and no one lives here, no one. A few rock holes hold puddles for desert bighorns for weeks or months at a time and the rains average three inches a year and sometimes forget to come for years at a time. In the summer, say from Memorial Day to mid-September, daytime temperatures scamper right past 100 and sometimes touch 120, 125 degrees or more.

This is the basic desert folklore, one uncluttered with annoying twentieth-century rest areas, water fountains, trail signs, and short cuts. For me, this is clearly part of the draw. I don't have to think much because everything is stated very plainly. I have found a place that skips the big words.

We do not know how many are out here with us this night. Before we left El Saguaro truckstop in Mexico hours ago, we watched men glide off in twos and threes and head north. But there are other spots for departure and many more are walking this desert. We are all heading for towns and points along the Interstate, places like Wellton, Tacna, or a roadside rest area at Mohawk Pass. Little dots of flesh inching north and probably by now all hurting.

We go up against seven border patrolmen who work days, the random war games of the gunnery range and full-time companions like hunger and thirst and heat.

Score-keeping is a bit haphazard. The Border Patrol body

count runs anywhere from two to twelve dead a summer but no one pretends to find all the bodies or have any real sense of how many rot undiscovered. There is a range here littered with bones and the desire to recover them is slight since a pauper burial costs the county $400. Over the past decade, I calculate at least 200 people have died on this stretch.

Jim Clarida, a Border Patrol agent at the Tacna station, tried to explain the power of the heat to me one day in late May. The afternoon before the thermometer had slapped 125 in the Tacna shade. Clarida patiently sipped his coffee, lit a smoke, and said, "Let me tell you about my son's pet rabbit."

The kid, he sighed, had raised this buck for a 4-H project and then you know how it goes. The rabbit became part of the family and stayed on. The animal lived in a cool hutch under thick vines.

Well, yesterday, he continued, the rabbit got out and ran about fifty yards before the boy caught him and put him back in the hutch. Twenty minutes later, Clarida went out and checked on him and the buck was thrashing about and heaving. Then he just died.

Clarida paused in his tale and snapped his fingers, pop! He died just like that, he smiled.

Of course Mexicans are not rabbits. Once, they found a dead man and the desert all around him was ripped up like he had gone berserk. They could see the marks on the ground where he had crawled on his belly swimming across the sand, acting as if the hot ground were a cooling sea.

Then there are those found with their shoes and clothes piled neatly beside them. Such men reach a point and decide the game is over and try to lie down and peacefully die. This is not an easy thing to do. When the cold takes a man, it is said to be like drifting off to sleep and not unpleasant. I have a friend who was drunk and womanless and depressed in a small pub in the Canadian bush. He walked out in the January night and hobbled off a mile into the snow. And then he lay down and began to fall into dreams. Calm and content, he waited for death. He eventually changed his mind and struggled out but he told me the brief taste of the grave was not bad, not bad at all.

With heat and thirst, death shows a different hand. The body temperature soars and the brain seems to cook. The flesh feels electric with pain as each cell screams out its complaint. People in such circumstances tear off their clothes in the hope of being cooled. They bury their heads in the sand in the hope of comforting their sizzling craniums. Sometimes the Border Patrol finds corpses with mouths stuffed with sand.

Strange thoughts and desires can be unleashed. A few years ago south of Ajo, a group of Salvadoran men and women crumpled under the heat and began to die. One man, staring at a death that seemed minutes away, tried to fuck a corpse only to find that he was too far gone for even this last pleasure. Dying in the snow and cold is better. On this everyone agrees.

But still they keep coming, day after day, night after night. Some will move only during daylight because they fear the snakes. Some refuse to wear hats. Almost all carry no more than a gallon of water. The desert south of Tacna and Wellton is probably the hardest sector of the American border to cross and survive. But they keep coming and I cannot help but wonder what kind of experiences produce people willing to take on such ground.

Almost always this particular chunk of the Republic is ignored. The 125-mile drive along Interstate 8 from Gila Bend to Yuma is universally decried as a vast boredom of sand, creosote flats, vicious-looking rock piles of mountains, frightening heat, and no decent restaurants to tease the traveler. Because the land south of the highway is locked up by the military and U.S. Fish and Wildlife Service, it is little known. There are no paved roads there, no picnic benches, no suggested scenic overlooks.

The statistics kept by the game rangers contend that 3,000 Americans a year peek into this country but the numbers are a bureaucratic fraud based mainly on those who drive a short loop road right next to Ajo. In a typical summer, maybe two or three Americans legally take out a permit and go into the hot country. And perhaps a thousand illegals who have other concerns than permits.

I was once having dinner with a woman who proceeded to tell me what a hideous drive it was to go to Yuma, to stare hour after hour at this God-forsaken wasteland. I lost my temper and told her she was a fool and she looked at me with disbelief. But I knew what she said rang with truth, that for almost everyone this country is a flat, dry tedium, something flaming past the window as the air conditioner purrs, the stereo sings, the cold beer sweats in the hand. It is not an idea or felt thing. No one sings its praises or spins legends from its emptiness. It is nowhere.

Now Bill and I are deep into this nowhere and by 2 A.M. we are facing our hurts. Our shoulders ache, our backs ache, our legs ache, and our feet ache. We drink constantly and nibble candy bars and yet our thirst never seems to end and our energy continues to decline. And we are maybe halfway.

The hunger is a fine thing. A month earlier I made a sixteen-mile night march out of this same desert with a half gallon of water and no food. The black sky flashed and sparkled with aircraft playing war and the air hung like a sweet drug full of carnal sensations. When I finally staggered into Tacna, the town's cafes were closed and I banged loudly on the kitchen door of one unit until a woman appeared and heard my plea. She sold me a small bag of M&Ms.

I tore the packet open and the little candies spilled out onto the gravel. I dove down to my knees and grabbed greedily at them in the dirt. She stood there towering over me and said nothing and I did not give her a moment's thought.

That kind of totally absorbing hunger is the basic menu here. It insists on your attention and yet is strangely sensuous like the feel of your hand caressing a woman's breast. It is not to be ignored.

Besides the aches and the thirst and the hunger, Bill and I

sense something else, something we refuse to discuss. Our behavior with the snake had a certain flair but does not seem terribly sensible. Why did he hunker down a foot or so from the snake and keep poking at it with a stick while he fiddled with his camera? Why did I sprawl out next to the snake and nap like I was sharing a bed with a domestic cat back home?

Something is happening at a deep level in our bodies, a revolt in the cells, a shift in the chemical juices, in the intricate synapses that fire information through our flesh and that organize our muscle into motion and purpose. Our will is dissolving as our tissue loses tiny trace elements, things with names I do not even know.

We skip the snake business, brush it off as a detail, and consider the containers of water straining our shoulders. Do we really need that much water? Maybe we should pour some of it out, cut the load?

Then we stop talking about the water and march on. We do not trust our minds any longer. They seem fine and even more interesting than is usually the case but there is something different now about the way thoughts come and go. And we do not want to speak of this feeling of unreliability. How can we even trust our perceptions of warning?

I drift back to our start yesterday afternoon. In that beginning there is warmth, confidence, and good spirits. We sprawl in the shade at El Saguaro truckstop, a dot along the Mexican highway between Sonoyta, eighty miles to the east, and San Luis forty miles to the west. A man, a woman, and a baby rest on pads under a flatbed truck and wait out the afternoon heat. The man is about thirty and he stretches out and smokes. His woman nuzzles against him. The baby gurgles and plays with the man's finger.

It is 105 degrees in the shade and rising.

The truck bears Sinaloa plates, a Mexican state 600 miles south and I imagine them homeward bound. El Saguaro has no electricity, and no cooling, no well. A few miles to the east is La Joya truckstop, another place of dreams. There electric lights hang from the ceiling, a television is mounted in a corner, and at La Joya also there is no electricity, no cooling, no well. Once I was there and I saw a dog eating a dead dog. The food in the cafe is simple but filling.

These two spots are the principal launching pads for the walks of los mojados northward. Water is sold to these travelers at about a buck and a half a gallon. At times Mexico can seem a little weak on compassion. A friend once asked an old patrón of San Luis what people did for a livelihood.

"They eat each other's bones," he smiled.

All my many Mexicos appear at El Saguaro. There are the tall Sonorans, fairer skinned than many of their countrymen and larger because they possess less Indian blood. Ricos, the richer members of the Mexican economy, pull in from time to time in new cars, windows rolled up to announce they have air conditioning. They buy a bottle of pop and a bag of chips, gaze at the slumbering throng with disgust, and then depart. The truckers and poorer folk from farther down are darker and shorter and look out on the desert heat with caution written across their eyes. Forty years ago this stretch of road was sand and many died when their machines bogged down and no help came. For years some residents of San Luis and Sonoyta made a tidy little income salvaging the abandoned cars and trucks. Once a man found the skeleton of an infant on a back seat.

The Mexican poverty that always catches my eye when I am deep into the country is here launching a war of liberation. The truckstops hold small groups of men, each man carrying a clear plastic, gallon milk container full of water and a bag or knapsack with a few cans of chiles for the hike north. I once hitched a ride on this road with a Mexican in an old wreck—we had to stop twice to pour in transmission fluid—and suddenly he pointed north to men going through the fence and laughed, "¡Mojados!" Then he asked, "How good really are wages in the states?"

I lie on a cement slab and stuff down potato chips and Cokes. My body is full of apprehension. Semi-drivers carefully string hammocks under their parked rigs and then climb in and sleep. Others sit in a small patio eating and drinking beer.

The baby starts crying and the man gets up, walks into the restaurant, and returns with a canteen of water. He sprinkles drops over the child's body and is very gentle. The crying stops. The woman sleeps on.

The landscape around the truckstop is almost empty of vegetation—some creosote, a few ironwoods huddling in a dry wash, but mainly rock and pale earth and glare. Behind us a road leads to a hilltop micro-wave station. We sit without electricity while high tech sings above our heads.

The Mexicans who travel this road fear the desert and fear the heat. I have walked out of this terrain and had them offer me free meals as if I were some wonder boy of the sands. Once Bill hitched a ride with a trucker on this stretch. When he asked the trucker to stop so he could hike off into the desert, the man refused.

He said, "If I let you go, you will die."

El Saguaro attracts people willing to give it a shot. Around 12:30 two men start north. They wear caps and each carries his gallon of water. Three hours later, some men get off a flatbed truck that has stopped. They carefully fold up the tarp for the driver as payment for the ride. Each of these men also has a one-gallon milk container and heads north. They wear no hats; their shirts do not cover their arms and are dark colors. For shoes, they favor sneakers.

Bill and I watch them depart into the heat. The Border Patrol has found that the men who die are usually in their twenties and quite strong. They do not fear the desert or the sun. They walk right through the heat of the day. And they die. We are both on the edge of forty. We wait.

I content myself with watching the people who must live with heat. They are drinking beer, sleeping in hammocks under trucks, sprinkling water on squalling babies.

Our preparations do not seem to be much as the hot hours roll past. We have run, lifted those weights, studied our safe little maps. Bill is basically a piece of iron, the survivor of thirteen marathons and a man who has run Pike's Peak four times. One room of his house is nothing but weights, the walls plastered with little admonitions to lift harder.

Our packs tip the scales at a little over thirty pounds and hold three gallons of water, some raisins, nuts and candy bars, extra socks, medicine, swatches of material for plastering blisters, flashlights, trousers and long-sleeved shirts, a sheet to stretch out for shade. Also, we have buried water along the route just in case we need it or run into someone else who does.

We wear hats, running shorts, t-shirts, and light boots.

Of course, there are some black spots in the training record. I sat up half the night before drinking and drinking and could hardly sleep at all what with the phantoms stalking my dreams.

The Mexicans train differently. They arrive after long truck rides and hitchhikes and carry their one gallon of water and little or no food. They wear shabby shoes or sandals, skip hats as often as not and sometimes are decked out in black from head to foot. According to the Border Patrol, about sixty percent have made the passage before and presumably know what they are getting into. The other forty percent are virgins.

The first-timers are often dropped here by *coyotes*, the border's smugglers of humans, and are told that the border is a few miles away and they will meet them on the other side. The other forty or fifty miles of the route is apparently considered a detail by these smugglers. The people ignorant of the area tend to come from the interior, from the jungles full of parrots or Sierras full of pines. They amble off into the hard desert and discover a different kind of world.

I watch them disappear one by one into the beginning of their education. The walls of the cafe are red and yellow, and a battery-powered radio blares, "Hotel California."

Men are busy working on the truckstop trying to install an air cooler. They fire up a tiny Honda generator to test it. The boss paddles over, a stout man in his fifties. He is dressed very nicely and makes conversation with us.

He explains that the lease on the place expires in fifteen days and he is making improvements in the hope that the landlord will renew it. He points to the big holes in the roof and sighs. Out back are two privies, and he dismisses them with a sweep of the hand. He confides that he refuses to use them.

The cooler is really his grand gesture. Surely, he feels, this will win his landlord to his side.

I am charmed by this Mexican Mr. Fix-it, but a little alarm rings in the back of my head. He moves with the unmistakable air of a Mexican official, a kind of predator seldom seen in the states outside the turf of the Chicago police force.

Suddenly, he demands, "Who are you and what are you doing here?"

He produces a badge and says he is an immigration official at San Luis.

He continues his questions with "Where is your car?"

Bill tells him that we are on foot, that we love this beautiful desert and wish to hike it.

The man brushes past such nonsense and asks, "Why are you taking pictures?"

"Oh," Bill smiles, "I take them for memories, Señor."

The official gazes with interest at our bulging backpacks and visions of loot, scams, busts, and bribes dance across his features. It would be difficult to exaggerate the roguery of a Mexican official. I know a man with a federal job in one border community who regularly drives up to Arizona and buys big appliances that are barred by Mexican law from importation into the country. Once, he was heading back with a load of microwave ovens when a friend asked him how he proposed to get them past the Mexican customs officials. Ah, he exclaimed, but they are for the wives of the customs officials.

The man with the badge continues to wait for our reply. Bill has brought an ice ax to use as a camera tripod and the agent's eyes light up when he notices it.

"Oh," he muses, "you are prospectors, no?"

He begins to babble of lost gold mines said to be in the area and the thought of ore brings pleasure to his face. Is that not why we have come?

We smile and laugh and shrug. He will not be dissuaded. He has seen the ax.

He punctures this moment of good cheer by noting, "I could ask for your papers right now, you know. I have the right."

This is kind of a sore point for me. The night before I could not find my birth certificate or voter registration card and in any event, I resent the paperwork demanded by governments that claim to own the desert. So I have entered the Republic of Mexico illegally and I start calculating just how much money this technical error will cost me.

We smile at the man.

Then someone calls him from inside the cafe, something about the new air cooler being installed. He nods and excuses himself from us for a moment.

We grab our packs and melt into the desert to the north knowing he will never follow us into such a country.

It is 5:30 P.M. when we step off and there will be some light for three hours. The border waits five or six miles ahead and many trails streak northward to the line. We follow tracks of tennis shoes, running shoes, soccer shoes, huaraches, and boots. The way is lined with empty cans of fish, nectarine juice, and chiles. Black ash marks where fires fought back the night.

The trails braid and wander and cross each other, a kind of stuttered beginning to a long walk. We move along the stone walls of the Tinajas Altas mountains, walking fast, eager to leave the Mexican immigration official behind and powered like all travelers on this path by the pull of the El Dorado to the north.

Then a white masonry obelisk spikes upward a couple of

hundred yards to the east. A bunch of stones on the ground at our feet spell out MEXICO/USA, and nearby a huge wooden sign stands there with its surface weathered and perfectly blank. Another and smaller sign warns that motor vehicles are forbidden.

This is the fabled border. There is no fence, just this boast of an imaginary line and footprints, everywhere footprints, and all heading one direction.

We move through the low hills, a gentle roll of land, and after a half hour, the view opens up and we can see across the Lechugilla to Big Pass. Beyond Big Pass, puffs of smoke rise from fields being burned off near Tacna. Everything looks close enough to touch. It seems impossible that the hike will take more than two, maybe even three hours. The light weakens from white to gold, the valley shines with perfectly spaced creosote and is lanced down the center by ironwood and palo verde lining Coyote Wash. We hardly speak now. The rhythm of our footsteps constitutes our language and to a degree, we are struck dumb by the order and hugeness of the landscape. The big valley could serve as the garden of a Zen monastery.

Two and a half hours out of El Saguaro truckstop, we reach a fork in the trail that leads off to Tinajas Altas, a series of nine rock tanks. All human footprints are away from the water. All coyote tracks race left toward the water. The small pools lie hidden from view on the steep rock side of the mountain. The rains fill them and historically they have been the only sure source of water between Agua Dulce spring sixty miles to the east, and Yuma, forty miles to the west. Once hundred of graves were visible around the tanks and the path was lined on both sides with the mummified carcasses of upright horses and mules. The federal boundary survey of the 1890s found a prospector dead just below the first tank. His fingers were worn raw from trying to climb the rock. He had been too weak to make it to water and died a few yards from his salvation.

At this place, a key medical paper on thirst was created in

1905. W. J. McGee, a nationally known scientist and renowned desert rat, was camped here in August while cancer ate at his body. Pablo Valencia dropped in.

Valencia had been lost for six-and-a-half days and for five days he had lived by drinking his urine. His bowels had completely shut down during this experience and for two days his kidneys failed. He had undergone change in what we moderns might call his values. He threw all his money away; he hallucinated a desert saturated with wet sand. He had dreams of dying and he spent days staying on the march. He made it to Tinajas Altas and was saved. McGee had heard this bellowing, this deep roaring, a sound he likened to a bull, and wandered out and found the man.

When Bill almost died because coyotes dug up his water supply, he was retracing Valencia's wanderings.

We pass Tinajas Altas without stopping and strike out across the desert for Big Pass, following the footprints of Mexicans. A little after 8 P.M. we stop and eat and drink. We have been drinking steadily, making no effort to conserve water. The problem is not running out of water but pouring it into our bodies fast enough. We sweat like beasts but we can only drink like human beings.

Bill checks his feet for blisters, the sun sinks, and the light goes from gold to rose to gone. We sit beside an ancient trail etched on a field of stone. Broken pottery fragments lie about. I smile and think of an Indian tripping, and I imagine strange curses in the air as the clay vessel smashes on the ground. The Lechuguilla wears the marks of many journeys. Aboriginal trails cross car tracks, tank tracks, game tracks, Mexican tracks, our tracks. Pieces of spent military hardware litter the ground. I can see traces in the sand of lizards, rats and sidewinders.

Big Pass is so near, so very near. We joke that this walk may be too easy, that Big Pass will be ours in an hour or so. But from Tinajas Altas to Big Pass is 13.5 miles as the raven flies. We are not ravens. We dodge clumps of creosote, fall into rat holes, stumble into washes, detour ironwoods, watch for cactus, and zigzag across the terrain.

The moon slams the ground with white light. At our backs, Cipriano Pass knifes between the Tinajas Altas and Gila Mountains, a cut the Border Patrol calls Smuggler's Pass. It is part of a shortcut to the Interstate and the town of Wellton, a nine-hour route. The various trails whipping across the Lechuguilla all have one goal: avoid capture. The Mexicans say that they come across this pan of sand and heat because they think their chances of evading the Border Patrol are enhanced. The Border Patrol denies this and claims such hikes are foolish risks. But then, their federal commitment to the game is not as complete as the Mexicans'—the referee never has the same feel for the sport as the lineman.

We stumble across the valley. The heat ceases to matter, not because it goes away, but because we go into it and join it and can imagine no life separate from it. The night is soft with warmth, the moon is up, and I feel my sweat as the air brushes against my flesh with a light touch. I have no desire to be cool and no desire to be elsewhere. I do not think of the Border Patrol or of snakes or of thirst, fatigue, thorns, blisters, hunger, and pain.

I think of my wife. I look at the moon and think she is looking up at the moon and we are together. This lunar unity strikes me suddenly as a great insight. The soil crunches under my feet and my legs bleed from the tears of thorns. I look at the moon.

The collapse of my marriage has not been tidy. I left; then there were no words. Then there were talks. She has seen a counselor and this, she tells me, has helped.

I am sitting in the living room, an exhibition hall of her taste and the sofa is soft and comfortable. My body is rigid, the muscles hard with tension. She speaks and the words pour out for more than an hour—angry jabs, blunt charges, an inventory of my sins. I do not disagree. I listen and I am mute. This is all necessary. The words must be said. She weeps.

We make love on the floor.

Then it falls apart again. The pattern repeats. We begin the process of divorce. Then we have dinner and laugh. I bury myself in work; I go through the motions of preparing for the long walk; I drink.

She has large breasts hanging from a thin body. She finds a lump. There are many tests and the results give different answers. I can see a blue vein just below the surface on one breast, a faint pulsing river of blood. There are more tests. After weeks, they decide: cancer. The breast must be cut off.

She tries to be brave but after awhile this ceases to be enough. She asks me if I can imagine what this means, if I can conceive of mutilating my sexual identity. Of course, I cannot.

The water sloshes in my pack, my feet pound along like a metronome on a grand piano, and I look up at that moon. In three days, she will be wheeled into surgery. I have had her schedule the operation so that it will not interfere with my walk, with this story. I am inflexible on this point and cannot be budged. My work has become my religion and I use it to keep at bay all demands and duties. She looks into my eyes and sees a sullen stranger there.

They will cut off the breasts and will search her tissue to see —to see if more must be hacked off her body. She stares at a fear much larger than Big Pass. She wants to make love all the time. The shambles of our marriage does not matter. She is like a gladiator about to go into the arena; she wants it all while there is still time.

She has never been more alive and her senses grow keen with this fact of cancer. "Can you imagine what this means to me?" she says. I hear her voice cutting across the Lechuguilla. She collects toys and stuffed animals; she collects images of pigs; she worships cats. As children we both happened to read the same edition of Hans Christian Andersen, one with intricate and magical plates by Nathaniel Wyeth. The illustrations promised a world far beyond my reach.

"Can you imagine?" she asks.

I enter a serenity of walking, dodging cactus and always those thorns on the small shrubs and large trees slice my arms and legs. I walk into the limbs, these I do not detour and I take pleasure in crashing ahead, in the sound of thorns raking across my nylon pack.

The moon—I draw power from the moon. I think—no, I do not think, I know with certainty—that I will make it and she will make it and that we are both looking at the moon and I will pull her through the dark cave of anesthesia and the knife and the pain and the bandage wrapped across where her breast once spread as a generous mound. My will becomes like iron and I know. I am a tiny dab of flesh dragging across a huge valley in the moonlight but I am larger than the mountains, stronger than hard metals, because I know. I know. I feel no guilt now.

Everywhere the earth is beauty. The mountains lift sharply off the valley floor, rock piles almost naked of plants. Beauty. The moon flashes off the stone walls. Beauty. The creosote, the much derided greasewood, stands spaced like a formal garden. Beauty. Stars crowd the sky and I can hear them buzzing with the fires of their explosive gases. I tear the wrapper from a Granola bar and crunch the grains between my teeth. I tip the plastic jug up to my lips and swallow. I lock on the moon. Beauty.

The desert tonight is an enormous theater full of tracks made by men and women and sometimes children inching north. The air is empty of sound. We all struggle toward Big Pass alone and this is necessary. We are always alone, everywhere alone, but here this fact cannot be denied. It is a condition of this place and other people cannot, this time, alter or obscure that insight.

A flare bursts over our heads. The military sharpens itself for war. We enter a cleared strip of ground, a target area. Something finned like a bomb fragment squats on the sand. And then everything turns blue. The mountains rise azure, the ocotillo waves blue wands, the creosote whispers by my feet, and everything is awash with a rich bright blue. At first the color is ahead and I enter it like water and the blue is everywhere. It does not coat the surface but seems to come from the center of things. I look at my hand and the skin glows with blue pigment.

I do not hesitate or wonder. I do not speculate that the sugar flow to my brain has declined, that the pangs of dehydration have addled my brain, that some vast chemical change in my body is altering my perceptions. I have entered this blue world and I accept it totally. It means peace. I long to see a coyote cutting across the flats on a night hunt, to see a blue coyote and hear a blue yell under a blue moon. My senses quicken and yet dull. The peace works deep into my muscle and my body works harder and harder and yet feels at ease. I begin to glide. Ahead Big Pass waits with dark blue jaws.

I glance at Bill ten yards off to my side and lurching as I must be over the uneven surface mined with holes, plants, and bad footing. But I glide. I know I glide.

Blue.

Other travelers have probably tasted a different, less serene Lechuguilla. In 1976, the Border Patrol found men harnessed to a cart equipped with auto tires for wheels. They were hauling it across this very desert where Bill and I now stumble. They were on no road or trail. The cart was full of marijuana.

Once Bill was walking a few miles to the south and discovered tracks made by wheels. He carefully measured the marks and realized they were made by wagons in the nineteenth century. I have a friend who served in this area during World War II. He says there is a wagon train lying in ruins in the sands, a relic of a party massacred by bandits a century ago. Men training for war sighted the wreck. No one has seen it since.

There is a mass grave near a big tree according to old accounts, a burying place for a man, a woman, and their children. The horse died, the wagon stopped, the family perished within ten miles of the waters of Tinajas Altas. People report visiting the site from time to time. Bill and I have tried to find it. There are so few large trees in the Lechugilla, the task should be simple.

We always fail.

To the north and west a ways, the military prepares to test a silo for the MX missile system. Giant doors will endure huge blasts to determine if this clever shell game with the Soviets will really work. Someday, future wanderers can search for this site.

Thoughts trip across my mind without obvious logic. They are soft, soggy clumps of feeling. They produce no argument or insight but seem like the pulps of fruit lying together in a bowl. I solve nothing and do not desire solutions. We are on a treadmill toward Big Pass. The rock walls glow under the fat moon.

Steps. Step after step after step. We tire, we stop. We time the break with our digital watches. Five minutes and no more. We must move, move, move. Move dammit, MOVE.

We must make Big Pass.

We do not ask why.

We do not speak at all.

About 12:30 A.M., Big Pass finally swallows us. We have drunk less than one gallon of water apiece. We are thirsty, constantly thirsty but we cannot seem to pour the fluid into our bodies any faster. My legs are tired, my shoulders sore, and I am beginning to feel the bones in my feet. We move on.

The tracks we lost at Tinajas Altas now reappear and I smile at the reunion. The soccer shoe is back. The running shoe also. We have all converged at the Pass and just beyond the gap. We all take a dirt road hugging against the Copper Mountains. Now the hunt begins in earnest.

The Border Patrol knows tracks. They can read prints on foot, from trucks and from aircraft. Once they pick up a fresh trail below the Interstate, they stay with it until the footprints tell them that the people have gotten out. In part this is because once the tracks make it to the freeway, the person is likely to hitch a ride and slip beyond the federal reach. And in part, this is because if the tracks do not make it to the Interstate, then the person is still in the desert and to the Border Patrol this means the person could be dying. Jim Clarida, the man who watched his son's rabbit die from the heat, once tracked a man for seventy-five miles.

The Mexicans in turn do their best to avoid the trackers. They walk backwards to confuse their pursuers. They drag brush to obliterate their footprints. They often stay off the roads. When caught, they ask the agents how they bagged them. The agents tell them. The game demands certain courtesies.

After Big Pass, the drag roads begin. The Border Patrol pulls old tires on chains to wipe the dirt clean. Then they know if any tracks are fresh. The drag roads are checked often, on the ground and from the air. When a new sign is spotted, the hunt begins.

Tonight, no one seems interested in hiding their tracks. The road shows clear sign. It is now 1 A.M. and the Border Patrol shift will not begin until 6 A.M. Perhaps, everyone counts on being past the Interstate by then. Or perhaps everyone is too weary to care.

The game is played seriously but without anger. If a Mexican cannot make it, his companions often go to the Border Patrol and turn themselves in so that help can be sent to the person left behind. The Border Patrol responds. If someone is trapped in the desert, they say he is down. And that is serious business.

The agents seldom face resistance. Some of the Mexicans have been caught many times in this sector. It is a game. Once Clarida cornered a man in the brush. Suddenly the man walked out and gave himself up. Clarida recognized him as someone he had once rescued. "Anyone else I would have run from," he said, "but I owe you this one."

By 2 A.M. I feel ruin in my limbs. It is not a question of being strong or fit. Such things no longer matter. Something is happening to my body and I cannot alter this decline. The rattlesnake briefly buzzes beneath my foot, the photo is taken, the incident filed but not discussed. We can now see the Interstate more than twenty miles ahead, a thin strand of lights beckoning.

A couple of years back, a nineteen-year-old came out and said his uncle and father were down. They had no water; the father had been snakebitten. The Border Patrol found them a few days later working on a ranch along the Gila River. The father and uncle had walked through their thirst and had drunk their urine. They had poulticed the snakebite with the flesh of a cactus.

The father was sixty years old. He was very angry that his son had gone to the Border Patrol.

We gaze ahead at Tacna, at the big road, at Mohawk Pass, at the twinkling lights of other people and the promise of shade, water, food, rest. We have twenty miles more.

We have entered the killing ground.

The people who come this way do not die in the heart of the desert; they go down near their goals. They go down because there is nothing left in them, not even a tiny spark to propel them one more mile.

We begin to consider dumping our water at a point up ahead. When we reach the mouth of a certain canyon. We will be only twelve miles from Tacna. Then, the water must go. Surely nothing can stop us from covering only twelve miles and to be free of the weight of the water would be an utter joy. Why, to keep carrying all this water is madness. We are sure of the fact. Dammit, we will get rid of the stuff. We are not fools. We will pour it out.

The calves in my legs tighten, the bones in my feet hurt, the hips grind and grow sore with each stride. My pack cuts into my shoulders and food no longer seems to work. I eat and walk a ways and the energy disappears. I drink but need more water. I envision drilling straight into my belly, auguring a big hole and just pouring the water in. I will use a funnel and not spill a drop.

The night is still a blue dream. The desert can never be better than what greets my eyes. The forms cannot be questioned. The night world brings no fears. Bats fly just over our heads and they are friends. I am certain of this. An owl lifts off a saguaro and I stop and stare with worship. Nighthawks sweep just off the ground.

Across the blue valley, the Mohawks glow. Once a woman lost all hope on the flanks of the Mohawks. She was just a few short miles from the Interstate and the roadside rest there with its ramadas of shade, its bathrooms, its tap water. She ripped her clothes off, article by article and walked up a canyon and then scaled the rock slope. From up there she could see everything and it must have looked lovely to her, seeing the green fields, the towns and snug houses, the traffic, the highway, the lazy course of the river. Behind she left her dress, her shoes, her panties, her bra littered along her trail.

They never found her body.

The night, the delicious night, denies such stories. The night insists on beauty.

But we hurt. Our bodies whisper: Yes, the stories are here.

At 4 A.M., we strike another drag road, wide and clean and hungry for our footprints. The moon is down and our pace is two miles an hour. We drift closer to the Coppers where we have cached water, all part of our grand strategy. Six gallons lie buried under the sand. We do not touch them and are amused by their uselessness. The water mocks our thirst. We possess this treasure but we cannot get it into our bodies.

We fall down on the road and eat and drink and watch a red glow grow in the east. We empty our packs of canteens and keep only a gallon. The rest we set out for whoever needs it, whoever comes after us. The brotherhood.

Originally, we thought we might stop at dawn in this area, wait out the murderous heat of the day and finish the following evening. We reject this idea now. We want out; that is part of it. But also we want to beat the Border Patrol. We want to win, to gain the big road before they can catch us. We have been playing the game too hard to be indifferent to the final score.

I walk off a ways into the desert, squat down, and take a shit. The sun comes on stronger. The literature of hiking is almost devoid of the simple pleasure of pissing and shitting at will. It is replete with tips on how to dispose of wastes, how to protect babbling brooks from pollution, how to leave a clean camp. But nothing on this pleasure, this return to infancy when there is no distance between the desire and the act.

I feel like I can walk no farther. I feel like I can walk forever. My body, my tired, sore body, is simply something I drag along and I cannot imagine the trip ever ending.

The traffic on the Interstate can now be seen clearly, trucks storming toward Los Angeles markets, cars cruising with the air conditioning blowing hard. I hear the rumble of engines and delight in the sound of machines.

Bill and I get up and trudge on. We must go twelve miles. We must. We cannot beat the dawn, but we will fight the sun; we will war against the rays. We refuse to stop. Every hour, we pause briefly, drink, snack, and lie down. Then we stagger up, our legs stiff as boards. Tacna seems just ahead but hour by hour comes nearer. We dream of Tacna, a hamlet of 100 people. Bill sees iced tea, and ice cream; he makes out a waitress holding up a cone and beckoning. We shuffle more than walk, our feet scraping across the soil.

The sun comes up with unbelievable force. I shudder under the rays like a vampire caught far from my coffin. All around us are the unmarked spots where the last dramas of the dying take place. One man went down a mile south of the Interstate. He set fire to a tree in hopes that the smoke would bring help. They found his body.

The dying can be very quick. A few weeks before a man left El Saguaro truckstop at 4 P.M. on a Saturday. By 9 P.M. Sunday he was in a body bag in Tacna. He was twenty-eight. Sometimes the Border Patrol finds people too far gone to risk the ride to the hospital in Yuma. They take them to a grocery in Tacna and put them in the beer cooler in hopes of lowering their body temperatures.

None of these tales stops the flow of people. There was an old man who crossed this desert with his son and nephew. The two boys died ten miles south of the Interstate. The old man was caught and shipped back to Mexico. A week later he was caught again crossing the same desert with a girl of eighteen. So far the Border Patrol in the Tacna sector has nabbed that old man fifteen times.

We walk on. We must have walked on. But there is no memory of this. We walk on.

We reach Tacna at 9:48 A.M. We have made the crossing in sixteen hours, seventeen minutes, drunk a gallon and half of water each, and have nothing to say. We have probably walked forty-five miles, but this figure, like our careful recording of the time elapsed, means very little. The weather has been very cool for this country, surely no more than 110.

I will write a story, the newspaper will print it, and there will be awards, the trinkets of the business. But this will happen later.

Now there are other tasks at hand. I must call Tucson and let them know we are out. I fumble at the push buttons of the pay phone and keep getting the operator of an overseas line. I persist and after forty minutes make the simple connection. I begin to grasp what has happened to me. My mind does not work in this world.

We enter a cafe and eat a breakfast and drink iced tea after iced tea. The food is flat. The cool drinks lack pleasure. We consume coffee, pop, ice cream, eggs, sausage, hash browns, beef, lamb, soup, beer. The gorging continues for hours.

I walk into a bar and order a Budweiser longneck. I cannot sit. My limbs ache too much. I recline on the floor. The bartender says nothing. The Mexicans are still out there. They were yesterday, they are today, and they will be there tomorrow and tomorrow and tomorrow. And they cannot walk in here. They are huddling by an irrigation ditch and drinking deeply and then walking ten more miles, fifty more miles, one hundred more miles, whatever it takes to find work. I feel the rush of energy that must be pushing such people. I hear this force pounding like a mighty heart somewhere to the south.

But mainly as I lie there, I feel it all slip away and my senses deaden under the blandishments and delights of my civilization. When I get home in a day I will write the newspaper story in four hours, a torrent of words, statistics, and suggestions on this illegal immigration problem. But I will not mention my wife. There will be nothing about the cancer, the scalpel incising the soft white flesh topped by the faint pink nipple. I will not find room for the insistent feeling that she will triumph, the conviction that everything can be overcome. I will skip my notion that we both looked up at the same moon. And I will write nothing of blue desert. Nor will I speak of that place to anyone.

I have exited the only ground where I truly trust my senses. Most of the Southwest is beyond my belief and strikes me as an outpost of American civilization with the exiled desert merely a faint, scenic mural stretching behind the powerlines and skyscrapers. But the Lechuguilla, the Tule, the Mohawk dunes, these places have a weight with me that makes the cities of my people seem light and insubstantial. There is no point in reasoning with me on this matter. When I touch the steel towers of the Sunbelt, they feel like cobwebs soon to be dispersed by an angry wind. When I touch the earth I feel the rock hard face of eternity

But as I lie on the saloon floor I can hardly believe in the country I have just left. I feel the bubbles of the beer against my tongue and savor the sour taste. I am busy killing experience with categories and words and leads, striking at it like it were a serpent to be slain and made into a safe skin, perhaps a belt or hatband.

And then I fall back again and see only one word. Blue. Always blue.

They play a game here. We play a game here.

POSTSCRIPT: I've never returned to the route I took that night. But then again, I do not think I have ever left it. For what it is worth, Kathy, my ex-wife (the woman I was thinking about as I crossed Blue Desert), survived cancer and ten years later is fit as a fiddle despite the statistical doom (70 percent chance of recurrence) preached by the doctors back then. So you see, people are not numbers.

*"Cousins from Kansas Looking for Cheap Tequila"*

## Max Aguilera-Hellweg

# La Frontera,
# Sin Sonrisa

'M A PRODUCT of the border. My mother lived in Juárez, my father in El Paso. When she was a teenager, she crossed the river and worked for my dad. They moved to California. I was born in Fresno. Farm worker country. But we lived in the suburbs. When we returned to El Paso to visit relatives, we'd cross the bridge into Juárez so my parents could drink, and me and my sister could buy bulls' horns, sombreros and velvet Jesus paintings. The streets were packed. I held onto my mom's hand for fear I'd lose her grip. But I did. I spun around, there she was. Mexico staring me in the face—a stump on a skateboard, amputated, her hand held out begging for pesos.

My sister has a photograph from one of these trips. It is of her and me, my mom and dad, taken in Tijuana in the early 60s. My sister and I are seated upon a pair of donkeys. The donkeys have been painted in black and white stripes so that they look like a couple of zebras. I'm wearing a sombrero that says LUPITA on the brim. I have a sad half-smile. My sister's expression is blurred and unreadable. My mom looks tense. My father's eyes look away, averted, not present. Years later my father told me he was mourning the death of Clark Gable that day, and we had gone to Tijuana so he could drink. In Mexico photographs are called recuerdos, memories.

The photograph was taken by a tourist photographer who worked with a wooden box camera, a crudely made 4x5, the Virgin of Guadalupe painted on its side. He used a bottle cap for a shutter and stuck his hand inside a sock in the rear of the camera which held a developing tray, a darkroom inside the camera. He developed a paper negative, made a contact print with the sun, developing the final image back inside the camera. Afterwards he submerged the print in a bucket of slime and told us to return in 15 minutes. Despite the technology and the eerie quality to the print, the image has neither stained nor faded. It stands apart from all our other family snapshots. It tells a story.

People often ask me when I take their picture, "What do you want me to do? What should I wear?"

"Do nothing," I say. "Just stand there."

"But what should I do?" they ask. "What are you taking a picture of?"

"Your soul," I say half kidding. "I'm going to take a picture of your soul."

In Mexico having one's picture taken is still an important event. The subject stands there, sin sonrisa, without a smile, as if saying to himself, "Look at me. This is who I am."

In the United States, El Norte, we don't even have our picture taken anymore. We are videotaped. Even our most sacred ceremonies—the wedding, the graduation, the barmitzvah, the birthday. Still, when we do have our picture taken we have learned to wear a mask. That mask is a smile. And the smile is a lie, a convention imposed. When we smile, in fact we are saying, "Don't look at me, the real me." When we are encouraged to smile, the photographer is saying, "Cover thyself." Afraid to look inside, afraid to reveal ourselves, we don the mask.

But when we look at the pictures of our grandparents, their

wedding photo for instance, they are not smiling. They are solemn. They are sincere. Their marriage has been taken seriously. The photograph is not only true; like their marriage, it endures.

In search of subjects that reveal themselves fully to the camera and in search of my self, I returned to the border as an itinerant photographer. It is a dying art, as most of these photographers who work the streets, the festivals and churches of Latin America have replaced the Virgin of Guadalupe boxes with instant cameras and color film.

Working in the manner of a Mexican street photographer, I set up my camera in the zocolos, the plazas, in front of churches, on the bridges, in Mexico City, in Lima, in East L.A. Using Polaroid Type 55 B/W film which produces a positive as well as a negative I'm able to give my subjects the print and take the negative home. This in itself changes the dynamic a photo documentarian uses. Instead of capturing the moment, stealing the photograph, the subjects pose themselves. The photograph is theirs.

Growing up a Mexican in America is to grow up an immigrant in one's own land. To be amputated at the hip without the language, without the culture, without a sense of history, continuity or belonging to the rest of Latin America. Although Mexican, I walk different. I wear my jeans different. My Spanish has a Cuban, an Argentinean and sometimes even a Catilan accent.

Nonetheless, with a black cape, a wooden tripod and a state of the art mahogany and stainless steel 4x5 field camera, I'm accepted as an ambulante, a streetwalker, as the itinerant photographers are called. I don't charge, but offer the portraits for free. Soon a crowd forms and others come up and ask to have a picture. The ones who had said no in the beginning would then ask too.

I wasn't always successful. Three teenage girls appeared in the plaza of Piedras Negras in communion dresses, torn and soiled. I asked them to pose. They declined. I pressed further.

They said no. The *coyote* appeared, who was going to take them across the border. They explained. They tried crossing three nights on their own. They'd lost everything, but the clothes they were wearing. These too now were dirty. They were from Mexico City. Their families were middle class. How could they arrive in the rich United States looking this way? No. No picture.

One afternoon, I had a man in front of the camera, Porfirio, an ice cream vendor. He stood hunched at the shoulders, staring straight into the camera, his feet planted firmly on the ground. I was all set to go, just about to snap the picture, when a ruckus broke out. Five men my age surrounded me.

"Why are you taking pictures of poor people?" A young man in Farahs and cowboy boots attacked. "That's all you gringos think of us. That we're poor and Indian. We got rich people too. Rich people and intelligent people. How come you don't take pictures at the country club? We're not all poor," he yelled.

Porfirio held his position waiting for me to shoot. Sensing I was about to get booted out of town, I turned and faced my accusers. "I'm Chicano. I'm Mexican. I'm Indian. I don't look at these people as poor people," I said. "I look at them as Mexicans. I just happen to be photographing this man, on this corner, on this afternoon. If you want to be next, ¡ándale pues!"

"Get out of here," the crowd yelled at my accuser. "We're having fun."

I turned back to Porfirio. Minutes had passed. He stood hunched at the shoulders, staring straight into the camera, his feet planted firmly on the ground. He hadn't moved an inch.

In Lima no one said no. If anything I had a problem keeping the frame clear. Mobs would form and step into the photograph. Starving for attention, wanting to be noticed. A policeman who helps me photograph a fortuneteller and his monkey expects his own photograph as payback.

There's a plaza in Lima where street artists, musicians and evangelists congregate. The plaza has strange magical power. Actors appear from nowhere. Instantly crowds emerge, encircle,

*"Profirio, Ice Cream Vendor"*

listen, watch.

A man holds out the centerfolds from *Playboy* and *Playgirl* extolling the sins of homosexuality and the virtues of the vagina and matrimony. A father and daughter perform acrobatic displays, rudimentary and unremarkable. A woman sells puppies from the pockets of her house dress. A photographer uses the bronze statue, a soldier on horseback, as the background for his portrait of a policeman.

I don my cape, kneel to the ground and focus. When I look up, a flock 200 strong has formed a circle around us. I realize it's my moment. I load the camera with Type 55 and snap the shutter. Still kneeling I pull the Polaroid and rise to my feet. I hold the instant print up high and make a slow 360 degree turn. "Aahhh," the crowd hums.

In Matamoros I wandered down the street and passed the door of an old photo studio. The door was open and inside stood an old wooden 8x10 camera, the owner and her son. Her father had been a photographer during the revolution. He had photographed Villa's troops as they hid in the North. He had been an itinerant photographer, as was her deceased husband, herself, her brother and now her son. I asked her if she would take my picture.

She went to a drawer and pulled out a 35mm late model Canon SLR.

"I want the old camera," I said. "Can we use the old camera?"

"We shoot in 35 now," she said. "In color. Cross the border and use one of those one-hour labs. But as you wish."

I stood still, tried my best not to smile and hoped my double-chin would not show.

Debbie Nathan

# Love in the Time of Cholera
## Waiting for Free Trade on the U.S./Mexico Border

SOMETIMES, before three in the afternoon, when my husband has wakened from his day of sleep after the graveyard shift, and the kids are still in school, and the two of us are in bed, we switch the telephone ringer to off, the answering machine to on, and we turn down the blinds.

The doorbell rings. He pulls out and I curse. We lie there, silent.

Come *on*, I say between clenched teeth. Just ignore her.

I can't, he says, I'm soft.

I kiss him. The doorbell rings again. It rings again. We lie very still.

But Perla knows what's up. She's got on her grimy Ghostbusters tee shirt. She's got her Fiesta cigarettes that have stained all her teeth dark brown. She knows the score. She's not going anywhere.

I throw on the Oaxaca wedding dress that I picked up cheap on Juárez Avenue. I answer the door. It's Perla all right. Today she's got mangos. I buy some, quick. She won't let me off so fast.

Oiga, she says in her reticent, confidential at the same time belligerent tone. ¿Me prestas diez?

The "lend" part is a joke, of course. Don't even think she'll be able to repay it. To me it's a miracle she and her family are even alive; that in itself is sufficient debt service. Still, the whole thing makes me queasy.

What's going on now? I say. Chuyito's sick, she says. He's had diarrhea for days. It's greenish. She needs to go get him medicine. Of course, I say. Give him plenty of water. Take this sugar and this salt, here's some lime, and this Arm & Hammer. Mix it up just so. Make sure he drinks.

Later I mention this to a friend of mine, a midwife up from Mexico City, with an almost mystical gift for coaxing and bullying tired, angry women in labor into expelling their babies without screaming. This friend listens to the facts about Chuyito's diarrhea. She looks sad and knowing. Can it be the famous cholera? she asks.

No, I answer. It cannot be the famous cholera. The famous cholera is not here yet.

SOONER OR LATER it will be. That's what the health department people are saying, and they're not fooling around. Cholera landed in Latin America earlier this year, apparently on an Asian ship loaded with infected merchant marines—then rapidly hop-skipped north from Peru to Brazil, Colombia, El Salvador, Guatemala. Mexico reported some one thousand cases, at least a dozen of them fatal. So far, the victims all live deep in the interior. But already, rumors are spreading about cases near the U.S. border.

El Paso is getting ready. Task forces are being formed to handle an outbreak. The talk is that city-county disaster preparedness personnel will be involved. Maybe even the military.

A Defense Department-style intervention is perhaps not

inappropriate. In classical history, cholera has the reputation of being Clausewitzian in its destructiveness. The biggest epidemic killer in the annals of humanity, it once was confined to Bengal. It used to spread through India during Hindu pilgrimages to the infected lower Ganges. Its very name means wrath: the wrath of God.

Under a microscope, the bacterium that causes cholera looks like a grain of cooked rice attached to a tiny, whipping and darting flagellum. It is an aquatic creature that comes in contact with people usually via feces-laden water—water that, in modern times, we call sewage. Sewage can be drunk or bathed in; frozen into ice; used to irrigate crops of fruits and vegetables. Historically, cholera has spread when, in the absence of hermetic water systems, human daily waste remingles with human daily life. Swallowed, the bacteria lodge themselves in the gut. If the gut belongs to a person who is malnourished and weak, the germs multiply and throw off a toxin. The toxin causes the intestine to swell and disgorge the body's fluid in stools the color and consistency of rice water. The stools go on and on. Daily, there may be gallons of them. Losing this much water, one dies very quickly.

To spread, cholera has always needed the commerce of business or war. By the mid-19th century, English imperialism and its steamships and railroads had exported the disease to Asia, the Persian Gulf, Southern Russia and the Baltic. In the 1830s cholera invaded Ireland, Canada, Mexico, and the U.S. Its toll was astounding: 30,000 dead Egyptians in one day; in a summer, ten percent of St. Louis. It liked newly industrialized areas, particularly their proletarian zones.

Not all victims were indigent though. Indeed, the random way cholera chose a body added to its shock value. The speed with which it killed was especially frightening, its symptoms terrifying. In mere hours, a victim would shrink into a dried-fruit, black-and-blue version of his former self. Cholera's quick, cartoonish representation of mortality reminded all who witnessed it of death's complete dominion.

Health authorities used to argue endlessly about whether the disease arose from germs or if it instead wafted silently from polluted "miasmas." Finally, everyone hedged their bets. By the end of the century, London, New York and all the other big North American and European cities had cleaned and sealed the water and sewerage systems thought responsible for both bacteria and noxious ethers. But Latin America never followed suit, and 90 years later, Mexico City, Lima and a thousand other places have swelled with people. Most come from the countryside: peasants whom governments and world banks no longer bother supporting with loans, fertilizers, seeds or commodities prices that might make it worthwhile to stay and farm the land.

PERLA drives me crazy. Well, my husband says, it's my own fault. She knocked on our door for the first time four years ago. I don't know why I talked with her as much as I did— illegal aliens come by all the time, selling avocados, asking for yard work, trying to make the busfare back south after the migra caught them hopping the freights to L.A.; or merely begging.

She told me her story in bits and pieces. They were field workers near their ranchito in Durango, she said. The family was there as far back as anyone could remember. But the cotton failed several years in a row and finally they couldn't take it— eating prairie dogs for food or nothing at all. They were practically the last of the extended family to leave. Perla came up with the four girls and Chuyito, then newborn, and they lived during February at the Juárez train station since they had no coats. Then they moved in with cousins and one of them lent Perla a grubstake to buy several kilos of avocados and limes, and showed her how to smuggle them across the Rio Grande into my neighborhood and sell them much cheaper than at Furr's, and at first she was scared but now she's used to it and the people around here know her and many are nice, though others chase you away like a stray cat and some even call the Border Patrol. Her husband joined her and they squatted on their own piece of land on a mountain near the Channel 44 TV tower and built a cardboard shack, and dug a pit into the ground for a toilet, and bought an old bucket to haul water in from the pipe down the hill. He picks up construction work pretty frequently (well yes it only pays Mexican minimum wage: about $4 a day, but he's deathly afraid of crossing into El Paso and anyway, there's so much new building going on in Juárez!). And now that Perla's got the fruit business down it seems more lucrative than working at the maquila, except when the Border Patrol and the Department of Agriculture grab her and take the fruit, or when the kids are sick and need medicine. Then the family budget goes into a tailspin. And now Chuyito's got diarrhea.

I N MUCH OF LATIN AMERICA, diarrhea—brought on by lack of clean water—is a major killer, particularly of small children. It's usually caused by gastroenteritis, but there are many other diseases related to dirty water: typhoid, hepatitis, amebiasis, schistosomiasis (a fatal disease of the blood caused by a species of flatworm). There are illnesses associated with lack of water to wash oneself: scabies, for instance, lice, pink eye; or illnessess borne by animals that breed in stagnant water (malaria is one).

In 1980, the UN General Assembly proclaimed the next ten years as the International Decade of Drinking Water and Cleanup. In 1990, the organization lamented that its goals hadn't been met. A fifth of Latin America's urban population still had no piped drinking water. Less than half had sewage. In the countryside the figures were much worse.

■ ■ ■

PERLA AND HER KIDS walk around encrusted with grime; their hair is stiff with dust. They love to use our bathroom, especially the little girls. They scuttle upstairs, lock themselves in and stay for ages. For an eternity you hear the shower running, running, running. Always when they come out their hair is combed and glistening; they look warm and drunk with pleasure. After they go I enter the bathroom. It's still misted with steam and I see they've helped themselves to the towels and the shampoo and creme rinse and the baby powder and Vitamin E lotion and Jean Nate; and for many hours thereafter, the bathroom reeks of cheap Mexican cigarettes.

IT WAS NO ACCIDENT that cholera hit Peru first. The statistics there on who has and doesn't have water closely fit the UN's drab numbers for the whole continent. Cities like Lima have mushroomed with outlying slums—places that a more hopeful and thus conscience-stricken era condemned as "marginalized," but which cynicism now cheerfully labels "pueblos jovenes." The poor in these "young towns" get their water, mere liters at a time, from trucks and buckets, or they poach from other people's pipes, which lowers the municipal water pressure and backs up sewage into houses. Chlorination systems don't always work, or they are prohibitively expensive.

Once, perhaps 20 years ago, Peru might have hoped for international aid to fix the chaos. But by the end of the Decade of Drinking Water, the World Bank, one of Latin America's two biggest lenders for water projects, had shifted funds away from health, nutrition and education projects towards schemes to stimulate economic development. Water, one Inter-American Development Bank official said, ceased being a priority because it wasn't "productive."

Neither did Peru's president help things when he suspended

most of the country's debt repayments in 1985. In retaliation, the IMF and World Bank halted loans to the country. When the Inter-American Development Bank loaned $3 million to South America for water and sanitation projects, none of the money went to Peru. Few were thus surprised when cholera did. In a few months, one out of every hundred Peruvians were stricken. Thousands died.

PERLA'S BACK. This time I'm trying to get ready for a conference over at the university. At least I've got my dress and makeup on when she rings the bell. She's still giving Chuyito water and the pharmacist recommended an anti-amebic medicine. It hasn't worked. Chuyito's stomach, she says, is hard and bloated. I'm worried. I give her money. I hurry so I won't be late to the university. Oh, and I buy two bags of avocados. They'll make a fine salad for tonight's dinner.

SOME OFFICIALS from the U.S. Environmental Protection Agency went to Peru this spring to check the water. In city after city they found fecal coliform and cholera in the wells, broken pipes and overland flows of raw sewage close to drinking water lines. People in the pueblos jovenes were sticking their dirty hands in their water jars. Fields of vegetables were being irrigated with sewage. Dirty ice—supposedly used only to chill raw fish—was all over the place; street vendors were dumping it into their fruit juice.

So far this year, there have been 300,000 cholera cases in Latin America. One percent have proved fatal. To eliminate the disease, it's estimated that $200 billion will have to be spent on new water and sewerage systems. No one knows where that kind of money will come from.

■ ■ ■

THE SEMINAR at the University of Texas at El Paso is slated to begin with an overview of cholera's history and epidemiology. Then the doctors and lab techs will learn how to identify the darting organism under microscopes. Dr. Nickey, head of the City-County Health Department, opens with a slide show, cumbersomely titled "Welcome to the Other America, or the Forgotten Texas. And Welcome to the Other Mexico."

Dr. Nickey, a native of El Paso and its unremitting sun, is an Anglo past retirement age whose face, nevertheless, still looks rosy and smooth. He has taken care of himself and he often sighs that when he was a boy, you could actually *swim* in the Rio Grande! At this conference he shows slides of current crossing spots in the river: sleepy little ranchos and burgs far from El Paso/Juárez, and then he contrasts these slow, quaint ports with our own frenetic, vehicle and people-ridden bridges. Last year there were 42 million border crossings northward, Dr. Nickey says (and these were only the *legal* ones, he adds).

With all this growth and busyness, the two cities have been unable to keep up with water, sewerage and health infrastructure needs, Dr. Nickey says. Especially water. Greater El Paso has 350 colonias—chockablock, illegal subdivisions out in the desert where you can buy a plot of land for maybe $160 a month and rig up a cinderblock dwelling or anchor an old RV in the sand, without water hookups or sewer service. At least 10 percent of metro El Paso's population are living like this, Dr. Nickey says.

He shows how these people try to make do with their own infrastructure. He flashes a slide of an illegal outhouse ("There are *hundreds* of them!"). A cesspool ("We have lots. They're not legal either."). An uncovered septic tank flowing into the Rio Grande. A rivulet of feces with children romping next to it. A pipe emerging from a house, draining onto a piece of plywood ("I don't have to *tell* you what comes out!").

All this is just El Paso. Over in Juárez, 400,000 people are living in similar conditions. There, even rich people's sewage goes untreated—the water from designer toilets and outhouses alike simply flows through stinking canals in the middle of town, then down through the Lower Valley, where it empties into fields to irrigate the crops.

The American Medical Association recently witnessed similar scenes up and down the border, on both sides. The group issued a report. It called the U.S.-Mexico line a "virtual cesspool and breeding ground for infectious disease."

CHUYITO GOT MEASLES during the epidemic two years ago. What happened was that first, Cristina (the fourth child) got sick. It started in El Paso. A Border Patrol agent had spotted Perla and the little girl with their fruit. They hid in an arroyo for three hours, waiting for him to go away. It was sunny and terribly warm, and when they got home that evening Cristina was hot and flushed. Perla was surprised because no one else near the Channel 44 tower had measles. She suspected Cristina caught them in El Paso.

Chuyito was next, and his case turned really bad. He was in the Social Security hospital under an oxygen tent for three weeks. The whole time, Perla and her family camped out on the concrete benches—all except 11-year-old Perlita, who stayed at her cousin's place. In the end Chuyito lived, but he's never really been the same (he stopped learning how to talk so well and he's developed the strange habit of banging his head repeatedly into the wall). When the family came home to their shack, they found the puppies dead (starvation) and an uncle had raped Perlita.

Also, someone had stolen the metal washtub.

■ ■ ■

EL PASO is booming. So is Juárez. We're in the midst of a bonanza of industrial development. Fortune 500 companies carpet the Mexican industrial parks: GM, Ford, Chrysler, Zenith, Packard Electric, Honeywell. In Juárez, all day and night, buses and vans rumble with mobs of people whipping and darting to and from the maquiladoras. In El Paso, upscale new neighborhoods bloom in the desert, and real estate ads in the Sunday paper lure twin plant executives to "Spanish" homes with sunken dens, xeriscaped yards, little enclosed gardens off the master bath, "maid's rooms."

Yet El Paso is poor, the poorest big city in the country, and things are getting worse. More than a quarter of the people here are living below the poverty line. Ten years ago, before most of these Fortune 500 companies arrived, it was *less* than a quarter. The poverty ratios are even worse when it comes to Hispanics. Besides El Paso, there are the statistics for Juárez.

Free Trade is coming. Who really knows what it is? Though since the start of the year the newspapers have been filled with headlines about Fast Track, about a New World from Anchorage to Tierra del Fuego. No more tariffs. In Mexico, you'll be able to buy a stereo as cheap as here. And lots of products that used to be made here will be manufactured there because the wages are so low. Here the garment workers will lose their jobs, sure. Auto workers too. But don't Americans deserve to work on computers instead of assembly lines? Free Trade will make work for everybody. It will bring democracy to Mexico. In the long run it will make things better across the board. If it's given time!

THE National Association of Hispanic Journalists Region Five Conference ("Free Trade: Redefining the Borderland"), held at the Marriott near the international airport, begins with a maquila tour in Juárez, sponsored by *Twin Plant News*. Lunch follows at Chihuahua Charlie's. The local Coors beer distributor furnishes food and drink in an afternoon hospitality room. An evening reception is provided by the Greater El Paso Chamber of Commerce. Continental breakfast comes courtesy of State National Bank ("El Paso's Bank Since 1881," their full-page newspaper ad says these days. "New opportunities. And one bank strong enough to see them, and to create more").

It is a curious conference. In the audience, journalists from El Paso and Dallas wear tags with their first names printed three times as big as their last names, and they have little to say about the topic at hand. The speakers, though, are a politically disparate group: fervid Hispanic businessmen and political consultants; earnest public relations men from Mexico touting their country's industry and federal government; border academics from places like UTEP who are riding theoretical shotgun for local free trade and twin plant lobbying groups; a humanist representative from the Quakers; a disgruntled local labor leader. They are eager to talk.

Oddly, much of what they say sounds the same. The labor man, for instance, is predictably hostile. How can free trade ever help El Paso, he asks, when promiscuous industrial development has failed to expand infrastructure like healthcare and housing, has merely made people's lives harder, dirtier, sicker, poorer? And really, now—corporations? Can one expect *them* to take the initiative with infrastructure: to clean the environment or the sewage?

No! answer many of the arch-developmentalists, and this is surprising, since just a few years ago, for them to agree with labor's point of view would have been unthinkable. But now the pro-Trade people talk a hybrid, half-chastised, half post-Perestroika-tough-guy line. Gordon Cook, former head of El Paso's Economic Development Office, agrees that yes, per capita income *has* fallen. And yes, free trade could have deleterious effects on the border. Then, sounding eerily like Karl Marx,

Cook warns the conference that "we are moving into a global economic situation. Capital is mobile…If it's more economical under a free trade agreement to move that plant from the U.S. to Mexico, that is what can happen. But then later on, if it becomes more economical to move that plant from Mexico to somewhere in Eastern Europe, that too will happen."

Still, Cook welcomes free trade. He only hopes things won't hurt too badly. Legislation around "social issues," he thinks, might bring "positive aspects flowing to local areas." The labor man says he certainly hopes for that, too. So does Mexico's ruling party think-tank sociologist, and so do various maquila developers who have never, until quite recently, advocated anything "legislative" except laws to hasten the creation of even more maquilas.

It is as though, in this New World Order on the border, populists and elitists alike are rechanneling their rhetorical effluents, processing them into one big verbal treatment plant, then emptying their words, cleansed and purified, into a deep reservoir whose waters will quench everybody's thirst.


ONCE, Perla told me, she rang someone else's bell and the man of the house came out and showed her his business card and on the back he had scrawled the telephone number for the Department of Agriculture, and he warned her that if she ever bothered him again he was going to call them on her and get her fruit confiscated. I wonder what that man was doing with *his* wife when Perla rang his bell.

Sometimes when she rings mine, I think of our time in New York, my husband's and mine, way before we were married, back when he lived in the loft in Manhattan and I lived in Brooklyn, and he worked in a cholera research lab at a hospital near my apartment, and in winter he would park in front of my place and take the battery out of the car so it wouldn't get cold, and carry it up four flights, and put it on the kitchen table, then get in bed with me.

Other times I would come after work to his lab. At that time cholera was still mostly confined to India and Asia, and in this lab near Flatbush Avenue they were typing strains from Bangladesh. This was done by drawing precise little grids, in purple ink, on the shaved backs of white rabbits. Cholera toxins were then injected into the squares. The squares puffed up, and when measured, the degree of swelling determined the particular strain of cholera.

The rabbits were then gassed.

"THE QUESTION isn't *if* it will get here," Dr. Nickey says, concluding his talk to the health people. "It's *when*."

The next slide show is presented by Dr. William B. Greenough III. He is a tall, patrician-looking gentleman, a professor from the Johns Hopkins University School of Medicine. Dr. Greenough has the instinctual grace and straightforward humor of a WASP physician who has done time among dark, chronically poor and acutely ill people, dosing them with antibiotics, serums and emergency regimens designed to save huddled masses of life quickly, and sometimes heroically. For many years, he has been posted in Bangladesh as head of its Cholera Research Laboratory.

Dr. Greenough's show is partial to images like that of a beautiful, sari-clad young mother with a haunted look on her face, pressing a glass of fluids to the parched lips of her sunken-eyed, sunken-skinned little daughter. Another slide, taken mere hours later, shows the child smiling and walking on legs whose spindliness obviously long predates her recent bout with cholera. The miracle of oral rehydration therapy, Dr. Greenough smiles.

His satisfaction is childlike and genuine, and he is not self-conscious about quoting nursery rhymes from author

Maurice Sendak ("Sipping once! Sipping twice! Sipping chicken soup with rice!") while explaining that the best oral rehydration liquid is elaborated not only with glucose and various salts, but also with starches such as rice, maize, potato, barley. And even, perhaps, with infusions of proteins and amino acids.

The best treatment for cholera is thus, according to Dr. Greenough, "like a milkshake or a soup." In other words, the best treatment is—to the chronically undernourished Indian, the starving African, and now to the enfamished Latin American— a medicalized version of a square meal.

THE WEEK before Christmas, I crossed the river with Perla. I knew if we were caught and the Border Patrol heard my Spanish, they'd figure out I was a gringa and not appreciate the joke. They'd probably bust me. So we had this plan. If we got caught, Perla and her companions would explain that I couldn't talk because I was dumb from "throat cancer." They thought that was funny. They nicknamed me La Muda and laughed.

I left my house dressed in threadbare corduroy pants, tennis shoes, two pillballed sweaters and a fuzzy polyester cap. For added authenticity, I grabbed a filthy plastic grocery bag that Perla once left on my porch for safekeeping. I walked to downtown Juárez, over the Santa Fe bridge to Victoria Street, where you catch the rutas to the river. Perla and her sisters-in-law and kids were waiting. I looked passably like them, which made them laugh even harder.

The river turned out to be colder than anyone had anticipated. A young man stripped to his underwear, carried his wife across, then returned for his week-old baby. The young man shivered and hobbled so violently from the cold that he could hardly keep his footing and the baby almost fell into the water. In the end, before he put his pants back on, the young man's legs were as red as boiled crabs.

A T THE JOURNALISTS' CONFERENCE, Bill Mitchell, a silver-haired black man with a portly build, answers a question from the audience, posed by a distraught young Mexican woman who has mentioned the impact of lack of infrastructure on the children of Juárez: children whose photos we see in the papers in the summer, intubated in public hospital beds, dying of dehydration.

Mitchell, formerly marketing vice-president for a Juárez maquila complex (the largest export processing zone park in the world) does not disagree about the infrastructure and about the children. "Thank goodness that this Free Trade, along with the unions, are finally bringing to light much of what has been swept under the rug!" he booms. Mitchell does not add that for years, he released lengthy annual reports to the press, each page rubber-stamped at a bottom corner with his signature, detailing the tremendous advantages created in Juárez and El Paso by the past year's twin-plant expansion, and never mentioning infrastructural items like sewage or dried up babies. But now things are changing. "Now is the time," Mitchell says earnestly, "for little people to get together. And get these problems straightened out!"

A man who speaks after Mitchell still works for the big industrial park, and he has his own notions of infrastructure. The problem, he thinks, is the international bridges and how very long it takes to move goods and workers across them. To resolve this dilemma, could not the interest on Mexico's foreign debt be returned to the border—to hire more customs agents? This would speed up traffic, the man says, and if we can only solve such problems, "Juárez and El Paso will take their respective well-earned places among the leading trade centers of the North American bloc and the modern world economy."

PERLA AND HER SISTERS-IN-LAW had no men to carry them over the river, and their shame was a problem because to have any hope of being dry and warm later that afternoon, they would have to remove their pants and hold them over their heads as they crossed. But there were men around, and the women were loathe to expose their legs.

The dilemma was solved when I looked into my filthy bag—which, by chance, appeared to contain the castoff slacks of every middle class adult in my zip code. We all scooted behind thorny bushes and weeds to change, and immediately I noticed that among the underbrush, human and animal urine and feces were everywhere. I hopped around barefoot, trying to avoid them. It was impossible. I felt nauseous. I wanted to wash but the river was no relief. A rat floated past. We crossed, discarded our rags, then ran across Interstate 10, and I was wild with fear for the children. We made it, though, then entered a wet sewer tunnel, bent over like crones, stumbling through the dark. Someone spotted a light and we climbed up through the hole. Suddenly we were in my neighborhood. Suddenly Perla and the sisters-in-law were yelling, "Aguacates! Limoneeees!" The sun warmed our legs, and some householders chased us away, but others were kind. We went onto the porch of one of my elderly neighbors. She gave us a bag of homemade tamales and bought produce from everyone. I had nothing to sell, so my neighbor, who didn't recognize me in my clothes or my silence, handed me a dollar bill. "Here, mija," she said in Spanish. "Buy your kids something for Christmas."

Soon I was home in my bathroom, running the hot water, furiously.

∎ ∎ ∎

D R. GREENOUGH III shows a page from a 1975 issue of a British Tabloid, *The National Tatler*. On the top is a large photo of Elizabeth Taylor draped ecstatically around an unidentified man. "The Tycoon Liz Hugs and Kisses Now," is the caption of this photo. Underneath, the *Tatler* informs its readership that "Cholera Will Hit America in 1975." Dr. Greenough and his colleagues were the source for this information, and now he shrugs gamely and laughs. They were wrong in making such a prediction, he says. In fact, cholera did not hit America in 1975.

But now, since it probably will, the doctor describes much of his job as "a reverse transfer of technology from Bangladesh to the United States." These days, he is here to introduce Americans to gruels made of sorghum or maize. And to an equally rude, and therefore equally brilliant invention—the cholera cot.

The device, as shown in a slide, is nothing more than a muslin pallet on legs, laid crosswise in the middle with a plastic drop cloth. Both the muslin and the plastic are cut with a large hole at the exact spot where the average subject, lying on the cot, would end up placing his posteriors. Underneath the hole is a large bucket. It is understood that the posteriors are to be kept unclothed, and that the bucket is there to catch the cholera patient's most fatal complication: his gallon upon gallon of watery shit.

"You may find the cholera cot useful in your community," Dr. Greenough says reassuringly.

There are Americans in the audience who gasp.

A FEW YEARS after arriving in Juárez, Perla and her husband have made great strides in infrastructural development: they have replaced their cardboard shack with a concrete house. It is one nine-by-nine-foot room with a wood and tar-paper roof and no windows. The pit dug outside in the sand reeks worse than skid row, and bits of stained toilet tissue blow in the wind.

Inside, lit by a 20-watt bulb, everything is the color of objects discarded on highways, everything smells like the sick and secret parts of bodies. The wood door locks from the inside with a rope. Everything is secure. Except the eldest daughter, Perlita, who is now twelve-and-a-half and living down the hill with her boyfriend, Adan, age 28. Despite Perla's angry imprecations, Perlita ran off with Adan after the rape by the uncle. Adan feeds Perlita and buys her clothes—even a little suit, matching tailored jacket and heels—and they have their own cardboard hut. Everyone admits that despite the age difference, they get along well, Adan doesn't beat Perlita, and there's nothing much to worry about now anyway, since she hasn't yet started menstruating. The Juárez police disagree. The uncle is in prison awaiting trial, but the police have told Perla they cannot prosecute him unless she separates Perlita from Adan, and that if she doesn't, the people who will be indicted are Adan and Perla. Still Perlita refuses to move back home. "I love him," she says with a pout. Once I went to Perla's house to deliver an old roller-style washing machine (from my neighbor who makes the tamales. I never told her it was me she gave the dollar to). Perla was in El Paso selling contraband fruit, so Adan climbed up the hill to help out. Turns out he worked in Las Cruces for awhile and even speaks some English. We talked about Perlita and their problems. "The biggest one is that we need water," Adan said. He pointed to the colonia's only supply: an algae-encrusted washtub under a spigot, leaking a few rusty drops per minute.

W E USED TO LOCK ourselves in the lab, after everyone had gone, and sit and do things in chairs. It was exciting. My husband said most of the rabbits had no personalities but that some did. The ones that bit and screamed, he gave little nicknames to, nicknames like "Fang" and "69," taken from gang graffiti on the New York subways. Around then, my husband (who of course wasn't yet my husband) developed the gnawing suspicion that every time I arrived late at the lab and said I'd accidentally taken a local train instead of an express—that this excuse was a lie, and that in fact I'd been detained because of dates with other men; and that his secret inner wrath sometimes drove him to frenzy. He confessed this one night while the white rabbits stared at us with their blind albino eyes. We got it straightened out and sat again in the chair, surrounded by the animals and by the toxins. There was a Jamaican cleaning lady who we always thought might barge in on us in the dark, with her hoary mops and buckets on wheels. We wondered what she would say, and what we would.

THE REGION FIVE CONFERENCE includes a panel called "The Free Trade Story: U.S. and Mexico Journalists' Perspectives." A woman TV reporter laments that her station cannot financially afford more than cursory coverage of this important issue. A dapper, Spanish-surnamed businessman then takes the floor—a man who has spent the bulk of this conference interjecting, as often as possible, that people of his ethnicity and people of the border are in a better position than any others to promote free trade and to profit from this world-historic opportunity. Now this man announces that his business association will gladly subsidize the reporter's TV station; all it has to do is broadcast a special program on free trade. He is greeted by polite silence and a quick change of subject. He does not seem to apprehend that his offer is seen as crass, as an insult to the objectivity of the media.

Perhaps that is because this man understands more about the local border culture than do people from interior Region Five places like Dallas. It is no secret, for instance, that Suzanne Michaels, El Paso's best-looking and highest-rated news anchorwoman, has been working a second job: at a trade publication financed, published and edited by maquila developers, that comes out monthly on cassette tape (perfect listening, the promotional literature says, for twin plant executives "waiting in line to cross a bridge").

Suzanne Michaels' crisp voice is promoted in this talking magazine as that of "news anchor for the ABC-TV affiliate station in El Paso." On the cassettes, she cheerily recites such events as "the recent visit of Mexican President Carlos Salinas de Gortari and U.S. President George Bush!" and "the just-concluded Border Trade Alliance Conference, held in Washington, D.C.!" It is not clear who writes the "news" scripts for this publication. Suzanne's own writing, however—in the magazine's "Bienvenidos" section—describes her view of the border. It is, she says, "an entity all its own, a curious combination simmering ethnicity, languages and customs into a blend as spicy as a bowl of chile." Suzanne invites her audience to read the magazine and listen to the tapes, since "There's nothing like a good bowl of chile."

THE Pan American Health Organization, which has assisted in the cholera conference at UTEP, distributes to journalists a xeroxed publication from its parent World Health Organization, titled *The Diarrhoeal Diseases Control Programme*. The programme, which has been designed for places like Bangladesh, advises the sanitation authorities of affected countries that "Funerals for those who die of cholera should be held quickly, near the place of death. Efforts should be made, through intensive health education or by legislation, to limit funeral gatherings, ritual washing of the dead, or feasting."

At the conference of reporters, I ponder this advice, thinking about our own gatherings, our feastings and washings. I thumb through the other programme, of the Hispanic journalists, and see that at the bottom some wag—no doubt from the

*El Paso Times* or the *Herald-Post*—has inserted a slightly misquoted quote from Graham Greene:

"How can life on the border be other than reckless. You are pulled by different ties of love and hate."

I go home, wondering if my husband is awake yet. Before I get a chance to find out, Perla is at the door. Mira, she says happily, pointing to her bag of limes. Inexplicably, the Department of Agriculture has just legalized their importation. They're a popular item in my neighborhood, and now Perla won't have to worry about having her wares seized at the river or about ringing the doorbell of the angry man with the business card. Now she's free to trade. Chuyito, unfortunately, still has diarrhea. But she has taken him to a doctor, and she is hopeful.

As for me, I plan to take Perla's limes and bake a pie, using a recipe I clipped from a newspaper section that used to be called Women, but now is headlined Style. My children tonight are invited to sleepovers at friends'. It'll be just us tonight, my husband and I. I plan to be with him and I plan to use the limes. I plan to wash everything first. Everything.

Luis Alberto Urrea

# None of Them Talk About Their Dreams

## Dompe Dreams

IMAGINE THIS: a muscular storm came in during the last days, and as we drove into the Tijuana dump, we were greeted with an apocalyptic scene. Let me try to describe it. The dump, as you probably know, is cheek-to-jowl with a rangy home-built cemetery. In fact, many of the graves are partially covered in trash. A section of this graveyard is a potter's field for poor babies and children, and many of the graves are decorated with the cribs of the dead. This is backed by a small village of shacks where the garbage-pickers live. So it's three rings of Hell: shacks, graves, garbage. The garbage used to be in a canyon about 150 feet deep; it is now a hill about 40 feet high. Above this hill is a seething crown of 10,000 gulls, crows, pigeons. But mostly gulls. Imagine, further, mud. Running yellow, brown, reddish wastewater. The few graves with cement slabs covering them glistening with rain. The mud is almost black. The sky is raging: knots of clouds speed by far above the gulls, and the gulls rise so high that they seem an optical illusion: from huge birds to nearly invisible specks in the sky, held in place by the violent wind.

Now, we drive in, and the muddy graves are pale blue and pale green and pale brown as their wooden crosses fade; the cement headstones are all white or streaked rainy gray. And from the hill of trash, hundreds, perhaps *thousands*, of plastic bags—tan bags, blue bags, white pharmacy bags and black trash bags, yellow bread wrappers and video bags—along with long streamers of computer paper, notebook paper, newspaper opened like wings, ribbons of toilet paper, tissues like dancing moths, even balloons, are caught in a backdraft and are rising and falling in vast slow waves, slow-motion, a ballet in the air of this particolored trash, looking like special effects, like some art department's million dollar creation, silent, ghostly and stately, for a half mile, rolling in the air, turning, looping.

And up top, exposed to the elements, the garbage is flying like a snowstorm. We lean into it at angles, held up by the wind. The garbage pickers are wrapped in bags to keep the rain off them. Huge tractors churn through the mud. My Jeep slides sideways, slipping through the mess. And the goo squishes up to our ankles. Boxes, panties, magazines, more bags, always plastic bags: flying and shooting off the summit to snow down on the distant village. I watch paper drift down onto the roofs, ads for stoves and dog food form sentimental white drifts of faux snow on the housetops. Beneath us, the slowly revolving magic bags. Above us, the infinite swirl of gulls. And garbage hurricanes lift off all around us: the photographer thirty yards away from the young woman and me is dwarfed by a whirlwind of trash—it rises twenty, thirty feet above his head, and he stands at the apex, shooting us with our arms around each other, holding on in the wind. Her breasts wet with running milk. Our eyes running tears from the wind. A pack of dogs tries to attack us, and an Indian woman name Dona Chuy heads them off;

one scraggly bitch with long dark teats has one eye ripped out of its socket, and pus is caked to her face, and she makes me want to throw up, but reveals herself to be the world's sweetest dog, and rubs all over my legs and grins and wags and generally demands to be petted. So I try to find a spot free of pus.

Behind us, as the rain begins again, a funeral procession winds its way down the narrow mud tracks, men in wet cowboy hats and boots pull shovels out of a station wagon and wrestle a coffin over the hillocks to a likely spot; ladies with lace veils are buffeted by the wind; endless plastic bags blow between them like fleeing ghosts.

And later, in the warmth, the young woman I have known since she was six nurses her daughter, and we smile as the little mouth gobbles the huge black nipple and this tired Indian mother and I hold hands as the rain hammers at the tarpaper.

Can you imagine such a scene?

▪ ▪ ▪

NOBODY KNEW what happened to the boys' parents. Not even the boys—Chacho, Elijio, Carlos and Jorge—could explain what had happened to them. As is so often the case in Tijuana, one day the boys woke up and their parents were gone. Papa had apparently gone across the wire, into the U.S. Mama blew away like a puff of smoke. The four brothers were alone in the Tijuana garbage dump.

For a few nights, the younger boys wept as Chacho, the fierce elder brother, pulled together a small homestead amidst the garbage. They went hungry for awhile, not having any dump survival skills. The trash-pickers gave them what food they could spare, but that wasn't much. And missionaries came into the dump with goodies, but Chacho didn't trust gringos, so he kept the boys away. Besides, the gringos gave baths and nobody was going to get Chacho naked.

One day, an old man appeared in the dump. He wore grimy old suits and had no past and no home. His left arm had come out of the socket years before, and he had wandered, half-crippled, from dump to dump, looking for young people to care for him. Chacho struck a bargain with him: if he would look out for the younger boys, then Chacho and Elijio would pick trash for them all. They had a new family unit.

The old man set up shop in an upended Maytag appliance box. Inside, the boys slept with him on a mat of newspaper and cardboard. They used cast-off clothes scavenged from the dump for blankets. The old man spent much of each day inside, where he often wept.

He had a passion for avocados, and he could often be found in a green puddle of muddy guacamole, drunk and sprawled in the fruit.

Chacho set up his own small shack on a low rise above the trash. There, he acquired a pistol. Then, he stole a pony from an outlying ranch and built a corral made of bedsprings and stolen wood. His brothers began attending the gringo bathing sessions, and Elijio brought home animals—unwanted puppies, piglets swiped or bartered. Chacho used his horse to steal cows.

THE OLD MAN moved on. He tied his floppy arm to his side with twine and rags, set his straw hat on his head, and wandered off with what few things he could muster in a plastic bag. Elijio, Carlos and Jorge were working the trash and came home to a silent box.

They went to Chacho, but Chacho was now a pistolero at twelve, too tough and macho to care. He told them to take care of themselves, that life was shit, that the brothers needed no one. So the boys went back to their box and crawled in alone.

Soon, they were used to it. Elijio, being the next oldest, kept watch over them. And Chacho, their legendary big brother, also watched them from his elevated compound. People knew to leave the boys alone, or Chacho would be there with his pistol. When he cut up a calf, he gave them meat. When there was money, he bought them Cokes. And he herded them to the baths every two weeks, where only one of them would submit to the water, but they all took home bags of doughnuts.

BOYS IN THE DUMP have their own playground of sorts. There is always something to do. Collecting trash is always hard work, yet it offers endlessly changing collections of strangeness. The boys could find clothes sometimes, or tins of food, water-damaged pornography, and even toys cast out by the ricos in the Tijuana hills. Once they even found a load of fetuses dumped in the trash by the city. "Dead babies," everyone was saying. "They left dead babies in the dump." People were afraid, able only to envision some desperately evil deed that would kill so many infants. To the boys, raised in squalor, the most squalid details became, by default, entertaining. Although Elijio loved animals, the sight of a diseased dog being eaten alive by a pack of other dogs was exciting.

There were always rats to kill, fires to set, food to steal. They could spy on the women when they went off to the side to urinate. And there were always drunks getting in fights: women beating each other up in rolling tangles, men flashing knives.

They even had their own private lake. On the hill above Chacho's horse pens, the city had built a huge pila to hold water for the community on the other, civilized, side of the dump hill. The part of the reservoir above ground was the size of a warehouse, and it didn't take long for the boys to break through the cement block corner at the top and climb in. They gathered inside the shadowy structure and swam in the water, diving from the maintenance catwalks and floating in the city's water supply.

Of course, the one game they most loved and that everyone—

from Chacho to the Mixtec Indians—warned them away from, was the most dangerous. The boys loved to ride the backs of garbage trucks.

ELIJIO THOUGHT he had a firm grip on the big ugly truck. Retired from San Diego, the truck was heavy with trash, its hunched back dark and rusty, its smokestack belching black smoke. The boys had spent the morning running up behind the trucks as they entered the dump and hopping on the back ends, hanging on to the hand-holds the garbagemen used. Sometimes they clung to the sides like little spiders, swinging over the wheelwells as the trucks banged over trash mounds.

Elijio had run behind the truck, flung himself at it and grabbed the edge of the open maw in back. The other boys shouted good-natured insults: "Faggot!" and "Coward!" He turned to laugh at them, hanging on with one hand and starting to signal to them. The truck slammed on its brakes. Elijio swung sharply forward, smacked into the truck and bounced off, falling on his back. The truck ground its gears and lurched into reverse. The boys yelled for Elijio to get out of the way. Carlos and Jorge stood staring. Elijio tried to scramble out on his back, but he was already bruised from hitting the metals and falling. He could barely move. The truck's vast double-axled rear wheels rolled up his body and over his chest, all eight wheels crushing him to death.

The truck driver shut off the engine and hopped out to unload the trash. He couldn't figure out why all the boys were screaming.

THE DUMP PEOPLE don't always knit together. Sheer survival makes it difficult to look out for their fellows. But death sometimes unites them. If the death is sad enough.

Everyone knew Elijio's story. They had all said at one time or another that someone should do something about those boys, but nobody had done much. Now, they were resolved to make good in death.

They came up with the money to buy Elijio a small suit. Some of the Mixtec men collected raw particle-board and hammered together a coffin. They set it inside the dirt-floor shack where the gringos had been bathing the kids. The wife of one of them took Jorge and Carlos in among her own brood. She had given birth to her last child in this same shack, cutting the umbilical cord herself with a steak knife.

Chacho took a bath. He stuck his pistol into his belt, got drunk, and wailed over Elijio. All the tough guys in the dump lost it over the boy. None of them knew how to deal with this tragedy —it was somehow worse than the other tragedies. The men wept openly, inconsolably.

Ironically, a bus-load of fresh-faced American Jesus-Teens pulled up and unloaded thirty happy campers to Minister to the Poor. The Mexicans stood away from them and muttered amongst themselves. The youth pastor sent the gringo kids inside the shack in small groups to see what life was really like. After they'd all looked in on the crushed Elijio, they mounted their bus and motored off, some other Good Works no doubt awaiting them elsewhere.

Jorge, the youngest brother, stayed outside the shack, playing marbles. He didn't show the least interest in Elijio's corpse. As Chacho stood beside the coffin, crying out his pain, Carlos snuck in and peered at the body. He reached out and prodded Elijio's face with his fingers, apparently to make sure his brother was really dead. He went outside and re-joined the marble game.


THE MEN OF THE DUMP hammered a lid onto the box and carried it outside. They mounted it in the back of a pickup. Chacho and the boys rode with the box. Directly behind the pickup was a flatbed, filled to capacity with standing men. The men passed a bottle. Bringing up the rear was a lone gringo van, with a couple of missionaries.

The procession headed off across the hills, into a region not seen by gringos, where there were no roads. They drove up a hill, where the dump people had created their own graveyard. Little crosses made of sticks dotted the sere hill. Bits of fancy garbage decorated a few graves.

"It's boot hill," the pastor said.

The men traded turns with the shovel, cracking, then scraping out the rocky soil. It took quite a while to make the hole, but between them they managed it.

They manhandled the box into it and stood around looking at it. Chacho almost fell in, he cried so hard. The men quietly went to work, pushing dirt and rocks back into the hole. Others who couldn't get close to the shoveling, went from grave to grave, pulling dry weeds and picking up paper. Some of the crosses needed straightening. A couple of guys made borders of rock around unmarked graves.

Jorge never went close to the grave. But if you paid close attention, you could see Carlos moving in behind Chacho's legs. Then, at the last possible moment, he grabbed a little handful of dust and pitched it into the hole.

## Pink Penitentiary

SOME OF THE CHILDREN of the dompes end up in orphanages scattered in the hills near their homes. In Tijuana, orphanages are not always really for orphans; they house "niños necesitados," or needy children. Children who cannot be cared for at home, children who have lost a parent to the border, or children who have been caught unattended by the police and brought in for care. Their other option is the children's prison, east of town.

One would think that a life in an orphanage would be preferable to a life on the trash.

SIX A.M. The dogs have been awake for an hour already, charging back and forth between the gates, growling at passing trucks and the drunks lurching home from all-night parties. In the compound, the chickens are clucking, and the voices of the boys can be heard. A cement basketball court lies upon the dirt of the big yard. On it, one small boy lies face-down, asleep. His partner, who is ten years old, is still up. He's swaying with exhaustion, but he's still awake because he knows if he's found asleep, he'll have to kneel out here all night again. The boys got in trouble. He stole gum; his sleeping buddy got in a fist fight. When these things happen, the orphanage director, who lives high above them in his apartment perched atop the building, comes down, scolds them, makes them read Bible verses, then forces them to kneel on the cement. All night. It happens to everybody, sooner or later.

Rubén, the eldest boy, is now in the kitchen, opening cans and cracking eggs. Rubén is worried—two of the other older boys have been sodomizing each other when they think the other boys in the dormitory are asleep. But Rubén is up later than everyone else. He wants to be a misssionary to the Tarahumara Indians, so he studies his Bible late into the night, and after lights out, he thinks about the scriptures.

Lying there, he hears the boys whisper, then the blanket on each bed rustle, and the sly creak of the springs. One of the boys has been reprimanded before for coercing littler boys to have oral sex with him. Rubén doesn't know what to do. He doesn't want to be a squealer, but he knows it's a sin. And it upsets him greatly to listen to the rhythmic creaking of the bedframe.

In the kitchen, he hauls out the huge frying pans. A young woman who lives at the far end of the compound with her husband comes in—the only female in the orphanage, save for the director's wife and daughter. And Hermana Conchita, a strange crone who lives in a small storage room beside the big room where they keep the clothes and shoes and blankets.

The cook rifles through the hundred loaves of old bread donated by the gringos, trying to find enough slices that are not moldy. If they're stiff and dried out, she toasts them. The boys won't notice. The bad slices can go to the dogs and the chickens. She melts lard and Rubén begins cracking over 100 eggs. This morning, there will be forty-two boys at the table, along with a couple of adults.

Some of the younger boys who worship Rubén, make pests of themselves as they scurry around behind him, trying to help.

EZEKIEL, who the boys call Cheque, is almost blind. He's sleeping in the nursery this week, keeping watch of the little ones. He changes their diapers and hustles them to the dual toilets raised on a pedestal to the rear of the room. There, pairs of little boys grunt away while the others watch. Cheque's thick glasses make him seem humorous, his eyes through the lenses are huge and seem to float beyond the plane of his face. Like a cartoon. And he jokes with them, able to be hip among the two-year-olds. "Oralé, morros—hagan caca, pues." (All right, little dudes, make that poo!) His brother is addicted to glue, and has melted enough of his brain so that he seems to slosh, somehow—his ideas loose in his head and runny.

Upstairs, the boys are stirring. Their bunk beds smell of urine. The boys are grumpy, dressed in their street clothes because they don't have enough blankets. Well, they have enough, but the director will not allow them to use them. He's saving them for future use. The one boy who gets two blankets has a bunk up against a shattered window. He sleeps year-round in the blowing air. When it rains hard, he sometimes tucks some cardboard in the hole to keep the water off him. The director applauds this. He likes to see such initiative. But he doesn't fix the window.

Radios are a sin, unless they're tuned to a Christion station. However, the Christian stations are sinful because they play music with drums. Drums in all their forms are evil: they convey the Satanic beats of Negro religion. All drums are instruments of voodoo and pagan cult activity. Hence, the so-called "Jesus-Rock" is a deception that is misleading the Saints in these Last Days. Likewise electrically-amplified instruments. Electric guitars are evil both in sound and intent, though country-western and ranchera music utilizes them, so the director is sometimes willing to make exceptions.

Rock'n'roll, as always, is more powerful than authority. It's everywhere. He's exhausted from trying to catch every demonic sex-inducing radio. Often, he just walks by the boys as they listen to the Devil's Music and shakes his head. They know what he thinks—maybe this Witness is enough. Later in life, perhaps his example will pull them away from some evil deed. He tells himself that the very fact that he's tired and can't keep up with rock music is proof of how evil it is.

Downstairs, there is a great commotion. Hermana Conchita is beating one of the boys.

Most of the older boys hate her. Many of them have never known a mother, or have only seen her on three or four weekends a year. Hermana Conchita is about it.

She uses a rubber hose. When she flies into one of her unexplained rages, she flogs the boys around the shoulders and faces with it, beating them into corners where they can't escape. The director, in his fourth-floor aerie, says it's not true.

She's got the hose now, and she's swinging.

Hermana Conchita has a problem, though. She didn't count on growing old—or her charges getting bigger. It's the law of diminishing returns. Many of her victims tower over her now, and they could easily break her arm. As she pounds one of the little boys, he's heartened by the jeers of the bigger boys, who she cannot hurt now. Her hose whacks the little guy across the shoulders, and he winces, then he starts to laugh at her.

"Witch," Cheque taunts. "Hag. Bitch." (Perra: female dog, not evil woman.) "Hit me now," he says, his headlamp eyes bright behind the lenses. "Hit me now." He's hopping around on one foot, hands held up as if to box. He is as cool as they get this morning. The other boys call out to him, urging him on.

Everybody's scuffling around in a loose knot, flowing up and down the big yard. The boy kneeling on the cement has yet to be released from his sentence. His buddy has awakened and blessed his good luck and struggled back up on his knees, undiscovered. To protect himself, though, he has had to throw bloody warnings all bout him: "You tell him I fell asleep, and you'll get yours!" he threatens. What they don't know is that the director is watching gringo television and eating donated waffles upstairs; he has forgotten all about them and won't remember till he sees them when he wanders down. They watch the Conchita-baiting with dull fascination.

"What are we doing in school today?" one asks the other.

But he doesn't answer. He has started to cry.

"Aw, come on," his buddy says.

"I want my mother," the boy says.

"Well," the first boy says, "she'll probably come this weekend. You'll see."

"Really?" he says. And he wipes his nose on his sleeve.

THE TOILETS ARE FULL to the brim. They are brown and solid, and of the four, two are running over. A thin slick of shit seeps across the floor and makes a scum at the drain-hole. The boys sometimes put their feet on the rim and let fly from a foot high. There is a sign written on the plywood partitions between the toilets. Someone has written it with charcoal. Maybe Rubén—he's thoughtful enough to have done it.

The sign says:

PLEASE DON'T SHIT ON THE FLOOR

PLEASE DON'T WIPE YOUR ASS WITH YOUR FINGERS
PLEASE DON'T WIPE YOUR FINGERS ON THE WALL

Ancient brown fingerprints and smears angle away from this notice, trailing to faint shadow. They look like paintings of comets, of fireworks.

FAUSTO has a chicken. This chicken rides on his shoulders. His father brought him in and said, "He's no good. I want nothing to do with him again." Fausto kept a stony face the whole time. "You can have him," his father said. "I don't care what you do with him."

Once, Fausto ran away to try to find his mother. He traveled deep into Mexico, knowing she was some sort of cantina girl. He was about thirteen, probably. Tall and skinny, with huge eyes that watered easily. He searched in whorehouses in the interior, sleeping under cars, in parks. He finally found his own hometown. When he found the cantina, they told him she had died the week before he got there.

Now, he keeps to the chickens. Sometimes he beats up smaller boys. This morning, he ignores the fight with Conchita. He hunches down in the small chicken coop the other boys have helped him build. He makes small kisses with his lips. The chicken steps on his wrist, then begins to work its way up to his shoulder, wings held open like the arms of a tight-rope walker.

RUBÉN COMES OUT and claps his hands. "A comer!" he orders. (To eat!)

Cheque is a little wild with the fight—his face is flushed and he's skipping around, cussing. His brother, still fried from last night's glue-sniffing, eggs him on. Rubén has to grab him and bang some cocos (noogies) into the top of his head.

Cheque goes in to eat, rubbing his head and wincing, making deadly threats all around. The boys kneeling ask,

"Can we come in?"

Rubén glances up at the director's apartment.

"No," he says.

When they complain, he says, "Next time, you'll behave better. Talk to the Lord."

At the huge tables, the boys cram in elbow to elbow. The director descends. They can hear him asking the boys outside if they're sorry for what they did.

"Yes, sir," they say.

Will they commit such sins again?

"No, sir."

Well, maybe he'll let them up...after breakfast. They can clean the kitchen.

They moan.

He comes in.

"Good morning," he says.

"Good morning," they all respond.

"How are we this morning?"

"Fine."

Somebody blurts, "Cheque got in a fight with Conchita."

Cheque's out of his seat. "Liar!" he shouts. "She was using the hose!"

"Cheque," the director warns. "What happens to trouble makers?"

Cheque sits back down, grumbling.

"We'll talk later."

Bold now to save face, Cheque murmurs their version of "I don't give a fuck." (Me vale madre.)

The director rushes toward him, a small burst of rage in his eyes that makes Cheque flinch. The director's son, somewhat of a hero to the boys, comes in.

"I'll handle it," he tells his father. He goes to Cheque and grabs his shoulder and says, "Let's go outside."

They exit.

"Ohh," the boys say. The director beams. He enjoys happy

highjinks. Boys will be boys.

"Let us pray," he says.

I T'S TIME for clothes distribution. Before school, the boys petition the orphanage director for shoes, or coats, or pants, or blankets. He stands in the doorway and inspects them.

"My shirt's torn," says one. "I need a new one."

"It's not my fault," the director says. I didn't tear it, did I?"

"But it's torn!"

"You should have thought about that before you tore it!"

"I'll throw this one away!" the boy threatens.

"If you're that stupid," the director quips, "go right ahead!" He laughs. The boys laugh.

"Can I have a new shirt?"

"No."

T HEY RUSH off to school.

The dogs take over the big yard. One of the bigger boys thinks it's funny to sneak into the coop and kill Fausto's chicken. Fausto won't know until this evening, when he comes home in his tired uniform.

One of the dogs, Capitan, has never had a ball to chase. He has learned to pick up a rock in his mouth and toss it, then chase the rock around the yard. Sometimes, he barks at the rock.

Tonight, while the boy sleeps, Capi, as they call him, will swallow the rock. He will choke on it, and they will find him dead on the basketball court. Even the director will cry. But for today, Capi has play and sleep and garbage-raiding and dog fights ahead of him. And this evening, he will be manhandled by at least thirty of the boys.

The cook stays in the nursery, playing with the little ones. They are a wild gaggle of tykes, and they sometimes descend on her as one, all of them wanting hugs at once. The two boys on the slab are allowed up. The one who fell asleep can walk; the other cannot. The director allows him to stay home from school today. He hobbles off to bed, the director telling him he's a good boy after all.

Cheque has put a t-shirt on under his uniform. It says "Dr. Zogg's Sex Wax." Cheque knows he's cool. He has a small radio and he plays it full blast as he be-bops down the dirt road, the speaker distorting the Devil's Music into an indecipherable gargle. He shouts out the lyrics and tells the little guys he'll kick everybody's ass if they don't do exactly what he says.

His brother vanishes half-way to school. They'll find him asleep after school. He'll be smiling.

WHEN THEY GET HOME, the meal cycle will begin again. Then basketball until it's too dark to see. Then bed.
None of them talk about their dreams.

Dick J. Reavis

# The Last of the Border Lords

O N A THURSDAY AFTERNOON in late 1986, a crowd gathered at the Church of the Holy Spirit in Nuevo Laredo to lay Octaviano "Chito" Longoria to rest. Longoria, 81, who died after a long and debilitating illness, had built the Church of the Holy Spirit and much of the economy of Nuevo Laredo and the whole Mexican border. But the service for him was a small one, limited to family and friends, nothing like the citywide show of mourning that had accompanied his father's death sixty years earlier.

When Chito Longoria died, a legend and the memory of a dynasty were buried with him. Longoria had headed the family that owned the border's largest industrial concern, its biggest banking chain, and its fattest portfolio of real estate. But he had played for high stakes and gambled at long odds. He had been bold, and most members of his family believed that for the past twenty years, especially since his marriage to the former Jeanette Jaffe of San Antonio, he had played too far afield and had caused loss. Their doubt stung him; even on his deathbed, Chito spoke to few of his family critics.

Intimates of the Longorias were impressed when Chito's widow and his estranged brothers greeted one another at the funeral with apparent civility. The new relationship between them was largely a result of Jeanette's decision to allow Chito to be buried next to his first wife, Alicia Penn, whom the family had regarded in a much more favorable light. "Everything went well at the funeral," one surprised observer said, "because Jeanette decided to give Chito back to the family."

But the story of the man and the family who were the border's most prominent institution does not begin with Chito or his marriage to Jeanette. Instead, it begins with his father, Don Octaviano Longoria, Sr., who came to Nuevo Laredo when both he and the city were adolescents and rose to become its modern-day father.

ON OCTAVIANO was a squat, bronze-skinned, square-headed man whose career more closely resembled that of a Horatio Alger hero than anything from the Mexican folklore or the literature of the times, which exalted generals and revolutionaries but denigrated men of business. He was born in 1871 to a provincial middle-class family in the village of Mier, just a few miles south of the Rio Grande on the road between Nuevo Laredo and Matamoros. Mier was a border town, but in spirit it was a hamlet of the interior, wrapped in its own insular traditons, indifferent to commerce.

Don Octaviano's mother had died during his childhood, and in 1887, when he was sixteen, he ran off to Nuevo Laredo to escape his stepmother. He lived with relatives who while not poor could not afford to fund his education. But Nuevo Laredo was brimming with opportunity. Six years earlier, two railroads had come to Laredo to connect with a line that ran south to Monterrey, and overnight the two Laredos had established themselves as centers for import-export trade. Their populations had jumped from less than two thousand each to nearly five times as much, and both were still growing. Mier's only business was farming, in the ancient way, but Nuevo Laredo's business was business. Young Octaviano found a job as a clerk in a combination dry goods and grocery store, and after a brief apprenticeship, because he had caught the spirit of competition, he opened a grocery store of his own. He then set himself up as Nuevo Laredo's distributor of beers from Monterey's burgeoning Cuauhtémoc brewery. When Prohibition was declared in the United States, Don Octaviano started an ice plant in Nuevo Laredo to supply the needs of the bars that were suddenly opening up all over town to serve thirsty gringos.

The bars took in dollars, and Don Octaviano added an exchange house to convert them to pesos. His grocery and exchange house brought him a lot of cash, and wholesale customers sometimes asked for credit, so he bought a floor safe and became a banker. Then he acquired ranchlands that had been collateral for bad loans. With a ranch in his portfolio, he could easily have retired to the courtly, leisurely life of a hacienda. But Don Octaviano was not cut out to be a hacendado.

On the border he had learned to think like an American businessman. When a drought came Don Octaviano, instead of seeing it as part of the age-old burdens of the gentry, saw it as an opportunity. He established a mill that made and sold cottonseed cake, a cattle feed, to ranchers on both sides of the border. Cottonseed could also be pressed, he knew, for oils that could be refined into a dozen consumer goods. The border in those days essentially was not a place where things were made but a place where things were exchanged. Don Octaviano, however, didn't let the border's traditions hold him back. On two square blocks west of Nuevo Laredo's train station, he built plants for producing cooking oil, lard, and laundry soap. Industrias Unidas, or United Industries, as he called his operation, was the city's first modern factory complex.

Don Octaviano had also taken advantage of opportunities in real estate. He had seen the caliche plots he had bought on a hunch turn into commercial properties as Nuevo Laredo grew to 10,000 and then to 20,000. He crowned his and the city's rise in 1929 by erecting Nuevo Laredo's most impressive structure, the Banco Longoria's limestone-and-marble home. His name was chiseled above its entrance in letters two feet high.

He had succeeded in domestic life too. In 1900, at 29, he had married Sarah H. Theriot, a delicate, dark-haired woman of 24. Sarah was a descendant of Confederate Creoles from Louisiana and Confederate Anglos from East Texas. Her father, Alcide, had come to Nuevo Laredo to shake his malaria and had founded the city's first pharmacy. His older brother, Shelby, became U.S. consul there. The Theriots also owned little shops that produced shoe polish, inks, and glues. Though the Theriots were more prominent in town than the orphan from Mier, by 1900 Octaviano seemed more golden than bronze, because his grocery was prospering. Sarah's family blessed the marriage.

Sarah Theriot bore five sons and three daughters for her husband, all of whom would be educated in the United States. By 1931 Don Octaviano was taking counsel in business affairs with his two oldest sons, Octaviano or "Chito," 25, and Federico, 24, young men of exceptional and disparate talents. Chito was the family's budding entrepreneur. As a child, he'd hawked jasmine blossoms from his mother's garden to the lovers and mariachis who came to Nuevo Laredo's plazas at night. He also salvaged cracked eggs from his father's warehouse and peddled them by the cupfuls in the city's open-air markets. As a teenager, he had managed the exchange house and grocery, even attended bankers' conventions. Federico, the family's second son, was less venturesome. Like a hacendado heir, he was as quiet and tradition-centered as his brother was spontaneous and daring.

Despite his considerable success and stature, Don Octaviano had never been a self-confident man; he was humble, even receding. He had earned a reputation of being hardworking, moderate in habits and opinion, shrewd but prudent with his money. He was nearly always serious, even melancholy. In his later years, as his two oldest sons took over his business affairs, Don Octaviano was always struggling to dispel forebodings of futility. Black moods overwhelmed him, his progeny say, moods in which his own defects and the smallest of difficulties of life took on frightening stature in his mind. Nothing he did delivered him from his gloom. Early in 1931, in an attempt to escape a wave of depression, Don Octaviano had begun sleeping in the little room above the bank. The change didn't help. On the morning of January 12, after he had finished shaving, instead of dressing in the suit and coat and vest he had laid out for the day, Don Octaviano reached into a drawer for his pearl-handled revolver, put its barrel to his forehead, and fired. Three pesos and a lottery ticket were in his pockets when he died.

WHEN DON OCTAVIANO'S BODY was discovered on the Monday of his death, Chito and Federico faced their first decision as successors to his legend. They had to decide whether to respond to his passing with grandiose Mexican grief and wailing, or to suppress their tears like gringos, remaining at their posts in the hope of dispelling a rush on the bank. They discussed their options, and agreed. With what San Antonio's Spanish-language daily, *La Prensa*, termed the "impassive frigidity of business," they kept the bank open—past normal business hours, all the way until midnight. Don Octaviano's corpse was sent to Laredo for embalming, and three days later was paraded south to a burial ground in an international procession that was twenty blocks and 170 vehicles long. The founder's funeral was the largest in Nuevo Laredo's history.

Don Octaviano had willed everything he owned to his widow, Doña Sara, who either gave or entrusted all of his businesses to her five sons. Reponsibility for managing the Longoria fortune fell upon Chito, the firstborn son, and Federico to whom deference was due. A new order arose in the Longoria family, with Chito as its head.

Chito saw himself as his father's equal, not as his heir. By his accounting, he had been the mastermind of much of the older man's success. Chito even claimed that he, not Don Octaviano, had designed the bank. His father's great weakness as a businessman, he told the family, was that he had made investments in a spirit both timid and slow. In Chito's eyes, Don Octaviano had left the Longoria family little more than a stake. Chito was determined to parlay that stake into an eternal estate.

His unbridled optimism and self-assurance led to incidents of foolhardiness. In the late thirties, for example, he decided that the family should have a weekend home on its ranch. He staked out the one-story design for workmen, then stood by to admire his efforts. "I like it," he told the construction crew. "Build me a second story just like it." Chito's workmen were faithful to his orders, even unto absurdity. The house they built had a kitchen upstairs, as well as a living room and exterior doors. But it had no staircase, because Chito had drawn none; in his excitement, he had overlooked that detail. He was amused by the new house. A little foolhardiness, he believed, was a small price to pay for genius. But for months the Longorias had to climb ladders to reach the second story of their retreat.

Keeping up with Chito became Federico's task, along with managing the bank. Federico regarded himself as a conservator, not as a spinner of schemes. His ambitions were limited, but in practical terms his power was great. Cautious and deferential by nature, he didn't challenge Chito directly. But as family treasurer, Federico could rathole capital funds or pledge them to dozens of safe, minor projects. In effect, Federico was able to pull Chito's financial reins.

The symbiosis of the two elder sons paid off in wondrous ways. During the next forty years, the Longorias became the royal family of Mexican cotton. They built or bought 52 gins, most of them in northern Mexico, and each year they brokered the sale and sometimes financed the production of nearly a sixth of the nation's cotton crop, an important earner of foreign exchange. With financing from Federico, Chito turned Industrias Unidas, their father's toehold in the food-processing trade, into a network of seven plants for refining cottonseed oil and four for milling flour. The family established nearly a dozen plants that supplied bottled gas to three northern states, and it acquired lumberyards, hotels, theaters, ice plants, and auto dealerships in Reynosa, Matamoros, and both Laredos. The Banco Longoria established 27 branches across northern Mexico, and the family added two finance companies to its portfolio, each with branches. Piece by piece, they expanded Don Octaviano's real estate empire to four hundred listings, including some 400,000 acres of Mexican ranchland.

Three business principles were the platform of the family's success. The first was self-financing. The Longorias sought only short-term credit for seasonal operating expenses. Because their loan applications were backed by production contracts and warehouse receipts, they did not have to open their books to auditors or account to bankers for their plans. The family's second principle was that of political obeisance. The brothers contributed to Mexico's ruling party, the PRI (Partido Revolucionario Institucional). They volunteered to aid and appease and even make sacrifices to the government, and when favors were offered in return, they accepted them, if their granters wished, with a public show of civic gratitude.

THE ULTIMATE SECRET of the family's empire, however, was not economic or political prudence or even the leadership of the oldest son Chito, as American admirers of the Longorias like to think. Instead, it was the Mexican principle of simple, traditional family unity. The center of family life was not Chito, the business chief, but Doña Sara, the mother of the clan. If Don Octaviano had learned to think like an American, his wife had established a balance by becoming a thoroughly Mexican matriarch. After her husband died, she referred to herself, not as Mrs. Sarah or Mrs. O.L. Longoria, or even as Señora Sara or Señora O.L., but in the old Mexican style, as Sara Theriot, viuda de Longoria—Sarah Theriot, widow of Longoria. She recognized the differences between Mexican and American culture and strongly exemplified those of her adopted land. Doña Sara paid attention to her family, not to her fortune. She was so indifferent to the status of wealth that she never opened a bank account; she kept her funds in a closet of her bedroom in the family homestead. Club, civic, and charitable pursuits didn't occupy her either. She spent her days tending to her gardens and clan, mediating quarrels, dispensing matrimonial advice, asking favors of one relative on behalf of another. The devotion she showed her descendants was matched by an equally Mexican mother-reverence. The family's inviolable reunion came every September, when Doña Sara celebrated her birthday.

While Doña Sara lived, all the family's business affairs were conducted in a very Mexican family way. Title to most of the Longoria enterprises rested in stock certificates that were the property of the bearer. Federico kept the certificates in a filing cabinet in the basement of the Nuevo Laredo bank. Ownership of commercial real estate was assigned to the five brothers or to any of a dozen of their children, almost on the basis of whim. Ranchlands were parceled out among family members or, to evade agrarian reform strictures, registered in the names of business associates and family friends. The assumption that kept the empire together was that stock certificates and deeds were fictions maintained for the convenience of the external world: real ownership rested not in individuals but in the clan.

During their dynastic years, every day at noontime the Longoria sons met for lunch at Doña Sara's house, and in her presence they discussed events of the day and plans of the week. Doña Sara rarely ventured an opinion on business affairs, but Chito and Federico frequently questioned their younger brothers, and when the elder sons disliked an idea it usually died or was revised to their satisfaction on the spot. There were, in effect, no rules of accountability in the Longoria family, only an unspoken primogeniture and mutual family trust.

The Longorias had established blood ties that were strong and vital, and their marriages were models of propriety. None of the sons had ever been divorced, nor had scandal touched them. With the exception of the youngest brother, Alfredo, who married a Mexican aristocrat, the brothers had wed women much like Doña Sara, middle-class Americans raised on the border, fluent in Spanish, content as housewives, able as mothers, and faithful as companions—Mexicanized.

In the late fifties, some 25 years after Don Octaviano's death, his descendants were leading what the orphan from Mier would have regarded as glamorous lives. They were wealthy and well-known in business communities on both sides of the border. Their children were being sent to the best American universities—Chito, Federico, and Shelby had been limited to brief business school educations—and spent their holiday like hacienda heirs, on family ranches. The brothers went on safaris together in Africa and vacationed with their wives in Europe.

THE ONLY BREACHES in the felicity of the Longoria clan, and in its respectability, were in the house of its commander in chief, Chito, and even those were hidden from public view. In 1927 Chito had married Alice Penn, daughter of Don Justo Penn, a Webb County judge and early-day publisher of the *Laredo Times*. Doña Alicia, as she came to be known, took to Mexico and her marriage as Doña Sara had. She became "more Longoria than Penn," Chito often boasted. Their marriage produced two daughters and a son and a fourth child who was a victim of crib death. The short, bright-eyed woman was popular with her in-laws as perhaps no other Longoria wife, and if she was sometimes downcast, she tried not to reveal her sadness publicly. The only problem with Alicia, her friends and in-laws said, was that she drank too much. Chito bore the problem stoically, as he bore everything else. Perhaps he bore too much. Between the ages of fifty and sixty, the span during which Don Octaviano had been pummeled by depression, Chito was also stricken. In both 1959 and 1962 he was briefly hospitalized for electroshock treatments in San Antonio. Members of the family feared that he was following in his father's footsteps.

Chito felt confined, like his father before him. Don Octaviano had been fatally content to change sleeping quarters; Chito had bigger changes in mind. He was weary of the border and the northern provinces. Doña Alicia's death at 58 in 1963 freed him. Whatever grief her passing caused Chito, it helped him break his ties with Nuevo Laredo. He began spending most of his weekdays in Mexico City and taking three-day weekends north of the border in San Antonio.

Chito had business and even patronly ties in San Antonio. During the fifties, he and Texan John Mecom, Jr., had established preserves for exotic game animals on their ranches near the two Laredos. To legalize the importation of their animals from a dozen countries, they had donated the parent stock to the San Antonio zoo, populating their ranches only with the offspring. Chito's patronage of the zoo had opened to him the doors of the social world, which was full of widows and divorcées. With his extensive English and even more extensive fortune, Chito Longoria was a highly desirable guest on the South Texas dinner party circuit.

It was at such a party, a Washington's Birthday celebration in the home of former Laredo mayor Pepe Martin, that Chito first met Jeanette Jaffe. Attractive and ambitious, she was at that time in her late thirties and married to Morris Jaffe, one of San Antonio's wealthiest and most influential citizens.

Jeanette Herrmann had been a daughter of San Antonio society, born in a home preserved at public expense as a landmark. During her marriage to Jaffe, she had done her part as a society housewife and mother, as an adornment to a man of wealth. But she wanted more. Not content merely to sit through coffee klatches and garden shows, she started the drive that built Santa Rosa Children's Hospital, and she sat on the hospital board. She had played a role in designing the Central Park Mall, one of her husband's real estate projects. In the fifties she learned to pilot an airplane, and in the early sixties she was hosting a television talk show. And she had done all of this while raising her six children.

In social affairs Chito was a propriety-conscious, staid Mexican conservative, and an extreme one at that: he always wore a business suit, even on safari. He had never known a woman as independent as Jeanette. As a frequent houseguest of the Jaffes, he may have felt a romantic attraction for Jeanette, but he kept it to himself. But in late 1964 he found a project whose success, he believed, required her collaboration.

Doña Sara had for years wanted to build a chapel in Nuevo Laredo, much as Don Octaviano had built her one in Mier, to show gratitude for her good fortune. After Doña Alicia died, Chito had taken charge of executing his mother's wish. His first decision—it was the signature of the man—had been to enlarge its scope. Chito envisioned not a mere capilla or chapel, but a full-fledged church. He picked a site for the church too: across from the public square that faced his mansion in the new Colonia Madero, or Colonia Longoria, as it was popularly called. He had commissioned architects to produce plans for the church he had in mind, but he hadn't liked their drawings. He thought that Jeanette Jaffe might have better ideas.

After marrying Morris, Jeanette had come to Catholicism with a convert's zeal. For their home at 300 Alameda Circle, she had designed an expensively appointed chapel at which under her enticement even bishops had performed private masses. She was also unimpressed by the architect's drawings Chito showed her, and she was disturbed by the name Doña Sara had chosen for the project, Church of the Holy Family. What bothered Jeanette wasn't that the church's name and the Colonia Longoria location would give wiseacres an excuse to quip. Jeanette believed that the appeal of the Holy Family was waning. She persuaded Chito that Holy Spirit was a more contemporary concept, worthy of the church's name despite his mother's wishes. The two sketched out a new plan, and within months the church began rising out of the ground opposite the Colonia Longoria's public park. Like the bank building, the church had a limestone exterior and floors of marble. Chito authorized Jeanette to select the decorations and furnishings for the church's interior, including its museum of Christian artifacts. He also gave her a checkbook with which to pay the costs.

Construction projects almost always move slowly in Mexico. It took four years to complete the church, and as work advanced, Chito was seen more and more with the Jaffes. He, the couple, and its brood took trips together, and as the months passed, Chito began keeping company with Jeanette and her female friends. In Mexico friendships across sex lines were still taboo, and Chito's family took a dim view of his new American acquaintances, even if under their influence, he had apparently beaten back the shadows of depression. Older members of the clan thought that they discerned in Chito a reemergence of the same reckless spirit that had led to the building of the stairless ranch house. They complained that Chito's new daring affected their lives too. When Chito gave Jeanette permission to write checks on his account, the Longoria woman felt envious, and the brothers felt betrayed. All of the Longoria women—Doña Sara, the three sisters, and wives—had lived on allowances, without the open-ended spending power that blank checks gave. The money for the Church of the Holy Spirit came from profits that belonged to a family pool that the brothers insisted should be disbursed only in the ink of blood. Chito's renaming of the church was viewed as imprudent, and the Longorias didn't share his sudden admiration for Jeanette, the self-willed married woman who spoke only maid's Spanish.

But Jeanette was enamored of Chito. While at the Jaffe home on weekends, he spent hours entertaining the children and sometimes slept in the same bed with them. Jaffe jokingly called him "the richest yardman in the world," because Chito also passed time tending the family's gardens. Her husband, Jeanette believed, was too preoccupied with business affairs, perhaps because he was still in his forties. But Chito, perhaps because he was past sixty, seemed to have the confident and paternal ease of a man who knows that he's already made his mark.

The brothers believed that Chito was courting ruin, not only in his personal life but also in his business dealings. The production of wheat and flour in Mexico was regulated by cartel and price-fixing agreements supervised by the Companía Nacional de Subsistencias Populares (CONASUPO), a federal bureaucracy. The Longorias had for years owned a flour mill in Monterrey, and in 1962 Chito had decided to refuse to renew the mill's pact with CONASUPO. He began making his own deals for wheat, including American wheat, and he laid plans to sell flour at prices below those of this cartel-aligned competitors. CONASUPO and farm groups close to the government protested. The National Association of Flour Millers published full-page ads in Mexico denouncing Chito for "unlawful disloyal competition."

When Chito's wrangles with the agriculture bureaucracy spread into the cotton trade, his brothers were alarmed. His initial defensive move seemed to be an act of pure, possibly American-inspired, folly: Chito had published an ad in a Mexico City daily, accusing the agriculture secretary of corruption. Although his brothers tried to restrain him, Chito pressed forward until the politicians he had been courting in Mexico City arranged, if not the victory he had sought, a victory of equal proportions. In exchange for cooperation with CONASUPO's programs, Chito won an exemption from the Mexican taxes that are usually levied on borrowed foreign capital. The tax break removed an obstacle in Chito's march to expand the Longoria empire at any cost.

The boldest of the tricks Chito had up his sleeve was a scheme to exempt the family from Mexican corporate taxes. The scheme was the masterwork of his financial genius, a plan designed in several steps. The first move, completed in 1965 over Federico's objections, required the merger of fifteen family-held agri-business firms into an umbrella corporation, Empresas Longoria, S.A., or ELSA, which Chito afterward headed. ELSA paid for the assets of the merged companies by giving the Longorias notes of indebtedness. The Longorias then traded those notes for bank stock in the Bahamas Continental Bank, a paper institution that Chito had created for the scheme. The Longorias received dividends from the bank, which were not taxable under Bahamian law while the corporation could demonstrate that it had made no profits and therefore could not be taxed. In short order, the ELSA-Bahamas gambit paid handsomely. In 1968, for example, a year in which ELSA claimed exemption from both corporate income taxes and the employee profit-sharing bonuses required by Mexican law, the stockholders of the Bahamas bank, all Longorias, pocketed $3.2 million in dividends.

Chito's expansion projects were only beginning to take shape in late 1967, when Jeanette Jaffe took a plane to Juárez for a quickie divorce. When Chito learned of this, he carefully considered his course. He was in love, and he had been in love longer than anyone knew. But his circumstances presented him with two options: he could offend his family or could deny himself. His Mexican heritage told him that families, like the haciendas they own, become the most stable fixtures in a man's life. But after seven months of waiting and deliberation, Chito could forbear no more. He sent a mutual friend to Jeanette's house in San Antonio, bearing a proposal for immediate marriage. Some two weeks later, on March 1, 1968, he and Jeanette were wed in a civil ceremony in Mexico City. The Longoria brothers did not attend. When the Church of the Holy Spirit was dedicated later that year, not even Doña Sara came to wish its patrons well.

Chito had more clout than ever as a business figure, but he was losing his family's support.

ARLY THE NEXT YEAR Chito drove Jeanette to an undeveloped thousand-acre tract in Mexico City and asked her to pick a homesite from the raw land. Jeanette chose the highest hill in view, from whose summit the whole city seemed to lie at her feet. The couple returned to the site with stakes and string and, as Chito had done at the family ranch years earlier, marked off a plan for builders. For the next three years construction crews and architects struggled with materials and the terrain to erect Casa Kismet, a $2 million dream home, 300 feet long, 35,000 square feet in size. The place had limestone walls and marble floors, as did the church and Don Octaviano's bank. Its interior featured a swimming pool with a retractable sky-light, three kitchens, a beauty salon, and basement quarters for the household staff. The home's furnishings included statues of Bacchus, in both youth and old age, and even Kaiser Wilhelm the Second's Meissen porcelain soup tureen. Outside were tennis courts, a gazebo, and two ponds stocked with fish and fowl. The spread occupied a square block and was surrounded by a high wall at whose entrance a doorman stood guard. Beyond the wall arose Bosques de las Lomas, today Mexico City's prime neighborhood.

Casa Kismet became an international party house. Cary Grant and Ricardo Montalban visited in 1973, and María Ester Zuno de Echeverría, Mexico's first lady, stopped in too. The following year Chito and Jeanette hosted a party for actress Merle Oberon at which members of two fallen royal houses were present. The Shah of Iran, Rufino Tamayo, Hulbert de Givenchy, and even California governor Ronald Reagan were guests of the house. Chito and Jeanette came to see themselves not as borderland provincials but as members of an international social elite.

Chito's brothers began to suspect that he had lost his sense of reality. In 1969, about the time he and Jeanette staked out their homesite, Chito had kicked off a program that in two years doubled the capacities of ELSA's oil and seed mills. The project cost $7 million, and Federico argued that it served no purpose: Mexico's food-processing industry was already overbuilt. Yet as soon as the project was completed, Chito unveiled the most ambitious plan of his life—a multi-purpose food-processing mill at Tultitlán, a suburb of Mexico City. The Tultitlán plant, designed as the largest plant of its kind in Latin America, was to be Chito's crown jewel. It would also seal his doom.

CHITO had deeply indebted ELSA to foreign banks at a time when the world cotton market was slumping. The cotton crash was reflected on the corporation's books by the rising totals of uncollectible debts from farmers who had contracted with ELSA to gin their crops. During the sixties Chito's political backers had given assurances that the government would guarantee the corporation farm loans. But in 1970, when President Luís Echeverría took office, ELSA was holding some $4 million in uncollectible notes, and the new regime, instead of reimbursing the Longoria family, did what Federico feared: it audited the corporation's books, then presented demands for about $3.2 million in unpaid taxes and profit-sharing benefits. At the same time, a monetary shift added to ELSA's woes. The deutche mark was revalued upward, adding nearly $1 million to the cost of the company's payments to European banks.

In desperation the Longorias turned for help to the Sociedad Mexicana de Crédito Industrial, or Somex, a government investment bank. Somex loaned the family $12 million, but in July 1972, with nearly $20 million in obligations on the horizon, ELSA sought protection from its creditors. In exchange for assuming responsibility for ELSA's continuing operation, Somex required the Longorias to hand over not only corporation stock but also stock and pledges from other family enterprises, including the Banco Longoria, which Federico headed. All five brothers were now in hock for ELSA's expansion, and the family's financial fate rested in the hands of Luís Echeverría's treasury secretary, José López Portillo.

Chito remained at the head of ELSA, determined not to let bankruptcy put a dent in his plans. When he moved ahead with construction of the $10 million plant of Tultitlán, Federico sounded an alarm to his brothers. His calculations, he told them, indicated that the family couldn't afford to operate the plant once it opened. He also argued that it served no national or Longoria purpose: Mexico couldn't produce enough wheat to feed its mills, and the family's existing food-processing plants, by his computations, were operating at only 30 per cent of capacity. In January 1974, when Chito ordered an additional $2 million in equipment for the plant, the brothers got together and asked Somex to halt Chito's spending spree. They also threatened to resign from ElSA's board if it didn't. But the government did nothing, pending a high-level visit to the plant.

On July 9, 1974, president Luís Echeverría, flanked by Jóse López Portillo, unveiled the cornerstone of ELSA's plant at Tultitlán. At a breakfast following the ceremony Chito made a speech lauding El Presidente, then led him and his entourage on a tour of the forty-acre complex. Though the plant impressed Echeverría and his crew, something about it troubled them. It was equipped with European state-of-the-art machinery, designed to limit labor costs. Only 27 workmen were needed to operate the plant. Chito's crown jewel promised to infuriate competitors in the milling trade, as well as Mexico's unions, the most faithful supporters of El Presidente's regime.

In a meeting with López Portillo in early August, the brothers renewed their demand that Somex replace Chito. As they had threatened, they also presented their resignations from the corporation's board. López Portillo's answer to their appeal was delivered on August 24 by Somex officials. They appointed Federico to take Chito's place at ELSA. Chito's days as the Longoria kingpin were over.

Following the purge, the brother's began negotiating a settlement of ELSA's accounts. In March 1975 their deal was consummated. ELSA's debts were paid, largely from proceeds of the sale of five of the company's industries to Chito's old nemesis, CONASUPO. The Tultitlán plant was part of the bargain. So was the old Industrias Unidas site in Nuevo Laredo, Don Octaviano's industrial homestead. Chito's crown was placed on the head of his enemies, and another link to the founder was broken.

Doña Sara died in April of that year in Nuevo Laredo, at the age of 99. Chito tumbled into a pit of depression: there was now little hope of working his way back into the family's graces. Heartbroken, Chito retreated to Casa Kismet, unable to conduct his business affairs. Lawyers defended his interests, filing suit in Mexico City for, among other things, his restoration to ELSA's throne.

Throughout 1975 and 1976 the Longoria brothers rained suits on one another on both sides of the border. Chito took shots in the press too. He described his brothers to a *Laredo Times* reporter as "country people who talk in centavos while I talk in billions."

The acrimony reached a climax in 1977, when Chito filed a pleading in Laredo state district court. In the suit he turned his back on the notion of a family holding and claimed sole ownership of the Longoria empire. He alleged that Doña Sara had given Don Octaviano's properties to him and that the brothers, after clearing the debt to Somex, had gone on a spree "recklessly buying in the United States city real estate, ranches, stocks, condominiums, restaurants, packing houses, oil and gas businesses." The allegation was, if not a calculated lure, a sure-fire come-on to Mexican officials, who are ever-sensitive to the export of domestic capital.

In response the brothers formally sought the opinion of Jóse López Portillo, who had become the president since the days when they had dealt with him at the treasury. López Portillo's answers made clear that he regarded the five brothers as equal partners, a blow to Chito's hegemony. They also brought charges in Nuevo Laredo against Chito's son, Octaviano Longoria Penn, for alleged abuse of power-of-attorney authorizations. Chitito, as he is known in the family, was jailed in his hometown in August 1978, and he remained behind bars, though in luxurious conditions, for nearly a month, a hostage to settlement of the Laredo suit.

The Dance of Millions, as the looming trial was dubbed in the press, attracted attention on both sides of the border. Most important, it got notice at Los Pinos, Mexico's presidential palace. On Sunday, September 10, 1978, a day before jury selection was to begin in Laredo, El Presidente summoned all five brothers to Mexico City. His was a mother's message: if you boys don't quit fighting, I'll spank every one of you. Talk toward a settlement began in earnest as soon as the separate Longoria planes touched ground that night at the Laredo International Airport.

No pact had been signed the following morning, and jury selection at the Laredo courthouse began on time. The first witness scheduled to testify, Chito Longoria, failed to show, citing nervous exhaustion as an excuse. Federico took the stand for two days, during which he answered "I don't know" to dozens of sensitive questions. Eduardo, the fourth-born brother, was slated to follow him, but he also became too ill to testify; the Longoria brothers and Chito were united, if by nothing else, by their desire to obey El Presidente and to settle out of court. Before other principals could respond to their summonses, a pact ending the suit was drafted in rough form with the help of Morris Jaffe, Jeanette's first husband and Chito's stalwart friend. It was finished and filed in court a week later, sealed from public inspection. Spokesmen for Chito say that he got only $9 million in cash and some 27 businesses and real estate properties; just which pieces he got, nobody will say. The settlement is rumored to have favored the brothers, but the Longoria fortune passed from the public view of the courts into the present, its family secrecy nearly intact. The only evidence that the myriad suits left behind was a boxful of financial documents and a handful of depositions. That, and a silence born of shame. When the settlement was filed, the Longorias were so thoroughly disunited that in a financial sense, they were no longer Mexican at all. Money had shown itself to be a force as powerful as blood, and the brothers, like Chito, had become Americanized. After dividing their holdings with him, they split the remainder of the family's assets. Don Octaviano and Doña Sara's legacy and the Longoria empire were dissolved.

THE SURVIVING LONGORIA BROTHERS will not discuss the rise and fall of their clan because both events are in a past whose memory is still a source of pain. Most of the family members also are wary because they felt stung a decade ago by *El Rey de Oro*, a sensational roman à clef about the Longoria legend by Mexican writer Mauricio González. They have other reasons for silence, reasons common to most of those who have made or inherited fortunes in modern Mexico. Eduardo, for example, was kidnapped for ransom in early 1986, not long after a picture of him ensconced in the luxury and apprarent security of his Nuevo Laredo living room was published in *National Geographic*. Even Sara Alicia Brittingham, Chito's fervently religious daughter, avoids the press because last March, when Mexico's leading daily published a list of alleged sacadólares, or capital-exporters, with foreign bank accounts of $1 million or more, her name was at the top of the billing. Taking capital out of Mexico has become a crime, and most wealthy Mexican families have begun dodging the public spotlight.

The third and fourth Longoria generations are rich, but not nearly so much as their parents, and nearly half of them are permanent residents of Texas. Like other Texans, their lives have been touched by divorce, child-custody fights, and estrangement from their origins; many of them are no longer Catholic.

Economic history has fragmented the Longorias, reduced their power, and begun edging them north across the border.

Chito Longoria spent the last few months of his life at Casa Kismet, an irascible invalid whose legs no longer worked and whose powers of speech had diminished to the point that only Jeanette and a few others could understand him. His health had begun to fail in 1982, after an accident at a constuction site. One of his remaining properties was a former gin and feedlot site in Nuevo Laredo, presumed to be of little or no value. Chito saw it as a setting for an industrial park to attract maquiladoras, American-owned plants that produce export goods on Mexican soil. Living in San Antonio at the time in the house Jeanette had been granted in her divorce settlement, he drove to Nuevo Laredo by himself, despite his advanced age. As he walked across the ground of the future plant, Chito's eyes were uplifted, his face as bright and confident as ever. His depression was gone: he was doing business again. Workmen had dug a trench across the property, on a line that separated him from his prospective client, an American leasing and locations agent. Unaware of the trench as he walked toward the man, Chito stumbled in. As he fell, he threw his arms out, as if hoping to grab a support. Instead, the fall left him with a broken arm. One medical complication followed another, and he never regained his strength. Chito's fall and his financial demise came about because, as always, his eyes had been on doing business, American style, and not upon the Mexican ground at his feet.

Guillermo Gómez-Peña

*Excerpts from*
# Warrior for Gringostroika

I LIVE SMACK IN THE FISSURE between two worlds, in the infected wound: half a block from the end of Western civilization and four miles from the beginning of the Mexican/American border, the northernmost point of Latin America. In my fractured reality, but a reality nonetheless, they cohabit two histories, languages, cosmologies, artistic traditions, and political traditions which are drastically counterposed. Many "deterritorialized" Latin American artists in Europe and the United States have opted for "internationalism" (a cultural identity based upon the "most advanced" of the ideas originating out of New York or Paris). I, on the other hand, opt for "borderness" and assume my role: my generation, the chilango (slang term for a Mexico City native), who came to "El Norte" fleeing the imminent ecological and social catastrophe of Mexico City, gradually integrated itself into otherness, in search of that other Mexico grafted onto the entrails of the et cetera ...became Chicano-ized. We de-Mexicanized ourselves to Mexi-understand ourselves, some without wanting to, others

on purpose. And one day, the border became our house, laboratory, and ministry of culture (or counterculture).

WE WITNESS the borderization of the world, by-product
of the "deterritorialization" of vast human sectors. The
borders either expand or are shot full of holes. Cultures and
languages mutually invade one another. The South rises and
melts, while the North descends dangerously with its economic
and military pincers. The East moves west and vice versa.
Europe and North America daily receive uncontainable migra-
tions of human beings, a majority of whom are being displaced
involuntarily. This phenomenon is the result of multiple factors:
regional wars, unemployment, overpopulation, and especially
the enormous disparity in North/South relations.

The demographic facts are staggering: the Middle East and
Black Africa are already in Europe, and Latin America's heart
now beats in the United States. New York and Paris increasingly resemble Mexico City and Sao Paolo. Cities like Tijuana
and Los Angeles, once socio-urban aberrations, are becoming
models of a new hybrid culture, full of uncertainty and vitality.
And border youth—the fearsome "cholo-punks," children of the
chasm that is opening between the "First" and the "Third"
worlds, become the indisputable heirs to a new mestizaje
(the fusion of the Amerindian and European races).

In this context, concepts like "high culture," "ethnic purity,"
"cultural identity," "beauty," and "fine arts" are absurdities and
anachronisms. Like it or not, we are attending the funeral of
modernity and the birth of a new culture.

OUR EXPERIENCE as Latino border artists and intellectuals
in the United States fluctuates between legality and
illegality, between partial citizenship and full. For the Anglo community we are simply "an ethnic minority," a subculture, that

is to say, some kind of pre-industrial tribe with a good consumerist appetite. For the art world, we are practitioners of distant languages that, in the best of cases, are perceived as exotic.

In general, we are perceived through the folkloric prisms of Hollywood, fad literature, and publicity; or through the ideological filters of mass media. For the average Anglo, we are nothing but "images," "symbols," "metaphors." We lack ontological existence and anthropological concreteness. We are perceived indiscriminately as magic creatures with shamanistic powers, happy bohemians with pretechnological sensibilities, or as romantic revolutionaries born in a Cuban poster from the 1970s. All this without mentioning the more ordinary myths, which link us with drugs, supersexuality, gratuitous violence, and terrorism; myths that serve to justify racism and disguise the fear of cultural otherness.

These mechanisms of mythification generate semantic interference and obstruct true intercultural dialogue. To make border art implies to reveal and subvert said mechanisms.

DESPITE THE GREAT CULTURAL MIRAGE sponsored by the people in power, everywhere we look we find pluralism, crisis, and non-synchronicity. The so-called dominant culture is no longer dominant. Dominant culture is a meta-reality that only exists in the virtual space of the mainstream media and in the ideologically and aesthetically controlled spaces of the monocultural institutions.

Today, if there is a dominant culture, it is border culture. And those who still haven't crossed a border will do it very soon. All Americans (from the vast continent America) were, are, or will be border-crossers. "All Mexicans," says Tomas Ybarra-Frausto, a Chicano theoretician in New York, "are potential Chicanos." As you read this text, you are crossing a border yourself.

■ ■ ■

## Intercultural Dialogue

THE SOCIAL AND ETHNIC FABRIC of the United States is filled with interstitial wounds, invisible to those who didn't experience the historical events that generated them, or who are victimized by historical amnesia. Those who cannot see these wounds feel frustrated by the hardships of intercultural dialogue. Intercultural dialogue unleashes the demons of history.

Arlene Raven, an artist and writer in New York, once told me, "In order to heal the wound, we first have to open it." In 1989, we are just opening the wound. To truly communicate with the cultural other is an extremely painful and scary experience. It is like getting lost in a forest of misconceptions or walking on mined territory.

The territory of intercultural dialogue is abrupt and labyrinthine. It is filled with geysers and cracks; with intolerant ghosts and invisible walls. Anglo-Americans are filled with stereotypical notions about Latinos and Latino-American art. Latin Americans are exaggeratedly distrustful of initiatives toward binational dialogue coming from this side/el otro lado. Bicultural Latinos in the United States (be they Chicanos, Nuyorricans, or others) and monocultural citizens of Latin America have a hard time getting along. This conflict represents one of the most painful border wounds, a wound in the middle of a family, a bitter split between two lovers from the same hometown.

Fear is the sign of the times. The 1980s are the culture of fear. Everywhere I go, I meet Anglo-Americans immersed in fear. They are scared of us, the other, taking over their country, their jobs, their neighborhoods, their universities, their art world. To "them," "we" are a whole package that includes an indistinct Spanish language, weird art, a sexual threat, gang activity, drugs, and "illegal aliens." They don't realize that their fear has been implanted as a form of political control; that this fear is the very source of the endemic violence that has been affecting this society since its foundation.

Border culture can help dismantle the mechanisms of fear. Border culture can guide us back to common ground and improve our negotiating skills. Border culture is a process of negotiation towards utopia, but in this case, utopia means peaceful coexistence and fruitful cooperation. The border is all we share/La frontera es lo único que compartimos.

My border colleagues and I are involved in a tripartite debate around separatism. Some Chicano nationalists who still haven't understood that Chicano culture has been redefined by the recent Caribbean and Central American immigrations feel threatened by the perspective of intercultural dialogue and Pan-Americanism. Meanwhile, sectors of the Mexican intelligentsia, viewing themselves as "guardians of Mexican sovereignty," see in our proposals for binational dialogue "a disguised form of integration" and pull back. Ironically, the conservative Anglo-Americans who are witnessing with panic the irreversible borderization of the United States tend to agree with Chicano and Mexican separatists who claim to speak from the left. The three parties prefer to defend "their" identity and culture, rather than to dialogue with the cultural other. The three parties would like to see the border closed. Their intransigent views are based on the modernist premise that identity and culture are closed systems, and that the less these systems change, the more "authentic" they are.

## The Border is...(A Manifesto)

BORDER CULTURE is a polysemantic term.
Stepping outside of one's culture is equivalent to walking outside of the law.

Border culture means boycott, complot, ilegalidad, clandestinidad, contrabando, transgresión, desobediencia binacional: en otros palabras, to smuggle dangerous poetry and utopian visions from one culture to another, desde allá, hasta acá.

But it also means to maintain one's dignity outside the law.

But it also means hybrid art forms for new contents-in-gestation: spray mural, techno-altar, poetry-in-tongues, audio graffiti, punkarachi, video corrido, anti-bolero, anti-todo: la migra (border patrol), art world, police, monocultura; en otras palabras y tierras, an art against the monolingües, tapados, nacionalistas, ex-teticistas en extinción, per omnia saecula speculorum....

But it also means to be fluid in English, Spanish, Spanglish, and Ingleñol, 'cause Spanglish is the language of border diplomacy.

But it also means transcultural friendship and collaboration among races, sexes, and generations.

But it also means to practice creative appropriation, expropriation, and subversion of dominant cultural forms.

But it also means a new cartography; a brand-new map to host the new project; the democratization of the East; the socialization of the West; the Third-Worldization of the North and the First-Worldization of the South.

But it also means a multiplicity of voices away from the center, different geo-cultural relations among more culturally akin regions: Tepito—San Diejuana, San Pancho—Nuyorrico, Miami—Quebec, San Antonio—Berlin, your home town and mine, digamos, a new internationalism ex centris.

But it also means regresar y volver a partir: to return and depart once again, 'cause border culture is a Sisyphean experience and to arrive is just an illusion.

But is also means a new terminology for new hybrid identities and métiers constantly metamorphosing: sudacá, not sudaca; Chicarrican, not Hispanic: mestizaje, not miscegenation; social thinker, not bohemian; accionista, not performer; intercultural, not postmodern.

But it also means to develop new models to interpret the world-in-crisis, the only world we know.

But it also means to push the borders of countries and languages or, better said, to find new languages to express the fluctuating borders.

But it also means experimenting with the fringes between art and society, legalidad and illegality, English and español, male and female, North and South, self and other; and subverting these relationships.

But it also means to speak from the crevasse, desde acá, desde el medio. The border is the juncture, not the edge, and monoculturalism has been expelled to the margins.

But it also means glasnost, not government censorship, for censorship is the opposite of border culture.

But it also means to analyze critically all that lies on the current table of debates: multiculturalism, the Latino "boom," "ethnic art," controversial art, even border culture.

But it also means to question and transgress border culture. What today is powerful and necessary, tomorrow is arcane and ridiculous; what today is border culture, tomorrow is institutional art, not vice versa.

But it also means to escape the current co-optation of border culture.

But it also means to look at the past and the future at the same time. 1492 was the beginning of a genocidal era. 1992 will mark the beginning of a new era: America post-Colombina, Arteamérica sin fronteras. Soon, a new internationalism will have to gravitate around the spinal cord of this continent—not Europe, not just the North, not just white, not only you, compañero del otro lado de la frontera, el lenguaje y el océano.

Tom Miller

# Discreets of Laredo

"I WORK in a small retail store. Someone comes in and buys twenty television sets. He pays cash, he gets a sales receipt, everything is clean. But he wants the TVs smuggled into Mexico, so he brings them to a man in town who seals them in a boxcar headed for Mexico City. I know the man smuggles because I deliver the goods to him. That's what I do for a living— I help Mexican shoppers get their purchases into Mexico."

The short man with the skin problem was explaining the facts of life, Laredo style. He had lived there since birth, seen generations of stagnant poverty among the townfolk, seen the wealth grow among the nouveau merchant class. Like so many others in this town of ninety-two thousand, he recognizes that shipping consumer goods into Mexico, in violation of that country's laws, can be a lucrative enterprise, condoned and even encouraged by pillars of the community. Mexicans spend so much money in Laredo that the city, whose residents earn among the lowest wages in the United States, ranks among the very highest in per capita retail sales. Mexican shoppers generally prefer U.S. products—televisions, clothing, stereos, appliances, blenders, furniture, cameras—to homemade ones. Superior American technology usually means a longer product life span. Many consumer goods are simply not manufactured in Mexico at all. Additionally, Mexican consumers often attach status to American products even if a similar item is available in-country. As the American town most accessible to the greatest number of Mexicans, Laredo, Texas, has become Mexico's shopping center.

Smuggling goods into Mexico is commonplace because of the prohibitively high import duties imposed by that country's government. The complex and well-established pipeline of Mexican smugglers imports items not only by freight train but over major highways as well. Aduana—customs—officials throughout the Republic receive systematic payoffs in the process. For Laredo merchants to sell goods to Mexican customers is perfectly legal. The merchandise becomes contraband only when it enters Mexico untaxed. Smuggled goods are called fayuca.

J. C. Penny, 80 percent of whose business is from Mexico, is located in River Drive Mall, a downtown shopping center virtually on the banks of the Rio Grande. Chiveras (literally, goatherds), or smugglers, come to town with shopping lists for a dozen or so families and fill the Penney's parking lot in the afternoons. They take their purchases out of the store wrappings and rip out any tags indicating they are new. Often clothes are worn immediately, two and sometimes three layers at a time. More clothes are crammed into suitcases—also just purchased for the return trip. The rest is concealed from the aduana in door panels, under seat covers, beneath trunk liners, and elsewhere. At La Posada, the city's best hotel, high-volume chiveras convert their rooms to warehouses, storing clothes for the return trip to the interior. Paper bags from shops all over town litter the hotel's hallways.

When the bridge is "tight"—that is, when high customs officials from Mexico are in town to monitor their underlings—

Laredo department stores such as Montgomery Ward will keep purchased appliances destined for the interior until the situation returns to normal. Sales clerks and chiveras throughout the city maintain a cozy relationship, each profiting from the other. In Laredo, clandestine activity is business as usual. The town has become an American Andorra.

To spot the chiveras, simply cross the International Bridge to Nuevo Laredo and watch Mexicans pass their own customs. Shoppers on foot carrying paper bags of new purchases often leave a ten- or twenty-peso note on top as la mordida (the bite), which is considered nothing more than a gift to speed things along. The aduana pocket the money, nod slightly, and move on to the next person.

Enrico, a friend from Monterrey, 150 miles south of Laredo, explained how the game is played when driving home. "You have to pull around to the rear of the port building where the aduana go through your luggage pretending they're looking for fayuca. Actually they are looking for their money. It's best to leave the mordida on top so they don't mess up your suitcase. For a little two hundred dollar television set, the aduana may get fifty dollars, but the total expense is still cheaper than buying a similar set in Mexico. Another aduana checkpoint is at twenty-six kilometers out, and another one as you drive into Monterrey. If Mexico City is the destination, there may be ten or twelve aduana payoffs along the way. The government is very lenient about this. These customs men retire very well."

Enrico's observations had historical precedent. John Russell Bartlett, the U.S. survey commissioner who traveled the border in the mid-nineteenth century, noted that "the duty...imposed by Mexico on many items of merchandise amounts to a prohibition. Yet owing to the laxity of customhouse officials, the law has been evaded, and goods regularly admitted at a nominal rate. Each collector knows that if he exacts the legal duty, either the merchandise will be smuggled in or some brother-collector, less conscientious and anxious to pocket the fees, will be ready to compound for a smaller sum. It accordingly became the practice...to admit merchandise for the interior of Mexico by paying five hundred dollars on each wagon load."

In one major appliance store, a twenty-four-inch color console television was tagged at $1,125. The store manager said he could deliver the set to Monterrey for another $315. "The bridge is still tight," he lamented. "When it loosens up, here's how we'll do it: You pay for the set here and we give you the receipt. When our chivera gets ready to deliver in Monterrey, he'll call you and you pay him the delivery cost. If the television is confiscated, we'll send out another one. We guarantee delivery."

In an office supply shop the story was similar. A new office-model electric typewriter cost $825. "Oh, you want it sent to Mexico? That will be an extra one hundred fifty dollars. Delivery guaranteed."

The pattern repeated itself in store after store. Each had its own chivera, each guaranteed delivery, and each undercut the legal Mexican price. At one store a salesman apologized that he had to delay smuggling because a new customs man was being broken in at the aduana station and the chivera had to negotiate his contract.

"A FRIEND OF MINE works in a discount store," recounted John Speer, part-owner of an electronics store. "A Mexican wholesaler put in an order for Polaroid film—a quarter of a million dollars' worth. An order that size in any type of business here is not unusual, because Mexican storeowners treat our shops like showrooms, ordering in bulk from demonstrator models on the shelves. A Mexican businessman may go into one store and ask what the price is on a nineteen-inch Sony color television. Let's say it's four hundred fifty dollars. He'll say, 'OK, what's *my* price?' The merchant will say three hundred seventy-five dollars. Then the businessman says, 'How about if I buy ten of them?' And the salesman will lower his price another fifty dollars. So the man from Mexico says, 'Fine. I'll take two at three hundred twenty-five dollars.' Then it's up to the merchant to decide if he'll let it go at that. The way things are on the border these days, he will. It's a chivera's market."

The "illegal permit" method is another way to smuggle goods into Mexico. The permits are available only through very special connections in the upper echelons of the aduana and cost a great deal, but they guarantee the chivera complete passage for his goods from border to destination, rather like prepaying a year's worth of bribes in one lump sum. The chivera is no longer smuggling. He has, in effect, legal contraband. One merchant whose chivera had just secured an illegal permit estimated that his sales would increase by $1 million annually as a result.

Storefronts on Convent Street, a narrow, seedy-looking thoroughfare running north from the International Bridge, give the impression that the shops have seen better days. The looks are deceiving. Convent Street real estate is among the most valuable in Texas. Business in the ten-block area adjacent to the bridge is so phenomenal that local realtors can't even recall the last land transaction there. Time and again, community boosters brag, "There's nothing you can buy in Paris or New York that you can't find in Laredo." A few stores stock only perfume and do very well. Even Gucci has a Laredo outlet. The city's leading haberdashery, Joe Brand, chauffeurs its well-heeled Mexican customers around in a Rolls-Royce.

Mexicans come to Laredo thinking that they are getting top quality, unaware that most of the large chain department stores use the border area as a dumping ground for irregular items. In-country advertising creates consumer demand, then shoppers come to the United States and buy. "A good example is Yashica cameras," explained John Speer. "You can't *give* them away in Dallas or Houston, but because they're so well promoted in Mexico, Yashica does an incredible business in Laredo."

Speer's method of shipping new televisions into Mexico is foolproof. Instead of being paid off to allow his goods past the checkpoints, aduana officers come into his store and drive the merchandise back into Mexico themselves. When the purchaser tells Speer the goods have arrived at the destination, he pays the customs men their delivery fee. "Because the aduana is involved from the point of origin, no intermediary payoffs are necessary. I deal with the jefes, the chiefs. Some very high officials are involved in this.

OF THE $4 MILLION WORTH of television sets that were exported from Laredo to Mexico in 1978, approximately $2.8 million was from smuggled sales. More than half of the contraband television sets went overland; the rest went by air. Flying contraband into Mexico from Laredo necessitates only a willing pilot and a safe landing strip. Because the goods are flying over all the payoff points, smuggling by air is actually cheaper than by land. One businessman who lives near the airport boasted that he can gauge Laredo's economy by how many Beech-18s and DC-3s he hears taking off.

Another merchant shed light on the air-smuggling operations. "There's a pilots' association, sort of like a club," she explained. "They'll fly goods anywhere you pay them to. The fellow I use makes the rounds of all his shops and then drives out to the airport for shipping, sort of like UPS delivery service."

At the airport a youthful pilot offered a guided tour. "This smuggling business can be dangerous unless everyone is square with each other," he confided as we drove down the tarmac. "The merchants tend to overload the planes because that's where the money is. See that one?" Before us was a grounded Twin Beech with both engines burned out. "One of the downtown merchants packed that sonuvabitch so tight that when it got about fifty feet in the air it stalled and came down—fortunately no one was hurt. But there's such a profit margin on these flights that businessmen can afford to lose a load now and then."

We drove past another plane which had had trouble, too. The

right side of a Lockheed Lodestar—an old World War II bomber —was buckled under and the wheel caved in. The propeller was damaged and the right wing tip was dented. By the time investigators reached the plane shortly after the crash, all the merchandise had been removed.

"These pilots establish their own landing strips in deserts, on mountaintops, in the jungle, and on the plains. You can usually tell where the planes have been by the type of soil they pick up. For instance, if there's good red dirt on the wheels and the belly, I'd guess that plane touched down north by north east of Guadalajara. You get to learn these things after a while."

A pilot flying a single-engine plane can clear $800 for a ninety-minute trip. Twin-engine pilots earn more, and sometimes make two trips a day. The Beech-18 is the best plane to use, my guide related, because of its agility and capacity. The biggest aircraft in the smuggling service is a DC-3 cargo plane.

My guide seemed just the type to fly cargo into Mexico at a moment's notice. "No way. No way! You couldn't get me to do that in a million years." He was emphatic. "These guys—their lives are on the line virtually from the moment they start their engines. The plane may not be in good condition. Going into Mexico they could get caught. The plane could crash and they'd have nowhere to go. So many people are involved in each trip a pilot never knows if someone's going to betray him. They're either crazy or without brains. I've been approached more than once—a guy puts five hundred dollars in front of me for a thirty minute hop. It's awful hard to say no, but I've never gotten involved. I don't have fuzzy enough nuts to do it."

A Mexican newspaper story told about one who did:

### American Plane Loaded with Contraband
### Shot Down Over Jalisco—One Dead

A small private American plane coming from Laredo, Texas, loaded with contraband televisions, tape recorders, and other electronic goods, was shot down in Jalisco last week, and the pilot died, authorities said. The U.S. Consulate in Guadalajara, the capital of Jalisco, refused to identify the dead man. Captain Carlos Fierro, Military Commander of the Guadalajara airport, said the twin-engine Beechcraft crash-landed completely in flames forty meters from a small country airstrip called Pacama. Nothing was left except the tail. The pilot burned to death....

The man U.S. authorities refused to identify was retired Air Force Colonel Phil Willer, a pilot who first learned the smuggling business while stationed at Laredo Air Force Base, which closed in 1973. The man most knowledgeable about Willer's activities was a Treasury agent who had been monitoring smuggling out of the Lower Rio Grande Valley. When I visited his office, he pulled out a thick stack of classified files on Willer and every other big-time smuggler. "There's a merchant in downtown Laredo who deals in volume televisions," he said, reaching for a photograph. "That's his brother-in-law there unloading a plane full of contraband in Mexico. He runs a store in San Luis Potosí.

"A lot of these pilots are ex-mercenaries who've flown for the CIA and Air America. When there's no war going on, they smuggle goods south of the border. We did learn one new thing about Willer after his crash: the lab analysis on his plane showed traces of marijuana. Evidently he was carrying freight both ways."

THE OFFICIAL MEXICAN POSITION against contraband is that if smuggling were reduced, more Mexicans would buy in-country products. The result would be more money in the economy, more manufacturing, more retail sales outlets, and less unemployment. With more people working, fewer would be tempted to migrate to the United States in search of work.

To reduce flagrant violations of its laws, the aduana service is ridding itself of a few obvious smugglers within its own ranks.

To investigate its own men, the aduana service uses volantes, customs inspectors who travel in unmarked vehicles, as mobile checkpoints on Mexican highways. "The volantes, they are more honest—that is to say, they are more difficult to bribe," one middle-class Mexican smiled. "It is ironic that smuggling helps individual Mexicans but hurts the country's economy as a whole. But we don't doubt that in the future, our technology will be as good as America's, and smuggling will no longer be necessary."

Emilio Reyes Flores is the number two man at the Zona Aduana Fiscal de Nuevo Laredo. The subjefe, whose office is next to the railroad tracks on the west side of town, was dressed in the height of fashion with a well-cut three-piece suit and alligator-skin boots. Hundreds of truck drivers and others needing his approval on import-export documents formed a line winding from his desk through his office, out the door, and down the hall. Before approaching Reyes' desk, each person left a few pesos with a man seated to the side, apparently a prerequisite to a fleeting audience with the subjefe. As Reyes initialed each form with a flourish, an aide would dramatically present him with the next.

"It is the uneducated who buy products in America," Reyes offered between pen strokes. "They are under the impression that American products are superior. They go to Penney's or Joe Brand or Frost Brothers and the American merchants give them credit. They can put a few dollars down on almost everything."

The line grew longer and longer. A haggard old lady inched her way to the front and begged Reyes to grant her a permit to bring American goods into the Republic. A phone call interrupted her plea, and the subjefe engaged in animated conversation while his assistant proffered more forms for his initials. He slowed down once when a man in an officer's uniform came in to whisper in his ear. Reyes arched his eyebrows and nodded sagely. The man smiled and departed. The old lady stood patiently to the side, ignored.

"We have two aircraft at San Luis Potosí which we use to

combat this aerial smuggling," Reyes went on. "Our men are getting better training now than they used to, and we have internal investigations going on constantly. We fire the men who are getting mordida."

Before leaving, I complimented Reyes on his suit and asked where he bought it. Flattered, he pulled back the lapel to show me the label. The inside right pocket said:

JOE BRAND
LAREDO, TEXAS

Everywhere I went they talked of the Silver-haired Fox, one of the pioneer air smugglers in the 1940s. Over the years he piloted every type of craft under the worst of conditions. He could take off on a dime and land on a peso. Was a stunt flier in Hollywood years ago. Started the cargo-smuggling business in the sixties. Been locked up in a Mexican jail for his troubles and lived to tell about it. There's never been anyone like him, all right. Retired Christmas 1977, but he still comes around. Full of piss and vinegar. A legend in his own time.

I wanted to meet him.


OUR PLANE had just crossed the Rio Grande and was gaining altitude. Behind us lay the United States. Spread out on all sides was Mexico. The Silver-haired Fox, George Gibson, now in his fifties, was flying me to some of his old landing strips. "We're now officially wetbacks!" he called back from the cockpit. A lively character who looks something like Kris Kringle, Gibson was in a mood to reminisce about his years as a contrabandista. The southwestern outskirts of Nuevo Laredo passed below as he began.

"I learned to fly in World War II. When I went back to southern California after the war there was an opportunity to bring lobsters out of Baja California. The fishermen always had lots more lobsters than they could sell through their regular channels, so I started buying some and flying them into California where lobster fishing wasn't allowed certain times of the year. I had my own connections, and my fishermen would supply only me. They were always so amazed that this gringo would come out of the sky and land near their village. 'Long about 1950 the California Fish and Game people busted me for bringing in lobster out of season! I told them that the season only applied to *their* coast, not Mexico's, but they wouldn't go along with that. So I moved to Las Vegas and continued. Word got around, and by 1954 there were too many lobster smugglers and they began to take the business far too seriously. There were shoot-'em-ups. I didn't want any part of it."

We were at five thousand feet and rising. The inside of the plane had a deafening rattle. The exterior paint job was vintage Korean War—natural camouflage, Gibson called it. He spoke with confidence.

"The world mercury market was going good, so through some contacts I got into the mercury business in the state of Zacatecas. I moved more black-market mercury than anyone." Gibson brought seventy-four pound flasks from his mines and sold them to New York mercury brokers at enormous profits. "I even had U.S. government pilots moonlighting for me.

"Every time I went back for more mercury, the miners would give me money and ask me to bring back little things like clothes or a camera. Their shopping list got so long I finally had to pay someone to take care of it for me. Later I learned that the guys in Zacatecas would turn around and resell the stuff I'd be bringing them and they'd be making a profit on it!

"Well, mercury was a good racket while it lasted. Then the goddamn Mexican government came in and took over.

"By the 1960s I had developed landing strips everywhere in Mexico, and merchants in Brownsville, McAllen, and all over the Rio Grande Valley started calling. They'd say, 'Oh, Mr. Gibson, we'd sure like to meet you. We have some merchandise we must move into Mexico.' So I got started in the cargo business—at the time I was the only one. My first few runs were clothing and Persian rugs. For a while I was carrying hardware items—drill bits, diesel parts, that type of stuff. Now the only cargo which carries enough of a margin of profit to make the flights worthwhile is electronics."

We were halfway to the first site, cruising at ten thousand feet. "The key to the whole thing is your landing strips," Gibson went on. "You need good, secure, isolated landing strips that are technically adequate to handle whatever type of craft you want to put on them. I figure I've established more than thirty strips in Mexico.

"The first thing I do is go down and tap the ground with the landing gear to test the firmness and buzz it a few times to see if I can get in real tight. If the strip is all right, I land and walk around to test it. Sometimes I have to move some brush. The next step is to find the nearest paved highway and see if any aduana checkpoints are close. The people who live near the strips pretty much mind their own business. They don't like officialdom any more than I do. Most of them are pure Indian."

We cleared the last mountain range and began our descent. "Each one of my flights was prearranged by telephone, but once I was in the air my receiver and I would have a signal in case anything went wrong at the last minute. If the hood of his truck was up, I'd go back. The one time I didn't pay attention was the one time I got busted.

"I was flying in Christmas tree lights. For some reason stores in Mexico don't stock them and every fall we fly down thousands of boxes of the darned things. Anyway, I was set up by a man in Laredo because I refused to haul his freight. As soon as I landed I was surrounded by Mexican authorities with machine guns. But the plane was stuffed to the gills and I couldn't get out of the cockpit—as a result *I* had to fly it out so *they* could put *me* in custody. They had me for seven months and eight days. I was released in May 1973."

The first strip of the day finally came into view. A finger of land jutted out next to a ranch house. Gibson turned in for a final approach.

"See those trees over there?" Two mesquite grew side by side. "The taller one is my target. The strip runs diagonal to it. I usually taxi over to those bushes and land right there."

We skimmed the ground at three feet going 130 miles an hour. "The strip looks a little damp today, we might get stuck in the mud." Instead of landing we S-looped around and turned south.

"I had a deal with some officials in Guadalajara, some years ago," Gibson continued as we gained altitude. One fellow was the aduana comandante of the zone and his partner was the jefe of the judicial federal police in the area. The head of the aduana would meet me at the airport in uniform, have one of his aides park me, and the federal police would unload the contraband. The jefe at the airport would drive me to the Fenix Hotel where I had my own suite and the run of the bar. I liked dealing with officials that way."

The second strip we visited was a dry lake bed. Once when George was about to land there he discovered wider tire tracks on the ground than those from his plane. Empty ammunition boxes lay next to nearby bushes. Someone had discovered the strip and was using it for himself. George stopped landing there for a month. When he came back the hull of a burned-out DC-3 rested at the far end of the strip. "I could tell someone had come in all wrong and couldn't get out. Well, if the plane had been seized by the Mexican government, the owners never would have collected insurance money. So they torched it." We circled again to catch a glimpse of the hull and returned to cruising altitude. We were north of Torreón where George had more landing strips, but darkness was approaching. We headed back.

"I don't know why you keep calling me a smuggler," The Fox said after a silence. "I'm an exporter. I'm not a smuggler until I cross the border. On the U.S. side I'm a law-abiding citizen. The general image of a smuggler is a dope runner. I'm very down on drugs.

"I got out of the cargo business a while back, but I understand last year at McAllen there was practically open warfare. A new breed of cat has gotten into the business and I don't particularly care to associate with them. They have no sense of honor. They don't have the expertise to fly some of these planes and they're strictly in it for the bucks. There's no *esprit de corps* left. Greed and avariciousness have taken over."

The Fox's face beamed with pride. "To me it was more than money. I liked walking a tightrope. I figure I've flown over three thousand cargo runs and I earned a good living doing it. I called my own shots. By now there're probably fifty pilots from San Diego to Brownsville in this line of work."

We touched down at Laredo International Airport a short time later. On the way back to town a twinkle flashed in his eyes. I still might move a little freight if the conditions are right. I admit it. I miss it. I like being up in the air looking around. To me, that's the biggest kick of this whole business."

POSTSCRIPT: The Silver-haired Fox and his colleagues played a colorful role in the border's endless drama, but their act began to fade in the late 1980s when Mexico started reducing tariffs on many consumer items. Although NAFTA accelerated the demise of contraband flying south, some local smuggling still exists, mainly to avoid a tax imposed on Mexicans who live in the zona fronteriza. *T.M.*

# Gary Paul Nabhan

# Cryptic Cacti on the Borderline

## Hide-and-Seek

WHILE DRIVING along the U.S.-Mexico border one scorching hot August day, I found myself falling under the spell of mirages once more. For starters, I had been letting my dreams drift toward a few scattered clouds. I was secretly shaping them into thunderheads, hoping that they would bring rains. I craved thunderstorms and the relief they carried with them; the air-conditioning wasn't working in my Jeep, and salty sweat was stinging my eyes, blurring my vision. On top of that, I had a headache pounding like a misfiring piston, making me more miserable than on most desert rides.

I was crabby, too, because it had just sunk into my weary brain that the ancient cactus stand that I had been wanting to survey wasn't in good shape. A few decades ago, someone went and put the border fence smack dab through the middle of it. Later, the Feds bulldozed a road next to the fence on one side, and the Mexicans bulldozed another on the other. I sensed that it was suffering other insults as well, insults I would soon learn about firsthand.

Up to that time, I had figured that the border fence was a pain in the tail only for humans and other migratory animals who had to cross it on a regular basis. Now, I reckoned, it was even wreaking havoc on sessile creatures like cacti.

I was supposed to be hot on the tracks of a night-blooming cereus cactus, *Peniocereus striatus*, which was considered to be a rarity. It is never that simple: when I followed the historic surveyor's notes I had been given, and walked the distance from the fence as specified, I ended up in the middle of a rutted road. I forgot about the directions and began to wander through the scrubby hills and valleys beyond the roads.

If any cacti were somewhere around there, I had not been fortunate enough to find many. Within the past ten months, I had found a measly seven plants south of the boundary. Slim pickings after more that fifty hours of cruising on foot through their suspected desert haunts. As I wove up one slope and down another, hitting upon one cactus every seven hours or so, I thought of the blues lyric, "If it wasn't for bad luck, I wouldn't have no luck at all."

The Sonoran cereus are cryptic, hiding their lead gray stems deep within the thorny mess of gray branches of the few desert trees and shrubs that offer any shade. You hardly ever find them out in the open. As if being in the shadows, nearly invisible, is the best way to survive this stinkin' hot desert. It must be, because they've given up the best defense that other cacti have stuck with—they lack needlelike spines to keep intruders away.

Instead, these spineless cactus stems are the same color, shape, and diameter as those of the creosote bushes all around them and not too different from the branchlets of ironwood and wolfberry. This coincidence has spurred cactomaniacs to talk of "cryptic coloration" and "protective mimicry," as if each cactus decided that it would be more fitting to cross-dress and live its life in drag.

It doesn't make much sense to me. Cryptic coloration must be aimed at fooling rodents, jackrabbits, and bigger browsers like desert pronghorn—discouraging them from eating a vulnerable cactus if it looks like an oily, unpalatable shrub—but most mammals are color-blind. I'm color-blind, too, but the seven cacti I had seen far outnumbered the ones that many of my color-sensitive buddies have scared up in the same amount of search time. All I know is that Sonoran cereus are harder than hell to see even when you've walked by them a dozen times.

After years of searching by various hapless biologists, only sixty plants had been found in the lands along the two hundred miles of Arizona-Sonora border falling within the Sonoran Desert. Multiply that batting average by my crabbiness quotient, and you can understand why my mind was turning every cloud into a harbinger of rain: I longed for relief from this heat and reprieve from my fruitless searches.

That August day, I was to have my two wishes granted: for rain, and for more Sonoran cereus cactus. By the time my Jeep had bounced down the rutted borderline road to reach the hills where I had seen the first seven specimens, a stray storm cloud had lingered long enough to dump a half inch of rain in a matter of minutes. Though it failed to turn the road into a running arroyo, the downpour was good enough to dampen the dust and drop the temperature below a hundred degrees for the first time in hours.

My headache lifted. Maybe it was the sudden rush of ozone in the storm-charged air. As my crabbiness began to disperse, I decided to circumambulate one rocky knoll once more, not far from the few plants I had already discovered. The entire scene had been transformed by that scant half inch of rainfall. The brief deluge had darkened the lead-colored stems of the creosote bush to a charcoal black. Beneath them, the Sonoran cereus cacti were showing their true colors as well. A powdery bloom had been washed away from the cactus stems, revealing a brighter green. Dressed up as dead stick moments before, the cereus had suddenly broken dormancy. Water had reached their roots for the first time in months and triggered their internal workings. The plants were breaking bud, but better yet, a miniature forest of cacti was instantly revealed between the rain-washed trees.

As quickly as the green cereus stems could reveal themselves against the black background of the surrounding shrubs and trees, I added plant after plant to my cactus count. In forty-five minutes, I spotted eleven additional Sonoran cereus, some of them under creosote, but others beneath small ironwood and paloverde trees. With the help of the rains, I had all of a sudden become a hundred times sharper at cactus hunting than I had been in all the previous months of the dry season. I had finally tracked down enough of the cereus on the Sonoran side of the line to compare their situation with that of their Arizona brethren a few hundred yards away.

# Different Sides of the Fence

THE RAINS CONTINUED that summer, bringing the good as well as the bad with them. The bad was my once-white Jeep getting mucked up regularly in the puddles along the borderline road. The good? I was able to tally up more than one hundred and ten Sonoran cereus plants on both sides of the border. Still not much cactus, considering that I had looked under every bush within a two-mile stretch along the border, going back at least another half mile on either side of the fence.

One day, while leaning up against the fence to tie my shoe, I began to ponder whether this cactus was naturally rare or merely a victim of what was known as the "borderline effect." I paused a moment and stared at the fence between my two study sites— three strands of barbwire that marked the boundary between two sovereign nations with capitals in crowded cities thousands of miles away from this desert. Those metal strands of barbwire shimmered in the desert heat. I suppose they were meant to be symbolic of political division; they didn't serve as any real physical barrier. I could hop across them in a flash. I've seen roadrunners zip through the wire and jackrabbits duck under it plenty of times. A buddy of mine once saw a Sonoran pronghorn jump clear over the highest strand without missing a step.

But the crazy thing was that the fence had started to shape out a clear "ecological edge." Soon after those strands of barbwire were pulled taut by some cowboy's come-along, the ways people treated the desert diverged on either side.

I plucked one strand of barbwire, as if twanging out a chord on a huge steel guitar. This ecological edge was not identical to the line of the fence but reverberated around it, like the afterimage of a guitar string struck, then watched until its sounding ceased. I was beginning to sense the fluidity of the borderlands—how phenomena on one side of the fence affected those on the other—rather than simply seeing one side cut off from the other by a static partition.

The ancient plants on both sides began their lives as one thinly scattered stand; now they were fragmented by the presence of the fence and the roads that run on either side of it. Trouble was, I had been ignoring how that demarcation had changed the uses of the land following the Gadsden Purchase in 1853. Perhaps two-thirds of the locally known cereus plants had become U.S. citizens, while the others remained under the flag of Mexico.

Before then and for some time after, I suspect that the plants and the people around them were not much affected by international politics. Historically, the O'odham Indians were just as sparsely scattered in the area as the cactus. For centuries, desert life moseyed along for them, more constrained by heat and drought than by the land-use trends in either country. Even the Hispanic families who colonized the region continued to run cattle in both countries. Gradually, however, the U.S. and

Mexican economies went their separate ways—former partners on opposite sides of the fence were forced to split the sheets. And each left his own peculiar imprints on the desert.

One of those imprints was in the shape of a hoof, and it sank deeper into Mexican soil than it did on the American side. Overgrazing was the norm on both sides for decades, until the U.S. government agencies began to force the Indians and their neighbors to reduce the size of their livestock herds. To this day, overgrazing in northern Mexico seldom gets held in check by anything more than the severity of droughts, which periodically decimate the wild corriente cattle hiding out in the brush-choked canyons and arroyos.

I had seen the effects of browsing and trampling by herds of cows, goats, or horses just the other side of the border, but I began to pay more attention to overgrazing of the desert scrub where the cereus grew. It was clear that livestock had browsed back much of the shrubbery beneath which the young cacti took cover. At the northern edge of its range, cereus cactus seedlings need more cover than farther south in frost-free areas.

Had the Mexican cattle snuffed out the hideaways required by the cereus? Sonoran cowboys run stock in densities two to five times higher than the desert's carrying capacity—that estimate I could confirm simply by walking around, year after year, watching how much vegetation was being eaten away. But what is odd is that borderline overgrazing can be seen even more clearly from thousands of miles away.

Waiting to have a beer with a buddy in Tucson one summer, I prowled around outside his office, looking at pictures on his wall. There it was, in a photograph taken from a satellite with infrared film: my little cactus survey site! The Mexican side of the border had been so badly denuded that I could see the border as clear as day. My friend later explained it to me: less red south of the line meant reduced plant growth on the Mexican side. He told me that climatologists up near Phoenix had figured out how the border had even changed local weather patterns. Where trampling and browsing had left the soil more barren and dry, wind speeds have increased markedly while ground temperatures have risen several degrees on the Sonoran side of the fence. These harsher conditions make it tougher for seedlings to get established. If they do survive, the maturing plants remain vulnerable to a variety of stresses.

I suppose I could have stopped there and blamed all the world's ills on cows. But I soon began to grasp that grazing was not the overriding pressure throwing the desert out of kilter. I had noticed that legume trees on the Sonoran side had scars from woodcutting on their trunks and branches. I decided to tally up the damaged trees, and in one week, I counted forty-eight trees with cut-up trunks or branches on a seven-acre hillside. The next week, when I arrived to tag those trees, I found that nine more iron-wood trees had been cut in the previous six days. Down in the washes below the hill, the cutting had been even more aggressive—stumps stood bleeding in the open where massive canopies had once offered shade. Woodcutting was dramatically decreasing the plant cover in which cacti could hide.

I was just beginning to fathom that deforestation in deserts can be as devastating as overgrazing, but it took me more months of reckoning to realize that the two threats were not unrelated to each other. For some reason, I thought that the local wood-cutting was for nearby grills and hearths of low-income Mexican households. As displaced campesinos from Mexico's south gravitate to the borderlands in the hope that American prosperity will rub off on them—or take them in—they build shantytowns in the desert lands harboring slow-growing trees. Border towns in the Sonoran Desert have grown sevenfold in size since 1950. In these borderland barrios, nearly all the fuel used is taken from wood collected within walking distance of the campesino's tar paper, cardboard, and plywood shacks. The desert's low yield of kindling is used for everything from heating tortillas to keeping flimsy-walled homes above freezing during winter nights. The stumps I saw, bleeding out their last gasps of sap, were victims of fallout from the borderland's population bomb.

Around this time, my Mexican friend Humberto Suzán helped me figure out what was going on. He immediately doubted that all the wood being cut was going for local home use. As tallies of pruned trees and stumps filled our field notebooks, we realized that well over half of the legume trees within reach of the cactus stands just south of the border had been cut back or killed by woodcutters. It wasn't long before we observed trucks coming down the borderline road with wood stacked ten feet high. The boys riding along with each load told us that the wood was destined for expensive restaurants in border towns adjacent to national parks, where American tourists came in for mesquite-grilled steaks and seafood. They themselves had only recently taken up woodcutting after the fields they had been working in had succumbed to whiteflies and to the prohibitive costs of pumping deep groundwater for irrigation.

What surprised us most was that the surge in wood gathering for restaurants had used up most of the local supplies formerly available to the shantytown dwellers, who could not match the firewood prices that the restaurant owners paid. Suddenly, the poor families along the border were forced to search for kindling in the United States, where professional woodcutters could not drive their trucks. The locals waited until it was close to dark, then illegally ducked under the fence with borrowed ax or rusty saw and cut an armload of wood in the U.S. reservations, refuges, and parks across the border. In one federally protected area, there was just as much woodcutting going on in its washes within two hundred yards north of the border as there was on the Mexican side of the fence. About a third of the legume trees still living had ax marks and saw scars, and three-fourths of the stumps we encountered were cut remnants of ancient trees that had not been given the chance to die natural deaths.

The borderline campesinos were hauling back home a variety

of desert legumes for firewood, but I was surprised to learn from them that paloverde had become one of their mainstays. Compared with ironwood and mesquite, paloverde seldom receives praise as fuel, and yet it was suddenly commanding prices of eighty-five dollars a truckload in the nearest Mexican town.

I asked one old Mexican cowboy about this. He grumbled, indignant, "I'd never buy paloverde if I had a choice. Paloverde is so punky, it burns as poorly as toilet paper." He reiterated that the mesquite he favored was being used up as charcoal and as fuelwood in barbecues and grills, but that another high-quality wood had also vanished—ironwood.

As these ancient trees have been cut up or burned, night-bloomers and a dozen other kinds of cacti—from towering saguaros and cardons to miniature pincushions—have been left without the protection of thorns and shade they depend upon. For a Sonoran cereus, having a woodcutter blow your cover means certain death.

## Into the Thick of It

NOT TOO MUCH LATER, while talking with several border town woodcutters, I learned that new markets had opened that were taking all the ironwood they could carry. "What markets?" I asked. "Well," one of them replied, staring at the toes of his cowboy boots, "all the remaining ironwood within an hour's drive of the border is being used to make 'Seri Indian' wood carvings. You know, carved animals to sell to American tourists.

"Why are the Seri Indians needing ironwood from up here on the border?" I asked. "Their villages are four or five hours to the south."

The group let my question hang in the air and went back to work. Later one of them took me aside and explained the situation to me. None of them had seen any "real" Seri Indians in years, but their wood was still going to make "Seri carvings." Then he smiled mischievously and added, "There are at least a thousand other Sonorans making carvings like theirs to sell to the tourists! An awful lot of instant Indians, no?"

The woodcutter was admitting a fact that few American tourists had fathomed: the majority of "Seri carvings" they were buying were not made by the Seri at all, although they were often advertised as such. Since the mid-1970s, the market for Indian carvings of animals had boomed, and nearly every Mexican beach town from Mazatlán clear up to the border now had non-Indian craftsmen who chain sawed, then carved and sanded ironwood by machine. The Seri themselves, who had begun selling handmade carvings to tourists a decade before, had lost out to this competition—only a tenth of the one hundred fifty carvers among the eight hundred remaining Seri still made ironwood figurines with any frequency.

The Seri had found that they could not undercut the prices that the machine-assisted carvers could offer to tourists, for it often took them a week of hand labor to make a carving their competitors could crank out in an hour. And the Seri preferred to gather only the dried ironwood on the desert floor, from long-dead trees. Woodcutters were now selling their competitors six giant ironwood trunks for one hundred fifty U.S. dollars, cut from live trees that were four hundred to twelve hundred years old. As wood became scarce near the carvers' villages, the cutters raised their prices even higher and ventured inland to cut virgin stands of ironwood. When non-Indian woodcutters began to be caught on Seri lands, clandestinely cutting live ironwood trees, the Seri arrested them and complained to government officials that they had had enough.

On a summer day Jim Hills and I drove the Sonoran coast into Punta Chueca, a Seri village that he had visited hundreds of times over the previous quarter century. He was not "Jim" to the Kunkaak people who lived there. He was "Santiago," a man who had clowned around with them, learned to sing their sacred songs, flirted with the community's women, and traded tools for carvings with two generations of Seri. They embraced him, tugged at his arms, pulled at his Hawaiian shirt, and teased him about how long it had been since his last visit, how poor his memory for Kunkaak vocabulary had become, and how many women were pining away for him.

Then, when someone mentioned competition for ironwood and crafts markets, the crowd calmed down and listened intently. "Why would anyone buy the Mexican carvings?" asked Ernesto Molino, a craftsman whose production had declined in the face of all the imitations. "We can shape animals so that they have a life that the Mexican carvers could never copy."

We sat around and threw out some ideas on how to deal with the dilemma. Finally, Santiago stood up and invited the Kunkaak of Punta Chueca down to the town of Kino Bay to meet more formally the next day. "If you don't like talk, at least come down for some food. There'll be a feast for everyone who comes." We got in his truck and left a trail of dust behind us.

The next day, the patio outside the Kino field station was loaded with Seri families, some shaping clay into figurines, others looking at carvings made out of barite, a stone that they carved when ironwood could not be found. Gradually, attention shifted to a table where Pedro Romero, the tribal governor, had invited his neighbors to voice their concerns over the depletion of trees central to their traditions and the resulting loss of economic options.

By the end of the afternoon, more than eighty of the Kunkaak had signed a petition to the Mexican government that explained how they had lost their livelihood, selling carvings of desert and marine animals that were part of their traditional lore. The mass production of machine-made ironwood carvings and the clandestine and excessive cutting of ironwood and mesquite for charcoal production were singled out as the major causes of that loss. The one government representative present conceded that it was time to legally protect the rights of Seri artisans and agreed to begin the paperwork to do so.

I looked around the table of men and women who had lived most of their lives beyond the reach of electricity, televisions, books and power tools. They knew the movements and postures of dozens of animals so well that they could effortlessly shape them from wood, clay or stone. I read down through the names on the petition, some of them signed by recently schooled children for elders who had never learned to read or write: Rey Morales Colosio, Rosa Montaño, Carolina Morales Astorga, Enrique Romero Blanco, Roberto Molina Herrera, and so on. Here were people who knew the animals—bighorn and quail and Gila monsters—ones just as likely as the cacti to be extirpated should the ancient desert forests disappear. No trees. No animals. No stories. No carvings of the animals in the stories. *Domino*. That simple.

Back on the border, I stumbled upon a hacked-up ironwood, with a heavily browsed night-bloomer beneath it, its young stems hacked back near ground level. The next month, it was gone. Such premature deaths have become a sorry fact of life in Mexico. I reckon they occur far more frequently there than al norte, on the other side of the fence.

That fact should leave no room for smugness among American environmentalists, as if night-bloomers north of the border are a whole lot safer. Not by a long shot: the fates of the cacti in both countries are as intertwined as the strands of barbwire strung out along the dividing line.

When I first went looking for those spindly cacti, it was during the winter, when they were dormant. Devoid of flowers, fruit, or any frills. It took me a while to really believe that night-bloomers are hot items up North, where such exotic flowers are painted, planted and panted over by the horticultural bourgeoisie.

Let me put it bluntly: they had the cuddle appeal of dead sticks. And so I snorted at the notion that anyone would want them for their greenhouse or front stoop. Even if they wanted to bag one and take it home, I doubted that they would go to as much bother to find the few plants as I had.

Then, in late August—not too long after the rain and its revelation—I stumbled into a cereus population just after dusk. At first, from a distance, I thought someone had left some flashlights on, dropped out among the desert scrub. As I walked closer to some ironwoods and creosote, the flashlights beneath them turned into flowers. I couldn't believe my tired eyes.

"¡Sonababíchi!" I exclaimed to myself. I had lucked upon one of four or five nights that they would bloom that entire summer.

They were gorgeous! The ugly ducklings had metamorphosed into swans! Silky white trumpets drenched with a perfume that I could smell before I could see some of them. The way the delicate buds and flowers were splayed out on the stems reminded me of some fancy floral arrangement in a Japanese painting.

In fact, the jazziness of night-bloomers had not been lost on Japanese floral fanciers. Black-market cereus cactus have been smuggled into Japan and sold for upward of ten thousand yen. No matter that the cactus trafficking is in violation of CITES—the Convention on International Trade in Endangered Species—wealthy hobbyists hold that agreement in contempt anyway, as if they're the only ones who know what is good for rare plants. Night-bloomers not only are flown into Japan but arrive in Germany and other northern European countries as well. The wilder they look, the more they cost.

Where were these plants coming from? I had a hunch that some were being dug up at a few of the places that scientists were naive enough to mention in popular journals. Some cactophiles have even published detailed maps to rare plant localities. More often, one hobbyist hand-draws a sketchy version to give to another cactus collector, who in turn passes it on to other friends. The inroads made by pioneering scientists had become rutted with the heavy tracks of corrupt collectors.

To make matters worse, most cacti are dug up on the lands managed by the government agencies that have the strongest conservation messages—the National Parks and Monuments, National Forests and Wildlife Refuges. I suppose they get visited more than the lands handled by the Bureau of Land Management or the state, but they must get more than their share of "git-me-one" tourists as well. Tourists to Sonoran beach towns also bring a mess of cacti back across the border hidden beneath seats, in the hulls of boats, or inside tires. Throw a bunch of empty beer cans and smelly trash on top, and the border guards let them sail through rather than wallowing in the smell.

From the plant's perspective, who owns the land or what country it inhabits doesn't matter. But over the long haul, night-bloomers growing near the limits of one landholding remain dependent on those living beyond such limits. The Sonoran cereus is seldom found in densities greater than five plants per acre, and they are often spread thinner—a single plant over several acres. Their prime habitat may cover only one hundred twenty acres per square mile.

They don't know who owns them when they start to grow— and the land can change hands several times over a century. Their habitat may be accidentally split between two countries or two land managers, and no one tells them.

Where I staked out my survey with Humberto, we stumbled upon seventy night-bloomer plants on the Mexican side of the border and another forty-five on the U.S. side. Other than the hundred-fifty-acre home ground where all these cacti cluster, there is no good habitat for a considerable distance in either direction.

Small patches. Low numbers. Low densities. Watchers of Sonoran cereus worry. Why? Because these guys need to be cross-pollinated to make any seed. Let me put it another way: if some pollinator does not find two plants blooming the same night within reach of each other, the whole effort is fruitless.

I wonder how they do it. About a third of all the plants in the stand bloom simultaneously on any single night, then close shop the next morning for good. Over the whole season, a single plant may have blooms on three or four nights, but hardly more than half of all the plants set any fruit at all. And many that start to ripen bite the dust before they turn ripe.

Now, put yourself in that plant's position: if you were a cereus flower, you would have less than eight hours of your whole blooming existence to attract a moth who has already visited one of the fifteen to twenty other bloomers scattered all over God's creation. If the moth fails to show, or carries no good pollen your way, you fail to pass on your genes. If you are a U.S. cereus, and a third of your mates are wiped out on the other side of the border, your chances of making sprouts become mighty slim.

Your meager supply of mates within reach may be enough of a worry, but what if your moths are being knocked out as well? When your cactus population sits smack dab in a valley with twenty-five thousand acres of irrigated cropland in it, some bugs around you will go with the flow. But what do you do when the five hundred acres closest to you are put under the plow and into cotton, and three thousand gallons of pesticides are sprayed out of a plane right when you come into flower? Sex under such conditions begins to look like risky business.

Remember the good old days? No lack of mates, no paucity of pollinators? Well, now your most frequent visitor is a common desert dweller, the white-lined sphinx moth. That's the good news. The bad news is that its larval form mobs irrigated fields as a notorious summer feeder on cotton foliage. The cotton farmer thinks that your sexual go-between is his biggest pest. The Parathion, Thiodan, and Azodin he's squirting on his cotton fields are aimed at controlling sphinx moth larvae—your connection for a hot date.

My mind is weary of trying to think like a flower. One notion after another has initially escaped my comprehension, and now this one—having a pollinator that is naturally abundant but attracted to cotton fields is a kiss of death. Why? The moth larvae become thick enough to attract pesticide sprayers.

The night I finally caught sight of a few sphinx moths buzz-ing from one cereus flower to the next, diving in from yards away, I had reason to relax. At least I could be sure that during that one summer, on that particular night, there were enough pollinators splashing about in this small binational gene pool to keep it flowing, from becoming too turbid. The sphinx moths had not yet been drenched with insecticides. There was still hope, perhaps, that the untamed desert nearby was still expansive enough to harbor enough moths to the service of this small cadre of night-bloomers.

Jazzed up, I took my friends, my wife, and our children out to see the last bloom of the season along the border. We were in luck, on time to be dazzled by the floral flashlights shining up from under the skirts of desert bushes. As the moths zipped around us, we spotted several additional night-bloomers that we had walked past numerous times but could not see until they were in bloom. Once again, patches of gray, static shrubs were transformed, for we could see the blossoms, freshly opened and fragrant, attracting an orgy of bugs, beetles, and moths.

By nine in the evening, it looked as though most of the pollen ceremonially offered up that night had already been spent. Exhausted ourselves, we began the bumpy ride along the border down the puddled, muddy Mexican road, overwhelmed by the chimeric nature of the desert: one moment seemingly barren and lifeless, the next, its garishness unmasked. Had I been sleeping, or had the desert?

A haze hung in a cool air pocket as the Sonoran road crossed a muddy arroyo. As my Jeep lumbered up out of the depres-sion, I thought I saw through the mist a cluster of men in the middle of the road. With instruments? In the heavy air and in the beam of the headlights, the men looked as though they held trumpets, violins, bassos sextos, and guitarrones.

"Mariachis!" I cried, startling the half-asleep passengers in the Jeep. As we peered through the windshield into the haze, the trumpets turned into pistols, the guitarrones into Uzi machine guns. An antidrug patrol, well armed, was on the prowl for loads of marijuana and cocaine.

"What are you Americans doing down here in the middle of the night?" the head of the Federales asked. He seemed bewildered by the presence of children in the vehicle.

"We've been out smelling cactus flowers," I tried. The chief grimaced, unconvinced.

Where cultures collide on the border, even cactus sniffing carries its own risks. As the odor of dust and firearms filled the Jeep, the fragrance of the cereus flowers vanished from our midst. We were like the cereus, caught without cover. If only we could reach across the border, reach and suddenly find some refuge. But the hope of immediate refuge drifted away like smoke, and we were frightfully exposed.

# Barbara Ferry

# Following Jaime

JAIME WORKED as a paralegal in a church-funded legal office that represented Central American refugees who got caught crossing the border. He had worked there for five years, earning $150 a week. The office was on the second floor of a shabby building on the main street of a small town in South Texas, above a dress store called Angel's. Directly across the street, the immigration court stood, bland and innocuous looking, with its Department of Justice seal on the door. The immigration service's intention was to send the refugees back to the countries they had left and the legal office's intention was to keep them here. The two entities were thus arch-enemies. They were also pretty much the only gig in town.

When I went down to join the anti-deportation forces as a volunteer, the lawyers in the office told me to follow Jaime around for a few weeks, until I got the hang of the routine.

He was wearing a green suit jacket that looked like it came out of the St. Vincent de Paul bin and old blue jeans the day he met me at the airport. He wore a shadow of a goatee and a small smile. The smile didn't seem to have anything to do with anything or anybody around him. It was an internal smile, the kind you see in old photos of Malcolm X, or paintings of religious mystics.

Jaime is the Spanish version of James, which was the name he was given at his birth—James Cushman. He was blond, well over six feet tall and fair-skinned, no more a Latino than I. His skin was tanned though, from spending so much time in the south Texas sun.

Some of the gringos who went down to the border looking for a cause or redemption from white guilt, or whatever it was we were looking for, adopted Latino names in order to identify with the poor and the oppressed. They wanted to "become" Latino. But I don't think this was the case with Jaime. I think he just figured it was easier for his Spanish-speaking clients to pronounce.

The first thing he did after greeting me was to point out the undercover INS agent waiting over near the baggage claim area, who was also wearing a green suit jacket, though his was less shiny and shabby than Jaime's. The two of them nodded cordially at each other.

Then he drove me to his house, a white and yellow A-frame on the edge of town, which he shared with a varying number of refugees, and was now also going to share with me. The house was sinking like a ship into the ground. Inside, the wooden floors sloped crazily and none of the windows or doors shut properly.

There was a hand-lettered sign posted on the kitchen wall. "Rules for guests" it stated in Spanish. "Number one: 'We will treat each other like brothers and sisters.' Rule number two was 'Do not spit on floor.'"

Mornings, we would climb into the office's blue station wagon and drive east, past the stinking pork rendering plant, past cotton fields and dry riverbeds. Thirty-five miles later we would arrive at the INS detention center, a group of low slung concrete buildings, on the grounds of a sanctuary for migratory birds.

The men and women locked inside called the detention center el corralon, the big corral.

WE'D PULL INTO the parking lot, walk past the men in orange jumpsuits playing basketball behind the cyclone fence, wait for the guard to buzz the door and pass through the metal detector. For the next few hours we'd sit in a beige padded booth that had the feel of a tiny confessional and listen to men with names like Epifanio and Eugenio. Jaime would ask them why they'd left their country, as he tried to fit their lives into the narrow spaces of a political asylum application. La situación allí está muy fea, they would often say. (The situation there is very ugly.) Jaime would write down: "I fear for my life due to persecution based on my membership in the social group comprised of Guatemalan Indians."

In order for Central Americans to avoid being deported, they had to convince an immigration judge that something really terrible would happen to them if they were forced to go home. Having relatives who had been murdered was considered good evidence. Scars from bullet wounds, which could be shown as courtroom exhibits, were even better. Whenever a new client stepped into our booth, I found myself hoping that he would tell us a really horrible story so that we could offer him some chance of freedom.

One time, after I had been there a while and graduated to my own tiny booth, Jaime called over to me. "I've got a good one. Salvadoran, a minor." The boy, 16 years old, had come home one day to find his parents' decapitated bodies lying in front of the house. "This is a great case," Jaime said, excitedly. "We're going to win this one." Then, hearing himself, he turned away, cursing under his breath.

After a few hours, we would step out of the coolness of the detention center, into the radiating heat, and head back to town. I was struggling with Spanish, which I knew only from high school classes. The subjunctive tense, the voice that expresses uncertainty, was giving me particular trouble.

Jaime suggested I listen to the lyrics of the Mexican songs on the radio. The songs were all about love and were, therefore, all written in the subjunctive tense. "Quiero que te vayas por el mundo," the singer would wail. "Que conozcas mucha gente. Que te besen otros labios." (I want you to go out into the world. For many people to know you. For other lips to kiss yours.) We sang along with the radio all the way home.

DURING THE AFTERNOONS, Jaime would sit perched on a barstool behind his desk, often talking on two phones at once, yelling instructions to a detainee on one line, while coaxing money out of a client's relative to pay a bond on the other. At the same time he would be shoveling down rice and beans out of a plastic yogurt container. This was the routine until six or seven in the evening, when we'd return to the corralon for a few more hours in the interview booth.

If you saw him walking down the streets of that small town in his second-hand clothes, you might think Jaime was one of the homeless men who wintered in South Texas, camping around the artificial lake near our house. But he wasn't like that at all. He was more like the guys you see on the floor of the stock exchange wearing splashy ties and beepers and waving their arms in the air. They seem to bounce along on their own single-minded kinetic energy. I often thought that if his clients had been people with money instead of refugees, he would have become a millionaire.

At the same time, he maintained this weird calmness, that small smile. It was an odd combination.

Jaime's triage methods sometimes irritated the lawyers, who wanted to stick to good cases they thought they could win. His idea was to clog up "the system" with as many cases as possible. He was against "the system," but he was very systematic about it.

I lived with him in the sinking house for about three months. I wouldn't say that we became friends, exactly, though we were constantly in each other's company. He didn't offer many details about his life. I found out that he was from Olympia, Washington, and that his parents owned a farm up there, and that he had a twin sister. I think that it was someone in the office who told me he was gay. He didn't philosophize about his work, the way the hippie lawyers and the Christian missionaries who worked with us did. He didn't talk about his opposition to U.S. foreign policy in Central America or his belief that the Christian should welcome the sojourner like it says in the book of Exodus. He did talk, quickly, moving his hands around, but it was usually about the details of a particular case.

I talked a lot. I complained. I could not, I told Jaime, listen to stories about people being tortured all day long, then come home to face a group of men I didn't know who smoked and drank and tried to con me into washing the dirty dishes, and then snored all night long. "I just can't keep up with you," I told him. Jaime watched me impassively with his pale blue eyes while I ranted, and said nothing.

One day, in a fit of rage against my squalid living conditions, I scrubbed the kitchen floor and made soup out of some broccoli and cheese and milk I found in the refrigerator. Jaime came home and ladled the soup into his plastic container of beans and rice and said nothing. Sometimes I didn't like him at all.

Then one night, an electric space heater tipped over while I was sleeping and set my bed on fire. I dragged the flaming mattress out into the yard, where it smoldered until morning. The next day I stomped into the office and demanded new living quarters.

They let me rent an apartment. A tiny hot box, with no shower and a pit bull next door—but all my own. My new home provided an outlet for one of Jaime's few indulgences— smoking pot, or more often, eating homemade oatmeal raisin marijuana cookies.

It was a strange habit, because pot didn't seem to make Jaime want to stare into space or giggle or watch TV reruns for hours. He would get high and then go back to the office and work at his usual frenetic pace.

The lawyers had forbidden him to keep his stash in his own house, because our clients, the refugees, were there. So he kept his cookies in the glove compartment of the office car, and sometimes drove around town smoking a joint. But that wasn't safe either. So when I got my own apartment he came over in the late afternoons to bake cookies.

Gradually I stopped measuring myself against him and began to think of him as a friend.

I knew of two other things that made him happy. He liked it when we drove away from the corralon with the back seat of the car full of newly-released detainees. And he liked to swim the Gulf of Mexico. On the best days we drove straight from the corralon to the beach and ran into the waves while the ex-prisoners yelled warnings at us—"The sun will punish you" —from the safety of the shade.

I think Jaime felt personally responsible for every one of the hundreds of people who ended up in the corralon. Faced with the enormity of the burden, he doled out his attention carefully. He couldn't afford to get bogged down with any particular sad story. But he indulged people sometimes. Once, I went along on one of his weekend shopping trips at K Mart for inmate provisions. He bought tube socks and cigarettes for the men, a home perm kit a woman from Jamaica had requested. We had a Honduran teenager named Rigoberto with us, who had lost his shoes when he crossed the Rio Grande. Rigoberto spied a pair of black leather sneakers that seemed to him the perfect fulfillment of the American dream. But Jaime saw another pair, bright yellow canvas high tops that were half the price.

Rigoberto balked. "Es color de mujer," he protested. "That's a woman's color."

Jaime stood his ground. He was paying for them after all. He came back from the checkout counter, yellow sneakers and a can of black spray paint in hand. If Rigoberto couldn't have his leather sneakers he could at least cover up the woman's color.

When Jaime first started complaining about seeing bright pink lights flash across his field of vision, 11 months after I first met him, we all muttered about too much stress, or maybe a batch of bad dope. It turned out to be a malignant brain tumor pressing on his optic nerve. Jaime said the pink lights looked like dragons.

When I saw him in the hospital he was propped up in his bed, tubes sticking out of his arm, a telephone receiver pressed into his ear, his list of clients resting on his lap.

"The telephone keeps ringing," he said. "Just like at the office."

The next day, two of the brothers I didn't know he had flew down from Seattle to take him home. They seemed like nice, normal people who knew little about his life in Texas. We seemed as improbable to them as they did to us. Surgeons in Seattle operated but discovered that the tumor had sent shoots of ganglia all over his brain. After the operation, his twin sister wrote and said he was blind and childlike. He died a year later.

Rubén Martínez

# Prop. 187: Birth of a Movement?

*EDITORS' NOTE: Proposition 187, a California voter initiative approved in 1994, sought to eliminate government services—such as health care and public education—for undocumented immigrants. Several civil rights organizations filed lawsuits against 187 on constitutional grounds. At this printing, it has yet to be implemented because of a federal court restraining order.*

POLITICAL PASSIONS are inflamed (literally) at the Peace and Justice Center, a quasi-underground youth hangout just west of downtown Los Angeles. As skateboarding daredevils go airborne and graffiti artists perfect spray can techniques on portable wooden canvases in the parking lot, about twenty activists in their late teens and early twenties plot pyromaniacal political theater in a meeting room decorated with posters of black and brown revolutionaries—everyone from Malcolm to Martin to Che and Marcos. The group approximates a politicized version of the forlorn ghetto waifs of Larry Clark's *Kids*—a multi-ethnic (though majority Latino) crew of youth who are creative, angry, idealistic, and unabashedly radical.

The demonstration being planned is set to take place at the federal courthouse where the fate of Proposition 187 is being deliberated by Judge Mariana Pfaelzer. "We have to be there, so that they will feel a serious presence," says César Cruz, a Chicano student at UC Irvine sporting the latest in 90s Chicano revolutionary chic: a dramatic black tejana (Stetson-style cowboy hat worn by Mexican banda music aficionados), a bandanna forming an inverted triangle from chin to chest, and a large leather medallion carved with the Aztec Sun Calendar hanging from his neck.

Nods around the room. "Yeah," says a blonde-haired, blue-eyed teen with a Chicago accent who, through one of those California transcultural miracles is now actually a Chicana who goes by the name of "Lucha" (in Spanish, "The Struggle"), "I think we should fuckin' take the streets!"

César charges forward with the adrenaline of an activist who knows that maybe revolution, or perhaps apocalypse, or possibly both, is just around the corner. "Logistics!" he cries out, furiously scribbling notes on loose yellow sheets that lie on the floor next to his copy of *The Diary of Che Guevara*. "Who's going to bring the bullhorn?"

They will take the streets. There will be civil disobedience. And, they hope, there will be massive media coverage because of the happy coincidence that the federal court building is across the street from the county court building, where every media organization in the country is presently camped out covering the O.J. Simpson trial.

The all-important discussion of march aesthetics begins. The members of the Four Winds Student Movement, La Resistencia (a wing of the Revolutionary Communist Party, USA), Youth Breaking Borders, the Affirmative Action Coalition of UC Irvine, and the Women's Action Coalition share one vision in common: they want to burn something.

"Let's burn those snitch forms!" someone proposes, referring to a draft from the California Attorney General's office of a form to be used—should 187 ever actually become law—to turn in "suspected illegal aliens."

The representative from the Women's Action Coalition offers, "I could make a big doll of Pete Wilson, cover him with those forms and then burn him." The idea is received with much laughter and immediate approval. (This is a far cry from the solemn Central America solidarity meetings I attended in the 80s, I think to myself. This generation appears to be actually having *fun*.)

"Let's dress Pete Wilson in a KKK outfit," César blurts out.

But Angel Cervantes, a student at the Claremont Graduate School and one of the most prominent youth leaders of the massive school walkouts just days before the 1994 election that saw the passage of 187, is concerned about timing. "If you burn Wilson first, the cops might arrest you and then the media won't get to hear any speakers. How about the speakers first, then burn Wilson?"

Several more proposals are tossed out; it's getting hard to follow exactly what is being burned when. "So what's it going to be?" asks Olga Miranda, a Belmont High School student leader. "Snitch forms burning, speaker, Wilson burning, or speaker, speaker, speaker, burning, burning?"

The WAC rep can't resist: "Speaker burn! Speaker burn! Speaker burn!"

After more deliberations, the group comes up with a slogan: "Wilson, you liar, we'll set your ass on fire!"

THE YOUNG RADICALS at the Peace and Justice Center and others like them throughout the Southwest represent the most important student mobilization in Los Angeles since the late 60s. Though they have yet to replicate the massive student walkouts and marches of 1994, this small but vocal and potentially galvanizing force represents, for Latinos, the most politicized generation since the Chicano movement born thirty years ago in the picking fields of California.

What neither no-nukes or greens could manage in the 80s, Prop. 187 achieved in a matter of weeks in 1994: a massive mobilization of inner city youth whose political voice had been virtually silent for over two decades. Most of the activists at the Peace and Justice Center are veterans of last year's protests—high school and college students who led walkouts, organized teach-ins, volunteered for get-out-the-vote efforts. Many were present at the pre-election October 16 march in Los Angeles which drew over 100,000 people, one of the largest demonstrations in modern California history.

"Proposition 187 affects me in every way," says Ana Vásquez, a 20-year-old student at USC. "My family is half documented and half undocumented. My mother's a citizen, my tíos (uncles) came across the river."

Indeed, most of the advocates for the undocumented are young Chicano and Central American *citizens* like Ana who feel that 187 paints all Latinos, regardless of immigration status, as welfare freeloaders, criminals, and the cause of the worst economic downturn in California since the Depression. In this, the activists of the 90s differ from their 60s forerunners. Latinos were once clearly and bitterly divided between native-born, mostly English-speaking Chicanos and immigrant, Spanish-speaking Mexicanos. Cultural differences and at times the appearance, if not the fact, of economic competition contributed to this rift.

Today, activists decry the line between San Diego and Tijuana. A popular slogan: "We didn't cross the border, the border crossed us." (Which re-imagines the old Mexico whose territory included the Southwest before the Mexican-American War.) And a growing Central American population, already politicized from the experience of the anti-intervention and sanctuary efforts of the 80s, has also informed and influenced what was once purely "Chicano" activism.

"We're trying to break down the image that this is the 'Chicano movement' of the 90s," says Angel Cervantes, a founding member of the Four Winds Student Movement (the group's name hints at Native American spirituality and a multi-ethnic worldview). "We want to bring in anyone who's been marginalized. A lot of organizers are moving away from race and ethnicity towards issues of class."

This post-nationalist rhetoric has yet to translate into political reality, however. While the crew at the Peace and Justice Center may indeed be a sign of a new coalition politics, the turn-out at the anti-187 marches in 1994 and the large protest in April 1996 following the videotaped beating by sheriff's deputies of three undocumented immigrants in Riverside, California, was practically 99 percent Latino. 1994's election results once again confirmed California's political and cultural balkanization. According to a *Los Angeles Times* exit poll, the divide between Anglo, middle-class California and the soon-to-be-majority Latino, mostly working-class population has become an unbreachable chasm. White Californians voted nearly three-to-one in favor of 187, while Latinos voted nearly four-to-one against. Asians and African-Americans wound up in the middle, nearly splitting even—perhaps a hopeful sign for coalition-minded activists.

The problem is, demographics don't match up with actual voter turnout, a situation that Mexican political scientist Jorge Castañeda has called California's "electoral apartheid." Had Latinos voted proportionate to their population numbers (approximately one-third statewide), 187 may well have been defeated. Low voter registration and turnout rates, along with the fact that a substantial number of Latinos are not citizens —documented and undocumented—have historically held back not only a possible swing vote, but a bloc that could, theoretically, become the dominant force of California politics.

NOT ALL the grassroots organizing going on around the issue of 187 is as visionary, or radical, as the admittedly fringe youth mini-movement at the Peace and Justice Center. Many

Latino institutions are focusing on political empowerment through more traditional channels, energized, like the students, by 187.

In 1994, community-based organizations like the Central American Resource Center, One Stop Immigration, and the Catholic Church-based United Neighborhoods Organization recruited people for marches, conducted letter-writing campaigns, and coordinated media outreach efforts. Latino newspapers, TV and radio stations went on an unabashed crusade. *La Opinión,* the country's largest Spanish-language daily, still regularly lists hotline numbers in stories about post-187 discrimination.

Nevertheless, there were deep divisions over strategy from the very beginning of the new Latino activism, and these remain intact today. Before the election, some elected officials counseled against massive demonstrations. "All those angry brown faces on TV, the Mexican flags being waved, it was exactly the wrong image to be sending out," says one political consultant. "It played right into whites' fears about being overwhelmed by Latins."

Others questioned this thinking, however. "It was a waste of time to pander to the angry white voter," says Gilbert Cedillo, general manager of SEIU Local 660, a union representing over 40,000 County of Los Angeles workers currently facing unprecedented lay-offs due to massive budget cuts. "The course we should have been following is to expand our base and create a social movement."

While the Peace and Justice Center kids dream of taking over the streets, many community-based organizations are focusing on voter empowerment. The Southwest Voter Research and Education Project estimates that some 100,000 amnesty residents are applying for citizenship yearly, a rate that is proving untenable for an agency primarily funded these days to "hold the line" at our southern border. At a recent INS swearing-in ceremony for new citizens in a football-field-sized room in the

Los Angeles Convention Center, it was evident that 187 has everything to do with the increased interest in citizenship.

"With the new laws that they're passing, I was afraid I'd be left defenseless," says Adelaido Vásquez, a Mexican immigrant who lived over a dozen years here and had heretofore resisted naturalization—an often painful process for Mexicans whose cultural ambivalence, given the history of conflict and discrimination in the Southwest, is legendary. "Today, they talk about illegal residents. Tomorrow, it could be legal residents." (Fulfilling Vásquez's prophecy, a plethora of legislation has made its way to Capitol Hill, virtually all of it restrictionist, and including some measures that would deny legal residents and new citizens public benefits.)

As the newest citizens exit the Convention Center, they are accosted immediately by partisan voter registration activists. "Republicans! Republicans register here!" shouts Yarda Scudder, a middle-aged blond woman wearing jeans and a red kerchief tied around her neck, attempting to approximate, perhaps, that ole' Ronald Reagan pastoral look. But the table that does the brisker business is presided over by the portly, Zapata-moustached Democrat Rudy Montalvo of the Los Angeles County Federation of Labor—a veteran of the demonstrations against 187. "Make your vote known!" he shouts in Spanish. "Let Pete Wilson hear the voice of the immigrants, of the workers, of the humble!"

The Catholic Church is active in the citizenship drive as well. There are 187 (eerie coincidence) Latino-majority parishes out of a total of 290 in the most populous archdiocese in the country. According to assistant director of Hispanic Ministry Louis Velásquez, half of these are helping the immigrant faithful naturalize. Sounding a clear liberation theology line, Velásquez says that the Church is "committed to the mandate of the gospel, which is less a matter of eternal life after death than living life here and now with justice, peace, and love."

(Interestingly, the Protestant evangelical churches, the Catholic

Church's arch enemy in the end-of-century battle for the souls of Latinos continent-wide, is equally involved in a grassroots effort at, the very least, keeping their brethren from being deported. At Iglesia Evangelica Latina in the Silver Lake district of Los Angeles, the church boasts an immigration office with several counselors and new computers. Over a 100 people a week seek immigration services here, according to church officials.)

Voter registration organizers are confident that political empowerment for Latinos is just around the corner. "We expect to have 2.1 million people registered by next year," says Antonio González, director of the Southwest Voter Research and Education Project. "The '96 election will be hot. California will be at the center of the country politically because of issues like immigration—and the Latino vote will increasingly be heard."

But, warns David Hayes-Bautista, director of the Alta California Research Center, Latinos will not be able to go at it alone. "The vast majority of the electorate will still be largely older and Anglo," he says. "Latinos must forge ties with African-Americans, Asians and progressive whites." It is a dream coalition that has yet to materialize.

Something else missing from the most mainstream institutions (and elected officials) is word on the fate of the undocumented, who are, at least ostensibly, the direct target of 187. While most organizations speak sympathetically of the un-documented—echoing the radical students' "borderless world" philosophy—the practical and political upshot of this solidarity is conspicuous in its lack of definition. When asked about the undocumented population (it is estimated that anywhere between three and 10 percent of California's Latinos may lack papers), one Catholic Church official said that the "Church still provides" healthcare and education through its hospitals and parochial schools to anyone regardless of immigration status, which sounds more like pious charity than forcefully advocating for more permanent solutions.

Admittedly, proposals such as a new amnesty to legalize the

illegals like the Immigration Reform and Control Act of 1986 is a political longshot in the current jingoistic climate. But many activists think that the mainline institutions have all but abandoned the undocumented. "The definition of political power only through voting is too narrow," says Leonardo Vilchis, a lay worker at Dolores Mission Church in East Los Angeles, a parish that serves some 150 undocumented persons through refugee and shelter services. "With that definition, you're ignoring the biggest problem—the undocumented." Vilchis notes that the undocumented have wound up advocating for themselves —forming street vending cooperatives and independent day-laborer unions.

Despite the recent high profile crackdown at the border, the incessant sweeps of la migra in the cities and the increasingly ill political winds blowing even in Washington, D.C., the undocumented themselves appear unfazed by the political storm. A visit to a day-laborer site on the corner of Sunset and Alvarado in Los Angeles reveals the eternal hope of the immigrant. By mid-morning, when most of the possibility of a day's work has evaporated, a handful of men wearing paint-flecked T-shirts, jeans and workboots respond to the situation with a shrug of the shoulders.

Yes, times are tough, several of the men say. "Work's less easy to come by," says Macario Moctezuma, a 28-year-old native of Mexico City who lost a job with a construction company when the boss came around asking for "good papers." Still, there's no going back, he says, prompting several men to nod in agreement. "We're still better off here."

Ricardo Martínez, a 21-year-old from rural Jalisco still believes in the promise of California—more than can be said for the supporters of 187. "I'm hopeful that all this will change," he says, "and that one day the politicians here are 100 percent Latino, so that we can be treated better in California. Why do they put us down so much when they're practically living off of the work we do for them?" As I'm getting into my car,

Ricardo comes up to me out of earshot of the others. Do I know of a good journalism school, he wants to know? "I know I have to learn English, and I'm taking classes at night, plus I bought one of those home study classes with the cassettes...."

Ricardo's optimism is the ultimate paradox in California's immigration battle. And, perhaps, a hint of a truth that few —certainly not liberal Latino politicians—can utter. "The undocumented are the most radical people we have right now," says Roberto Lovato, executive director of the Central American Resource Center. "They defy Pete Wilson and [former INS Western Region director and 187 proponent] Harold Ezell. Despite all kinds of restrictions, they're taking over housing, selling on our streets, thumbing for work on the boulevards, taking care of the children and cleaning the homes and gardens of everyone from movie stars to the Governor."

Lovato, a Salvadoran-American and veteran activist from the days of Central American solidarity, can't help but quote Monseñor Oscar Romero, the martyred Salvadoran archbishop, to offer a moral justification for the undocumenteds' "criminal" activity: "You don't have to follow an immoral law."

Meanwhile, the political temperature continues heating up in 187 California. The fallout from the Riverside beatings and the continuing violence at the border, including two fatal highway accidents involving the Border Patrol in early 1996, has helped to re-mobilize the forces initially unleashed after the 1994 election.

The immigration debate, after all, includes issues of race relations, class disparity, and the global economy. Three decades after the civil rights movement brought us both fire on the streets and major change to our public lives, a new, and, perhaps, just as momentous struggle is upon us. At the center of the controversy are the newest Americans—and their blood relatives who have been here for generations.

Teresa Leal
with Nadine Epstein

# Recipe for a Radical

EDITORS' NOTE: When this article was published in 1988, Teresa Leal was running for mayor of Nogales, Sonora. She lost that race, but she keeps trying, she keeps "throwing rocks at the sun." As an unrelenting social activist, she works with Proyecto "Comadres," an organization she co-founded with her friend Nadine Epstein in 1987. Comadres is an alliance of local women who are struggling to empower women and children in the barrios of Nogales in their everyday battles to better their lives. Immediate environmental/health issues are among the most important that Comadres confronts: for instance, contaminated drinking water, lack of health-related infrastructure, and toxic wastes issuing from local maquiladora plants. Persons interested in knowing more about Comadres may call 1-520-287-6317.

M Y MOTHER brings this young man, whom I've never known and never seen, and she says, "I've got this young man, he's very Catholic, he's very correct, and he's a very good son, and I want you to marry him." So when I met him, I already knew what I was going to do. And I did it. I did it with the feeling that I will marry him and will be "free." At the same time I'll be pleasing my mother and she'll be through with this feeling that I'm being brought up in an American society where women are very loose and have no scruples. Two weeks after I got married, I approached my mother and I began by saying, "Well, you know he's not all that I expected." Then she stopped me short and she said, "Listen, if you have any complaints, anything, I don't want to hear it. You married him, you gave your word to God and to me, and you'll keep it. And if you don't, you don't have a mother, and, of course, you don't have a God." I just clammed up and for sixteen years I never complained to anybody. The only solace I could find were my children and my books and my ideas and my work with the poor.

Nine months and fifteen days after I married I had my first baby. So a month or two after I first married I began having morning sickness. And the bastard, the beast, would bar me from vomiting because it made him queasy. He would get me before I got to the bathroom and he would say, "Don't do it, swallow it."

PERSONALLY, I was having babies every year (eight in all) and coping as best I could with a beast—for fourteen years. My excuse for putting up with it was that I had given my word to both man and God (and worst of all, to my mom) and I was going to keep it if it killed me. It almost did. The only problem is that after I broke up the marriage, he moved in next door. The hassle of an ex-husband waging war from a permanent and short distance wasn't easy.

My husband would come and break windows and the whole neighborhood would be witness to it. Finally, around three o'clock in the morning, this was the last time I called the police, the captain said, "Listen, if you call me one more time, I'm going to put you in jail." I said, "why?" He said, "You're just wasting my time, I have other things to do." I said, "Well, the guy's got a butcher knife, can't you see that?" And he said, "Yes. Listen, if he comes into your house, you kill him. You have a right to defend your house. Knock him over with a chair. Whatever. And you're protecting your children."

So I went back home and the guy was still yelling away. Then he started breaking the windows. I have a crossbow. I could see his knife. I started getting it together. I'm going to put a dart through his foot or something. There are darts with a rubber end to stun, darts to inject tranquilizers. I reached for a thin dart because I was going to put one through his foot, and then I thought, I'm just going to make him into a victim. I grabbed a long, very pointed thick dart and I said I'm going to kill him. This had been going on for such a long time and nobody did anything. I'd been asking for help for such a long time and— my mother she comes to visit me in Nogales and she says I was such a nice little girl, she doesn't know what happened to me. I don't go explaining to anybody. He explains it. Everybody says he's such a nice person. He goes to church every day, to Mass every Sunday, he goes to confession. I grabbed a big one and I was going to kill him. I'm a very good shot. The minute I put on the dart, he fell through the window he was so drunk. I felt so desperate and the guy is laying face down and I try to wake him up and he is out cold. I didn't know why I wanted him to be awake when I killed him, except maybe a sense of honor. I just couldn't bring myself to shoot him right there. I put the crossbow on the table.

Early the next morning I gave it to a lawyer friend and told him not to let me have it. I went to the police again and the man I had talked to on the phone said, "You should have killed the bastard."

I HAVE THE POTENTIAL for a very short life. Seven years ago when I had Roberto, my last baby, I fell on the floor and my skull was cracked. From that I got a tumor and it began to grow. At first I thought the headaches were just out of the disgust I had. I had blackouts. I was walking down the street one day with Roberto, who was a year old, and three or four of the other children. I blacked out in the street and I could have been killed and they pulled me to the side of the street. I went to the doctor. The doctor said what you have is an aneurysm. It's not cancerous. An operation would probably leave me handicapped. Or I could die right there. I decided I would just live it out, whatever it was. He told me that I could live maybe a year or two, at most. But if it stopped enlarging, I could live to a ripe old age. I didn't have anybody I could run to. I was dealing with a divorce, with earning enough money—with chopping wood because I didn't have electricity or gas, even hunting because I didn't have enough money to buy food. I decided that, okay, I think I'm going to die. Which means that I haven't much time. I recorded some messages for my children. I talked about when they would have their first relationship, when they would face their first opportunity to give a bribe, when they would be shunned by others. I asked to be cremated. I went to see a priest because my mother and children are Catholic. I went to see coffins, I laid in some coffins—they are very uncomfortable. I told the people at the funeral home it was for an aunt of mine. I put my organs up for donation. That way my children wouldn't have to spend on a funeral. Then I said, What is the best way of dying with dignity? What am I going to do?

What really pushed me to think that I would not go by myself when I died was that I had been working with a lot of social justice issues. One of the big things that is marring Mexico is the corruption. What do you say to people about what is happening in Mexico? All these Americans who don't go to my country, they say—You're a bunch of marijuana growers and there is a lot of corruption in your country, your government is corrupt and gone to pot, literally.

Then comes this total overwhelming sensation that the good weren't the good, that justice just wasn't done to those that I cared about. There was a lawyer, a writer, there was the attorney general, and there was me. We all were concerned with this one thing, the injustice, and had this tight-knit circle. Then, the attorney general was himself framed and brought down in shackles. Everybody freaked out. The lawyer armed himself to the hilt and headed for the United States. The writer, he just barricaded himself and waited for them to come and pick him up and kill him. And then there was me and what was I to do? I was having these tremendous problems at home. I was totally disenchanted with society. I still had an inclination toward change through politics. I couldn't sneak off to the United States, I couldn't do what the writer was doing. That's when I figured I'll do it: I'll take a couple of very bad politicians with me.

I think maybe it's in the genes. My family came from a social activism that has been going on for many years, for many generations. The reason my mother couldn't take it was that my father and his family helped form, in the '30s and '40s, a party called *Partido Populare Socialista*, which is a popular socialist party dedicated to bringing back the origins of the Revolution— agrarian reform and a bettering of the impoverished masses. Then it evolved into a really social element to create change. My mother never liked that—that they used arms to get their politics through.

A friend of mine visited, and he was from the underground, a left-wing courier. He told me about this way of dying, about how you could go out in a big way, you could go and place yourself next to somebody who really is the root of all this evil, get next to this great big guy and blow yourself up with him. I said, "I don't know how to go about that." And he said, "Well, I have some friends who could teach you."

He invited me to a school—one was being set up in northern Mexico, he said. First, you have to be recommended, he said, but that's easy because I can recommend you. Then you have to be willing psychologically to do this—you have to be screened.

He gave me a contact and then the man on the phone said, Come to this city, and he gave me a phone number. The man said, "You have been recommended for our institution. We would like to see if we have the curriculum necessary for you to come." So I arrived from a bus station and I called and they said go to such and such a place and then just wait there.

I wasn't prepared for it. It was on the beach and I sat there for quite a while. A very sedate looking person comes over, very scholarly, longish hair, a very non-aggressive looking person. He said, "Teresa?" and we sat on a rock and talked. He asked about my eight children, he couldn't believe I had so many, and he said, How could you dare get a divorce? It's so hard, he said, to feed just his two kids. I was asked repeatedly why I had got my divorce and I told him the whole story. But he just kept asking why. What were the faults, he kept asking, that my husband saw in me? He kept alluding to the fact that I was a coward, that the reason I had stayed with my marriage such a long time was that I was afraid to drop it. That the reason I had even accepted this was that I did not want to say no to my mother. That my whole life was one cowardly situation after another. I was afraid to face the end as it would come naturally.

I was bombarded with all kinds of questions: What if you're just a CIA agent trying to penetrate? How many men do you sleep with? Do you prostitute yourself? Things like what tastes do you have in sexual play? I began to falter because the questions became so personal and I would sometimes shoot back a lie. I didn't want to come out like a prude. But, of course, he noticed. Finally, I would say, I don't think that's any of your business. He would say, "What's wrong with you? You've got to be totally honest, that's what the revolution is all about." He said, You're playing games just to get through the screening. He kept asking me if I thought the training was going to make me a hero?

He said, "Why don't you just shoot yourself?" I said there were a bunch of creeps around here who weren't worth remaining on this planet, creeps who just make hell for people. He said, "That's your anger: they're going to keep on living and you are going to die." I said, "No." He said, "What if after you go through this program and have an assignment, you discover that you're operable? Are you going to drop everything and maybe denounce us? And you go your own way and you are safe and you live on for years. What then?" I said, "I find it highly improbable that that will happen." And he said, "Well, it's very possible with modern medicine. How about us? You'd drop us and forget all about us?" I said, "No, I think you have a place in life, a place in this struggle. I don't think that you're going about it right. That's one of the reasons why I don't beat my kids. I've never laid a hand on them. When we've lost our reason, then we are admitting we have lost it all. And that's your role, when we've lost it all. That's when you will come in. But not yet. Except for me, because I've lost it all." I was questioned on the beach for four hours.

That night we met again and he fingerprinted me. He wanted medical proof that I was really going to die. I had an X-ray of my head. After that, he eased off. Then he started in again. I was very angry. He had torn down all my explanations. That night he questioned me for three more hours. I figured the guy was just out to unmask me. And the truth is, he was right. So I just left and went to the bus station and went back home. I thought for sure that I had failed this job interview. About a month later, the same voice called me and said, "All right, do the same thing again, and we'll be expecting you." I said, "What do I take?" And he said, "Some overnight things, take some paper that will identify you." And I did.

When I got there, I checked into a hotel and then I called and they asked what room I was in and who I was with and who I had talked to and who I had told. What reason had I given for being away from home? Who had bought the bus ticket? Who did I talk to on the bus? Had I been approached at the inspection point twenty-one kilometers from Nogales? They told me not to talk to anyone or to call anybody. And if I did talk to anybody to remember what I had said, because I would be asked. They told me I would be monitored.

So I went to the same area as before, the beach, and was picked up. There were about fifteen people on this desolate beach. They were people who seemed like students or professors or professionals, all Latinos from various nations in this hemisphere—there was one who looked Oriental. People from many places and groups who would go back to their own countries after the program. Some were in little groups like they came together and knew each other, and some just stared off. The majority did not talk. Nobody had any bags—I was told to leave everything at the hotel, and not to leave it at the desk and to bring my key with me. I pretended I was walking down the beach. Finally, a car came in and all these people flocked to the car. Then a truck came by and picked up people. Some had books and papers and pencils and they were piled up and burned. Everyone was frisked, everywhere. Our shoes were taken off. They told us to unhook our bras and shake them. And they said, "No padding, no padding," because padding is made out of paper and you can take notes with paper. And they checked our body cavities. All jewelry and watches were taken away. The labels on our clothes were checked. One woman had Calvin Klein pants and she was asked where she bought them and how much they cost. Then they wrote that down—I guess they were going to check. I had on some khaki pants and a T-shirt and some walking shoes and the inside sole was taken out. No dark glasses were allowed. We just went off with nothing and we did not know how long we were going off.

I wasn't afraid. I knew by the body language that some of the people had done it before. We went down a ways and then back again and then down dirt roads and finally ended up on another strip of beach way back. There were two trailers and none of the vehicles had license plates. It looked like an isolated tourist group. Then we were split up in groups, blindfolded and taken to other places. I tried not to speak too much because I had learned they could spot my American accent and I thought that a bunch of people that leery about the CIA...well, it could

be terrible. I've always had this thing about my accent—
anybody who is a Mexicano can tell right away if your first
language is not Spanish. I've always had trouble with that. When
I first didn't speak very good Spanish, I was dubbed a chicana
(chicanas are very looked down upon in my country) or a
CIA agent. And by God, I didn't want to be a CIA agent, not in
this camp anyway.

They all stared at me and would talk to each other. Two
or three days later, I realized that I was the only one being
considered for a suicide mission. I finally realized that they
thought I was very brave. One guy told me I was highly
regarded because I was going to give it all.

We were told right away not to have sex. Not to drink when
we were outside the camp. Not to make any phone calls. Not to
talk to strangers. If the sign was ever given, we were told to act
like tourists. We had bathing suits underneath our clothes, we
had beach balls, snacks, beer on ice. There was a table with cards
already laid out. There were fashion magazines laying out. We'd
stay at hotels at night and go out to the camp during the day.
There was this big camper with electronic equipment—
they taught how to man a short wave radio, how to make a
short wave radio. They had a big box of first-aid. They had a
projector with a camera, they had arms, they had charts. We
saw films on how to clean a pistol, how to make a gun, what
chemicals are needed for making this or that, how to mix them.
You were told to sit there and take it in, you were not to take any
notes. The arms were given out inside the trailers and we did
things repeatedly, practicing and practicing. When I started doing it, they didn't really care if I did it well. They kept looking at
me. They decided I didn't have to learn those things. I wasn't
going to have the time according to the budget in my life.

There was a lot of harassment. If somebody didn't know how
to do something, they were told that they were stupid, retarded.
This woman started to cry and she was slapped. At first I asked
questions, and I was told to shut up—no questions. I thought,

this is very infantile. I thought, I don't have to take this. But then I thought, with these people, if I back off, they will all sneer. It was a very competitive thing. I was never watched as much because they didn't care if I really learned anything. There were about seven teachers and they were international. There were other students who didn't look like students. When we were taught how to handle a machine gun, they were already doing it. We'd been told we'd have observers who would be monitoring us. Why would anyone come to the school who already knew the material—just to get the credit? Terrorists are seeking diplomas and credentials? In fact, that's why they become terrorists, because they lost their faith in credentials.

It was supposed to be for ten days. The first day we were given a series of hypothetical situations and each of us was asked how we would deal with them. Our answers were taped and then they would go back and replay the answers and the whole group would then put in some criticism. The second day we were given the methodologies of different groups and their results. The third day was the arms and chemicals. We were told to study the equations, the amounts, and the results.

The people around me were from a long tradition of political activism. I was looking for an elementary way of dying. They weren't people who were newcomers. They were very human. There were two lesbians who had very strong rhetoric, using a lot of machismo and all that, and they fought with each other. They fought over what couples fight over—the guy drank too much and the woman was frigid. I tried to ignore the rule about talking. I would come up to people and say, "My name is Teresa, what's yours?" and people would give me this stony look. So I listened to them talk, and some of them knew each other. Some people talked about their fear about what was going on in the world—with the growth of fascism. We talked about the plight of the environment, the whales for example, because we were close to the sea. The irony of the whales killing themselves— you know that's never been explained. One of them thought that maybe that was a cosmic response to a genocide that was going on, that to let people see what was going on they would do it themselves.

There was a scattering of currents there. There came a time when their rhetoric couldn't be fit into a left wing appreciation of what was going on. Somebody mentioned the Gray Wolves in an exalted way and then somebody told me he belonged to the Gray Wolves. The Gray Wolves are a group in Germany and Austria, a terrorist group, a right-wing group. They are like a sect, they kill. When I would go back to the hotel at night, I would realize some of the people admired people like Hitler. Che Guevara wasn't talked about at all—he was bland compared to the people talked about. Here I am thinking about saving the masses and making everybody happy and not giving up until everybody has a swimming pool and a limousine and all these things are going on around me. This was a terrorist camp open to all ideologies. People were there to kill and learn the art of killing. Here we were among wolves and we were part of it.

One woman asked, "How can we know the ratio of people killed? How can we lessen the possibilities of killing innocent people?" One of the students said right away, "That has nothing to do with it." The others nodded their approval—they had heard the answer they wanted to hear.

Before we left every night we were taken into little groups and some of us, according to what they observed during the day, were taken aside and talked to directly. The somebody I talked to, I guess was a German, but he spoke very good Spanish. He told me that I seemed a little confused. I said yes. I started to tell him what I felt and he said, "Stop that. I don't want to hear that." I said maybe there is something wrong here or I'm wrong. He said, "No, no, it's just that you don't fit into this. Tomorrow you're going to come and we start on your program. Right now, all this time, we've been preparing the basis for the different groups that are going to go off. You'll be the only one—I'm going to be your instructor."

And I said, "But if I don't feel comfortable about this...."

And he said, "You don't have to feel comfortable about this because you're only going to do this once. These people are militants, they've had commitments for a long time to the groups that have sent them, to the groups that need them."

That night I hardly got any sleep. I walked. What he was telling me was that I was more of a tool than the rest—a tool for a one-time thing. That night I went looking for my friend in the camp and we talked. He said, "You can't get out of it. They could even do away with you." We had been told that if we wanted to get out of it, we could be killed.

That night we talked all night, and he gave me the good excuses because he knew where I was coming from. He said, Be as truthful as you can because they're going to come down hard on you. He said, I can't get out of it but you may be able to because they know from the start that you're a square—that you're not really a hard-core professional.

And so I went on the following morning, the fourth day, and as nicely as I could I told the original guy who had contacted me. "I couldn't sleep at all last night," I said. "I'm very nervous. I don't think I'm ready for this project." He asked, "Are you sick?" I told him I just didn't think I could do it. I'm not ready for it.

He just stared at me, there was this long silence after I finished. I said, "Any questions?"

"I knew you were a damned coward," he said. "If you're going to die, why wait until you just erode?"

He asked me if I could take a course to psyche me up for self-destruction, would I be willing to do that? I said no. He told me to go join the others for a while and he would talk it over with the other people. About two hours later, he came back and he told me this was a very special assignment and they were to blame him for choosing somebody who wasn't really committed to a cause. I had to bite my tongue to keep from saying, "Did they have a cause except just to promote violence?" He asked if I would like to continue the regular program with the rest of the people. I said yes. That night, before I went to the hotel, my friend warned me to be very careful, they may harm you, don't sleep in your room, sleep out in the park if necessary. So that night I didn't sleep in the hotel. There was a scientologist who had been expelled from the United States who lived there close to the shore and I went and knocked on his door. I told him I had been stranded there and was going to Nogales and he gave me a place to stay.

On the fifth day when I walked up, the guy I had originally contacted said, "No, no, no, you have to go right now." The word, he said, had got out and the rest of the students were very angry. They were disappointed in me and my life might be in danger. There was a truck waiting. I was taken to a beach near to there and told to wait. My friend came with me. He said he would wait with me—I think he took great risk because that was the first time we were really seen together. Then he went back and I worried about him, whether he would be made responsible for what had happened. Months later, I finally heard from him.

I left with a lot of mixed feelings. I learned that I hadn't exhausted my resources in dealing with what life is about. There isn't any miracle cure for my head or for my life. My aneurysm hasn't progressed, I still get headaches. The issues are still there. I think human beings aren't made for killing. They're made for trying and trying and trying. I keep losing. But there is no other way.

I AM RUNNING FOR MAYOR of Nogales, Sonora—the election is July 6th. We don't have the money or the mechanics to finance a good campaign. We're trying and trying and trying. We're dreaming again. Someone told me that if you don't dream, you have nightmares. We're scared out of our wits to think that we could again become cannon fodder as we were in 1910 when one million Mexicanos were killed in the revolution.

My mother is like a little dove. She says, "Teresa, stop arguing, stop writing, stop saying all those things. Get on your knees and pray to God that this all changes." And she means it. She prays a lot. I can't oppose her, it's just not there. She is my little dove. She calls me her yucca—it grows out in the desert and is full of thorns. She grew one in a pot and gave it to me. She calls it "Teresa." She says, "It looks very nice, but it's arid and it hurts."

Alan Weisman

# The Deadly Harvest
# of the Sierra Madre

THERE WASN'T MUCH MORE the old Tarahumara Indian healer, Agustín Ramos, could do for the man taking refuge in Pino Gordo, high in Mexico's western Sierra Madre: All the medicine that grows in the Sierra couldn't reverse the damage that automatic weapons had wreaked upon 30-year-old Gumersindo Torres. Nevertheless, he entered his dream to ask his god, Onurúame, what might bring the broken young man some relief.

Presently, the One Who Is Father appeared behind his closed eyelids, looking much like Ramos himself: headband, single-thonged sandals strapped to bare legs, breechclout secured by a tasseled girdle covering his loins. Onurúame directed the old man to prepare poultices and teas of verbena and chuchufate, plants found in Pino Gordo's ancient forest, to soothe Torres' bruises and restore his tranquillity.

Torres had come because his own ancestral village, two days away either by foot or truck via the new logging road, was now the most dangerous place in the Sierra. His community,

Coloradas de La Virgen, lies at the edge of a monstrous abyss in the Mexican state of Chihuahua called the Barranca Sinforosa, about 250 miles south of El Paso, Texas. Tarahumaras have lived and gathered there for at least 6,000 years, but until the family of murderers who now ruled the area could be brought to justice, no Indian in Coloradas de La Virgen was safe.

On that chilly night in November 1992, when Torres was left for dead, two of the killers had burst into the church where Tarahumara men and women were swaying to the violins and drumbeats of their ritual prayer dance. First the gunmen shot Torres' brother, the local Indian vice-governor, just as they had slain his uncle, a commissioner, a year earlier. With Torres, who they suspected was involved with environmental groups lately meddling in these mountains, they took their time, blasting him in the right shoulder, then the left, then shattering one of his hips with an AK-7.

He survived because their parting shot to his head, fired as he writhed on the floor, only creased his scalp. Afterward, unable to walk in his fields or chop firewood, Torres was taken to Pino Gordo and then given a small stipend from funds that had trickled down to the Indians through a succession of international environmental organizations. Among his objectives: to help this community resist the scourge of opium and marijuana that had poisoned his own village and whose spreading cultivation now threatened one of the continent's most crucial ecosystems and its people.

But how? The bullet holes that Torres insisted on showing me, sprinkled around his broken body by Coloradas de La Virgen's narcotraficantes, were sickening reminders of how defenseless one of Mexico's largest Indian tribes had become. For centuries, the Tarahumara, who today number 50,000, had mostly known peace and seclusion. They lived in tiny enclaves dispersed through the Sierra's labyrinthine terrain, which they bridged by becoming the world's greatest distance runners, often covering 60 miles between settlements in a single jaunt.

(In their own language, the Tarahumara call themselves Rarámuri—foot runner.) Now I was hearing that many non-Indians who had invaded this precipitous country in recent years to steal the Tarahumaras' timber were also clearing their land to reap a growing harvest of pot and raw opium gum.

Indians who protested have been routinely shot, and local authorities have been either too intimidated or too implicated to protect them. Few of the mild, agrarian Tarahumara own firearms or would use them on humans if they did. Had any of their dream-healers, I asked, pressed God for a cure for the narcotic-induced death now spreading throughout the Sierra?

In fact, old Agustín Ramos told me, he had tried several times: lately, the dreaded plantíos were blossoming even around his remote Pino Gordo, among freshly charred remains of some of the oldest trees in Mexico. Each time, though, he got the same frustrating answer:

"Onurúame can't destroy plants that are also part of his creation," he said. "We will have to save ourselves from narcotráfico."

W HEN, for whatever divine motive, Onurúame created opium poppies, enabling humans subsequently to manufacture heroin, he did so not here but in Asia. Chinese traders who settled in the town of Culiacán—today northwestern Mexico's leading cocaine distribution center—brought the first seeds during the 1930s. The vast mountain range that paralleled the Pacific coastal plains seemed a logical, virtually unpatrollable place to cultivate both the colorful flowers and another Far East import, *Cannabis sativa*—marijuana. Few human beings then realized the troubling implications, not only for Tarahumara Indians but for the Sierra itself, because no one yet understood that Mexico's Sierra Madre Occidental was the richest biosystem in North America.

Some 50 million years earlier, this region had simply exploded, spewing enormous quantities of volcanic dust into the atmosphere, which settled and metamorphosed into powdery layers of gray tuff and pink rhyolite. Then, as the shifting Pacific plate ripped Baja California away from mainland Mexico, runoff draining toward the widening trench that became the Gulf of California rapidly eroded the soft cap rock into a network of deep canyons. At the same time, huge blocks of crust were collapsing along innumerable faults as western Mexico continued to thrust upward. Eventually, all this tumult left a jumble of colossal barriers interspersed with immense chasms.

Within the myriad riches of this elaborate landscape evolved a woodland like no other. Here grow more different pines than anywhere else on earth and more than 200 oak species. Recently, biologists have realized that for sheer diversity, the western Sierra Madre surpasses even Mexico's cloud and rain forests. In pockets of human habitation, ethnobotanists have discovered an unprecedented genetic repository here: scores of heirloom strains of beans, squash, gourds, chiles, melons, herbs, medicinal plants and, especially, corn. Indian farmers instinctively had assured the success of nearly 20 distinct races of maize by cross-pollinating them with stands of teosinte, corn's prehistoric ancestor, found growing alongside their fields.

This splendid cache remained relatively isolated until 1962 when, 87 years after construction commenced, the Chihuahua al Pacífico Railroad finally succeeded in spanning the tangled Sierra Madre. The route instantly became famed for thrilling vistas of the geological complex known collectively as the Barranca del Cobre, or Copper Canyon—a system of four gorges bigger and deeper than Arizona's Grand Canyon. Bird watchers and backpackers thronged to view collared trogons and magpie jays with two-foot tails; oaks whose leaves ranged from slivers to giant, velvety lobes, and pines with drooping needles so long that Indians wove them into baskets. The fabulously picturesque Tarahumara themselves—bronzed, beautifully muscled—formed an idyllic portrait of indigenous people thriving in pristine innocence as they trotted easily up steep canyon trails, entire haystacks of corn fodder strapped to their backs.

But by 1988, when I first saw the Barranca del Cobre, the purity was becoming sullied. For two weeks, five companions and I had hiked over snow-covered rim country and descended into barrancas more than a mile deep, where green parakeets flitted through tamarind and citrus trees. When we finally reached the town of Batopilas, site of a Jesuit mission to the Tarahumara, we promptly located a restaurant. But inside we found a white-faced cook sitting with a pile of metallic blue automatic rifles heaped on his trembling knees. At one table, four men wearing reptile-skin boots and clumps of gold jewelry regarded us with silent stares, and nobody moved for the next 45 minutes while they finished eating.

The next morning, a priest whispered that the two Tarahumara families huddled in the mission chapel were hiding from these men: five Indians, he said, had just been massacred for refusing to tend illicit crops. Down river, the captain of a Mexican army patrol, his olive-drabs brightened by the addition of lizard footwear and half a pound of gold chain, reassured us that all was serene. We trudged on; a day later, four men on horseback, leading a string of well-laden mules, nodded politely but kept their weapons trained on us while we passed.

Just last Christmas, a group of Tucson naturalists I knew unwittingly strayed where they were not welcome; two of the men were pistol-whipped and one woman raped. Now I was in the Sierra Madre again, this time in the back of a four-wheel-drive Ford pickup, flanked by three Mexican federal police officers carrying Chinese-manufactured AK-47s equipped with 35-cartridge banana clips. Wedged into nylon holsters on their belts were 9-millimeter Smith & Wesson semiautomatic pistols. Our mission: to find where marijuana and opium growers were burning this precious forest to sow illegal crops, terrorizing Indians in the process.

Since Mexico's federales are famed more for collusion than combat with drug thugs, my escorts did not instill great confidence, but I had no choice. They were sent by Teresa Jardí, the new federal attorney general for the state of Chihuahua, who assured me that I was in trusted hands.

"These are fresh from the police academy. It takes a few months before the narcotraficantes contaminate them."

"And then?"

"I get rid of them and bring in another batch."

In Mexico, any attempt to accurately gauge progress in stemming the unmeasurable tonnage of drugs that flows across the border each day is effectively undermined by such systemic graft. According to recent U.S. State Department reports, drug trafficking has declined here since 1990, but locals in Chihuahua scoff at such pronouncements, pointing out that they're based on figures supplied by the Mexican government.

Just last February, Jardí, then a veteran human-rights advocate, was leading a campaign to throw the federal attorney general's office out of Chihuahua, so thoroughly polluted had it become by drug money. Then, in the wake of the drug-related slaying of the Catholic cardinal of Guadalajara, her old law school classmate and founder of Mexico's Human Rights Commission, Jorge Carpizo, took over the country's legal system. As national attorney general, Carpizo assigned Chihuahua to Jardí: Mexico's biggest state, with 480 miles of largely unguarded border with the United States and regarded by U.S. drug-enforcement officials as a lawless void. By August, Jardí had purged more than 50 corrupt federal commandantes and district attorneys, and, she now boasted, was actually "fielding police without entire jewelry stores hanging from their necks."

A petite, graying woman in her early 50s, Jardí was especially proud that Chihuahua's jails were no longer filled with peasants and Indians coerced at gunpoint to plant contraband, then nabbed during bogus raids while the true mafiosi roamed untouched. But this past fall, the week before I arrived, her success began to wear thin. Jardí had requisitioned three helicopters from Mexico City and invited Tarahumara leaders, whose pastures lately had been filling with poppies, on a search-and-destroy mission. The pilots dutifully sprayed several small patches with defoliant. But when the Indians directed them to a field that stretched for several acres, two of the choppers fled. When Jardí ordered her pilot to continue, he landed next to the plantation's isolated headquarters and told her to discuss it with the people inside. She refused to leave the helicopter, a decision that possibly saved her life, and the poppy farm remained intact.

Back in Chihuahua City, Jardí soon discovered that she had a rat among her new police officials. She had assembled her commandantes to meet with Edwin Bustillos, director of the Consejo Asesor Sierra Madre, a nonprofit group promoting environmentally sound farming and timber practices. Bustillos, a 29-year-old mestizo agricultural engineer, grew up among the Tarahumara and credited their healers for his recovery from a near-fatal accident. Now he was trying to help them preserve their shrinking resources, but lately he found himself spending more time saving humans than trees.

It was Bustillos who took Gumersindo Torres to Pino Gordo and then collected enough testimonies from witnesses that bloody night in Coloradas do La Virgen to actually jail two gunmen, Tacho Molina and Agustín Fontes. Now, in secret meetings, he was requesting Madame Attorney General to pursue Fontes' uncle Artemio, whom he alleged to be the real strongman behind illegal logging, cattle rustling and dope growing on Indian lands around Coloradas de la Virgen, as well as the ruthless author of many murders.

The accusation surprised no one. Artemio Fontes was a well-known and well-connected cacique of the Sierra, whose powerful but reckless family had yanked themselves violently from rural poverty. During the early 80s, Artemio Fontes' brother Alejandro was named head of the Chihuahua state police, a position he enjoyed until the army shot him down in a plane stuffed with marijuana. Fontes' men often engaged in blood feuds with outsiders and frequently with each other. Each week, wealthy Fontes widows could be seen driving fine four-wheel-drive vehicles into town from the rancho to shop.

Attorney General Jardí called another meeting to examine information that Bustillos claimed linked Artemio Fontes to several Tarahumara deaths in Coloradas de la Virgen. Caciques elsewhere in the Sierra, he warned, were increasingly emboldened by Fontes' impunity. Artemio Fontes could be seen frequently in restaurants in Chihuahua City, where he now resided in an elegant neighborhood: a man with silver-flecked hair and gold-tipped boots, in the company of friends like former Chihuahua Governor Fernando Baeza. Meanwhile, three to four Tarahumara and neighboring Tepehuán Indians were being killed each week. Bustillos again had a stack of testimonies with signatures or thumbprints. Jardí was sufficiently persuaded to order a formal investigation. Someone else at this confidential gathering apparently was also impressed: a day later, gunmen shot up Bustillos' house in the Sierra.

The next day, in Chihuahua City, Bustillos met with his U.S.-based funding partner, Randall Gingrich, director of the tiny Arizona Rainforest Alliance. Gingrich, who wrote his master's thesis on deforestation in the Sierra Madre, had garnered a small chunk of USAID money administered through a coalition of World Wildlife Fund, the Nature Conservancy and the World Resources Institute, earmarked for easing biological impacts of Third World Development. But the threats to the environment listed in their proposal had not included the armed men they now could see parked outside their office.

They managed to slip away and headed for the border. Gingrich tried to convince Bustillos to lie low in Tucson awhile, but within a week he was restless and returned to Mexico. Now, seated on an ammunition box between me and the federales, he was heading off to find some flowers.

VIDAL VALENCIA had drunk a lot of tesgüino, the corn beer that accompanies all Tarahumara gatherings, before he finally raised his hand. The occasion was an assembly of Redondeados, his community deep in southern Chihuahua, where human-rights workers were asking whose lands had been invaded lately. Valencia wasn't sure which was more frightening: the new poppy fields he found every time one of his cows strayed, or what might happen if he reported them. But Edwin Bustillos had promised that the police now intended to help Indians, not to beat and jail them as in previous dope raids. And they knew of the risk Bustillos, a marked man, was taking to come here.

We were driving in a light rain through the wedge between the states of Durango and Sinaloa known as Chihuahua's Golden Triangle. "Pick your gold: our richest forests or richest drug crops," Bustillos said. Severed from the rest of the state by the great canyons to the north, the region was tied closely to Culiacán, source of the weapons and South American cocaine that were luring more young local mestizos into choosing narcotráfico.

A World Bank loan recently proposed for this area, intended to make Chihuahua's timber industry more competitive, had been delayed by international protests when road building began before required environmental assessments were made. Bustillos, originally hired by the Mexican government's regional manager of a World Bank-funded forestry-development program, was one of the critics, because new roads would enter virgin Indian lands. Now, after two slapdash impact studies were successfully challenged, the World Bank was ready to resume disbursements, as soon as Mexico came up with its matching portion, $48 million. Besides the predicted habitat damage and erosion from increased logging, Bustillos feared that better roads would be a gift to narcotraficantes, currently bulldozing their way into places once never imagined.

Mexico, however, was in enough debt already and not inclined just yet to turn these primitive Sierra lumber trails into passable highways. The fractured bedrock and slick rhyolite clays we were bouncing over had already eaten one of the police vehicles, a Chevy Suburban van, that was supposed to take us up to Vidal Valencia's mountain pastures. A backup four-wheel-drive pickup had arrived from headquarters in Parral, Chihuahua, 10 hours away, without a spare tire. His budget was so thin, Comandante Serafin Cocones of the narcotics squad told us, that it wasn't just tires: he and four men had to buy their own ammunition.

Now we were following a borrowed Datsun with a cracked chassis, crammed with Tarahumaras, as well as a contingent of five municipal police armed with hunting rifles and ornate pistols, whom Cocones had mustered that morning simply for more firepower. Since most local police are assumed to augment their $200 monthly salaries with narcotráfico themselves, there was some question as to which way they might aim in the event of a shoot-out. "What choice is there?" Cocones lamented. "If someone really wants to defend these plants, we'll need 50 men against their weapons."

The road dissolved into a giant gully. We continued into the forest on foot, which made the Tarahumaras much happier. I half-walked, half-ran to keep up with Vidal, a thin, taciturn man in a red plaid shirt, and his 80-year-old cousin, Tirso Téllez, who leaped over outcroppings and scrambled up mountain arroyos where we stopped to drink from streams and catch our breath. These men had grown up playing rarajípari, Tarahumara kick-ball, over courses that sometimes stretched 50 miles. Their great-uncle Tibursio, Téllez told me, once ran the 110-mile round trip to Culiacán to deliver a message the day before an important match and returned in time to pace his team to victory.

Above us, thick-billed parrots frisked through the Chihuahua pines, showering us with droplets that hung from the elongated needles. We heard the triple hoot of a Mexican spotted owl but saw no mammals except for the flash of a white-tailed deer's rump. The last grizzlies were killed here some years ago, but, Telléz was telling me, jaguar and Mexican gray wolves still stalk this pine-oak-juniper maze. Suddenly, Vidal stopped and pointed. At his feet was a steaming pile of fresh dung, surrounded by mule-shoe prints. Instantly, Comandante Cocones motioned for the police to fan out.

They spread across the hills, running silently along the ridges. The rest of us crept behind Cocones, scanning the perimeter and treetops for snipers. We inched forward and listened. Nothing. Finally we crested a small rise and looked down. Even the Indians gasped.

Below us, a swath of miraculous color burst from the dark green forest: pinks segueing to purples, pale lavenders, bright crimsons—big papery flowers that intermixed nearly the entire blue-red spectrum, fluttering on waist-high stalks. To see a field of poppies such as these is to begin to grasp the irresistible, addictive nature of opium. These plants did not belong here, and their presence signified great danger. But for a few moments everyone simply gazed at their beauty, so soft and seductive, like lotus blossoms floating atop the blood and violence.

We had found roughly an acre of blooms, surrounded by three strands of new barbed wire, in a clearing of downed trees that had been burned. A ragged shirt and a pair of old jeans tied to a stick served as a scarecrow. There was a moment of confusion: The federales had forgotten wire cutters, but I had a pair on my utility knife. As the fence tumbled, the police and the Tarahumaras picked up sticks and began whacking the olive-green stems.

Whoever tended this field evidently had just departed, because the round bulbs left on plants that had already dropped their petals had been freshly scored. One of the local police, looking a little bereaved, showed me how to cut and squeeze the bulb until milky white syrup bubbled out every drop of which harvesters collected in vials made from battery casings, where it coagulates into brown gum. In Parral, he said, the goma brings 10,000 pesos per gram: slightly more than $3.

Resting that afternoon on a log in the 10th field Vidal showed us, while the police built a bonfire of 200 pounds of marijuana they'd also discovered growing there, Bustillos and I did some calculating. About 10 poppy bulbs yield a gram of opium gum, and a bulb can be milked from three to 10 times. Bustillos, who had paced the boundaries of each plantío, reckoned that we'd destroyed about 12 acres. Figuring 10 bulbs per square yard, that represented at least 150,000 grams of opium gum, worth $450,000 at its crudest stage.

About 10 grams of opium gum produce a single gram of heroin, which brings anywhere from $80 to $500 in the United States, depending on the city. In a few hours, I realized, we had removed millions of dollars' worth of untaxed goods from the market, plus at least another hundred grand for the pot now going up in flames. No matter at what point in the processing and shipping Artemio Fontes took his cut, I guessed that he would be upset, because we had just relieved him of a small fortune.

"These plants don't belong to Fontes. He's from over there," Bustillos replied, pointing northwest toward Coloradas de la Virgen.

"Whose then?"

He shrugged his thin shoulders. "Who knows? There are so many growers now."

Behind us, the Sierra Madre dropped into Arroyo Hondo, a minor canyon compared to the barrancas to the north, but sufficiently vast to convey the impression that no one could ever eradicate dope cultivation here.

"Frankly," Bustillos said, "I don't care if they do. I just want growers to stay out of the last hidden sanctuaries and stop bothering the Indians who know how to care for them.

"But they choose those places because growing dope is illegal. How can you keep them out?

"Simple. Legalize it."

BEFORE WE LEFT, I asked Vidal Valencia, who now looked a little worried, what the Tarahumaras thought of legalization. After rephrasing the question twice, I let it drop: The concept of plants being unlawful was alien to him. All he knew was that, despite the Mexican constitution that recognizes Indians' rights to defend their land, someone was going to be mad about this. "When the police go, they could grab us," he observed.

For the next two days, we struggled up 40 miles of atrocious roads toward Pino Gordo, where Teresa Jardí and another helicopter were meeting us for more raids. At times we passed through deforested stretches where loggers had taken the best pines; without sufficient cover, the smaller trees left for seed stock had dried up. At lumber mills, we saw Tarahumaras working the worst jobs, hauling sawdust and dragging huge trunks to the blade. Supposedly, Bustillos' funding was designated to help Indians gain control of and properly manage wood resources that were legally theirs, but the fallout of drugs had become a constant distraction. In every village, we heard of shootings.

The road rose through spruce and aspen, then traversed hairpin ledges where waterfalls gushed between enormous boulders. We were nearing Pino Gordo, which has the largest stand of old-growth forest left in the Sierra Madre. Comandante Cocones grew edgy because of a rumored 5-million-peso ($1,600) bounty on policemen in the area. In the valley below was Coloradas de los Chávez: Some members of the extended Chávez family were reputed to be as charming as the Fontes. Last year, the Tarahumaras of Pino Gordo had found their first marijuana plantation. By this spring there were nine, and by autumn, 17. Armed men from Coloradas de los Chávez were appearing in Pino Gordo, offering money and corn in exchange for labor in the plantíos. They arrived over the same new road we were traveling, illegally opened by loggers, and made it plain that they were coming in with or without the Tarahumaras' cooperation.

In the past, it wasn't unknown for a Tarahumara to agree to plant a little pot in exchange for food or a few pesos, but with people dying and large chunks of their forest disappearing, the situation was now getting out of control. That afternoon, the men and women of Pino Gordo gathered at the log cabin schoolhouse. They hoped to see Bustillos and the federal attorney and police who promised to help rid them of narco-terror but by then we were long gone. Teresa Jardí and the helicopter had never appeared. Later I learned that, despite her livid denunciation of the pilots she had recently flown with, she had been sent the same crew again. Without air support, Cocones refused to destroy any plantíos here.

"There's only one road," he said. "Without air cover to get us out of here, they can roll a tree trunk or boulder across one of those ledges, then pick us off like pigeons.

To raid Pino Gordo properly, Cocones added, would require 100 men on the ground and 20 giving air support. It would take a week here, with tents and sleeping bags—things he didn't have. There was no budget. Cocones, with a plastic right shoulder joint as a memento of his last drug shoot-out, was getting no argument from his green troops. "I'll try to return with reinforcements," he told the Tarahumaras.

Yet if he did, I realized, these Indians would then be sitting ducks, and Pino Gordo would become another Coloradas de la Virgen. Cocones couldn't refute this. "Then how can you ever stop the killing?" I asked.

"Easy," he said. "Legalize drugs. They'll lose so much value that they won't be worth killing for." He snapped open the folding stock of his Galil. "It's the only way. Instead of public safety, we have shootings. We shoot one narcotraficante and another steps into his place. Instead of prevention and rehabilitation, out budget goes into uprooting plants. And they just keep planting more."

I had heard this proposal a few years earlier, in Colombia, where so many people were dying that the government in Bogotá openly contemplated decriminalizing drugs simply to halt carnage. The United States warned that such a move would put diplomatic relations at risk. Since then, however, Americans such as former Secretary of State George P. Shultz, columnist William F. Buckley Jr., economist Milton Friedman, several federal judges, the mayor of Baltimore and, most recently, U.S. Surgeon General Joycelyn Elders have argued that too much time, money and blood are being wasted in a futile war on drugs. Legalization advocates cite the example of Holland to show that decriminalization doesn't cause a surge in addiction, any more than ending Prohibition here increased alcoholism, and that drug-related crime actually drops. The potential tax revenues from legal drugs could help pay for a massive national drug education program, to say nothing of reallocation of the United States' current $8.3-billion drug-enforcement budget.

U.S. Drug Enforcement Administration officials counter that legalization would fill our highways and workplaces with stoned drivers and employees and needlessly jeopardize the mental and physical health of future generations of productive citizens. The DEA also denies that the war on drugs is hopeless, citing Department of Health and Human Services figures showing that usage in fact is declining. When I inquired about the source of these figures, however, I learned that they are derived from door-to-door samplings of households, a seemingly dubious measure of illegal activity. An HHS statistician defended the methods, which uses an anonymous questionnaire, but admitted that the polls were probably worthless in monitoring heroin abuse, which even the DEA admits is rising.

For or against, none of these arguments mention the human sorrow and ecological loss being wreaked upon neighbors beyond our borders. I decided to ask Artemio Fontes, whose number I found in the Chihuahua City directory, what he thought. After several tries, one of his bodyguards told me that, "Señor Fontes says anything you want to know about him, ask the attorney general. She seems to have all the facts." This apparently didn't trouble Fontes: weeks later, a 64-page file Jardí submitted to a panel of judges, charging Fontes with both homicide and drug trafficking, failed to produce a warrant for his arrest.

"They tell me they are very behind," Jardí explained. How long? "Months. Maybe a year. Who knows?"

I took a taxi to Fontes' house. The watchman said he was out. Standing there, I realized that Artemio Fontes certainly wouldn't want drugs legalized if in fact their value, bloated by virtue of being forbidden, had afforded him this agglomeration of carved wooden doors and shiny white brick, surrounded by rosebushes and iron bars.

O N MY LAST DAY in the Sierra, I accompanied Edwin Bustillos to his home village, Guachochi, where he broadcasts a weekly radio show in four dialects to educate Indians about their rights and their priceless environment, encouraging them to unite against unscrupulous lumber caciques and narcotraficantes. He was pleased, he told me, because he had obtained from witnesses the license number of the truck whose occupants had fired at his house, which he was passing along to Teresa Jardi.

We walked outside. The truck with offending license plate, from the state of Sinaloa, was parked next to his car.

"We'd better get out of here," Bustillos sighed.

---

*Persons interested in making donations to Edwin Bustillos' efforts to preserve the environment should contact: Sierra Madre Program for Human Rights and the Environment, P.O. Box 41416, Tucson, AZ 85717, 520-326-2511.*

Linda Lynch

# Beauty and the Beast
## Trashing the
## Texas/Mexico Border

EDITOR'S NOTE: *Linda Lynch is an artist, a painter. I have known and admired her art for years. Stephen Vollmer, Curator for the El Paso Museum of Art, says of her work:*

> *The paintings and drawings of Linda Lynch reveal the powerful, spiritual vision of a woman who knows her kinship to nature, to the land.... It is the land that is Lynch's greatest concern, the underlying theme in all her work. The earth is not a silent, inanimate object providing a foundation for life: The earth is life.*

*In May 1996, at a conference in Juárez, Chihuahua, I encountered Linda in another role—she is a passionate and articulate defender against using her homeland as a dump for nuclear waste and urban industrial sludge. This role is not a guise, but is rather an outgrowth of her upbringing in rural West Texas and of her life as an artist. Big government and big business had targeted Hudspeth County—just east of El Paso County and bordering Mexico—as a suitable dumping ground for much of the country's toxic wastes. Linda and her community have been struggling against that intrusion for the last 13 years. We as editors felt that their struggle—because it is similar to many others which are occurring along the U.S./Mexico Border—needed to be documented in this anthology.*

*This report is a collage built from the speech that Linda gave in Juárez and from an interview that Susannah and I had with her.*

—Bobby Byrd

■ ■ ■

*Linda, can you tell us about your relationship to the landscape of West Texas, the place where you grew up.*

I grew up in Hudspeth County, near Dell City. My father was farming and ranching and so I grew up farming and ranching. From the beginning I was living mostly outdoors. Dell City is a small town. We still only have about 500 people there and maybe 1000 in the valley surrounding the town. My understanding of that landscape is from spending a great deal of time inside of it, horseback riding, walking and hiking. I have many memories of how that landscape looks and what it feels like. I grew up totally involved in all the different moods, all the different light, all the different conditions, good and bad, of that particular landscape.

So I love the desert. A lot of people whiz through there in their automobiles and see *nothing*. They don't understand that it is a landscape that reveals itself slowly. It is phenomenally beautiful.

HUDSPETH COUNTY is one of Texas' largest counties, yet it numbers only about 3,000 residents. Approximately the size of Connecticut, it is sparsely settled, with under half of its population registered to vote. More than 60% of the residents are Hispanic, and approximately 40% of the citizens live below the poverty line. Spanish is a first language among most of the residents. The agrarian-based economy (farming and ranching) has been seriously depressed since the 1970s and in the area of the town of Sierra Blanca, that economic depression is older. Much of Hudspeth County is characterized by a tremendous underground water table, which has supported its agriculture.

*Linda, you are a visual artist, a painter. You describe your work as being heavily influenced by the landscape of your childhood. How so?*

It was natural that I started looking at elements in the landscape with the eyes of an artist. Both of my parents are creative.

My mother is a painter. All of my life my parents have made and built things. My mother still paints very beautiful landscapes of the Guadalupe Mountains. I remember specifically a time when I realized that not everyone grows up with art in their lives. I was surprised. I had always assumed that having art in your life was normal. My sisters and I would go out and find beautiful pieces of driftwood and unusual looking rocks and odd looking plants, bones left over from dead animals, turtle shells and things like that. We would bring them home. That started a long creative interest in my life.

Now, in my paintings, I refer to that place of my growing up far sooner than I refer to, let's say, the human figure. In the visual arts, the human figure is usually a central component, but my work has always first reflected an interest in nature and in landscape. I am entirely indebted to the days that I spent in the desert of West Texas.

ECOLOGICALLY, Hudspeth County is a prime example of high Chihuahuan Desert spread generously between its three small communities—Dell City, Fort Hancock and Sierra Blanca. Existing on only 7 to 9 inches of rainfall per year, it is an ecosystem which supports a miraculous range of species, including migratory pathways for many coastal birds and cranes. At its northern edge are the very beautiful Guadalupe Mountains, and to the south, the Eagle Mountains and Victorio Canyon. Typically fragile, the desert has suffered from overgrazing and development-related habitat loss near the communities, as well as air pollution from El Paso/ Cuidad Juárez and, more recently, the Carbon II plant at Piedras Negras in Mexico. River contamination, much of it from the maquiladora plants in Juárez and from El Paso, exists along its southern border at the Rio Grande.

*In the early 1980s you went to New York City to pursue your work as an artist full-time. But, then, over the last 13 years a great deal of your time and energy has been spent as an environmental activist. How did that happen?*

Well, I was living in New York City in 1983. I was looking

forward to working in a new studio that I had just rented in Greenwich Village when I received a phone call from my mother. My mother has published the *Hudspeth County Herald* and *Dell Valley Review* for the last thirty-one years. She received a phone call one morning from a journalist with a Texas newspaper. The reporter asked, "What do the local people think of the nuclear waste dump planned to open near your town?"

This was the first news any of us had heard about the plans of Texas officials to open a nuclear waste dump in our home. And the project was well underway. As I listened to my mother, I was overwhelmed with the sinking realization that I would never be able to use my new studio. I had a very clear understanding of what nuclear waste was because when I lived in San Francisco I worked with Greenpeace to fight the dumping of nuclear waste off the Farallon Islands.

Ever since my childhood, the landscape of West Texas, the Rio Grande river, its mountains and deserts, have been deeply rooted in my psyche. Those roots had become the central component of my work as an artist. Nothing could have been more disturbing to my work than the destruction and abuse of that landscape. The nuclear waste dump felt like a very personal violation. It felt like watching my sister be raped. I had established a very close relationship with this place and then some guy comes in from Austin and says, Well, we're going to dump our waste here. There was no question that I had to react. Within a month, I had moved back to West Texas.

*Alert Citizens for Environmental Safety, or ACES, was born to address the issue of the nuclear waste dump. How did it start?*

Our little community scrambled to a defense. After we learned about the plans that the Texas officials had, a few of us—about 10 or 12 people from the community—got together to discuss what we should do. There were some farmers' and ranchers' wives and a couple of school teachers, my mother, myself, and some nuns from the Catholic Church. So there was this small group that was very alarmed. We decided to hold a public meeting. That was in Dell City in 1983. The state officials attended to try to explain what they were up to. At that meeting there were about 350 to 400 people. It was standing room only and it was very, very testy.

*So about one third of the population came to that meeting? Those are good numbers.*

Yes, people were outraged. Now everyone is tired of fighting. I don't think any one of us thought that we would have to sustain that kind of energy for years and years. One of the worst aspects is that every time we beat this project down, it comes back again and again.

OUR GRASSROOTS STRUGGLE, which has been fraught with many disappointments, has demanded that ACES grow more sophisticated in its effort to stop the dumping in our county. But the people in town have become weary and unable to respond. Years of depressed agricultural industry in Hudspeth County had already weakened their resolve when the dumping enterprise began. Fear related to intimidation and censorship, political corruption and chronic apathy have developed, creating a mood within the community as challenging to overcome as the problem of radioactive waste dumping itself.

*How did it evolve that you started partnering yourselves up with organizations in Mexico?*

Just out of logic. It just seemed so obvious. We were concerned about a problem that will affect the state of Chihuahua on the other side of Rio Grande. We also went into Mexico because we wanted to increase our ranks. We wanted to get more of the population concerned. We are in the same region, and Mexican people have a right to know about the dumping. I had learned about the La Paz agreement so we started working with Mexican ecological organizations.

IMPORTANT INTERNATIONAL agreements, such as La Paz, are blatantly ignored. The La Paz Agreement was signed in 1983 by the presidents Miguel de la Madrid of Mexico and Ronald Reagan of the United States. It stipulated a 62-mile zone of environmental protection on each side of the U.S./Mexico Border where no new sources of pollution are to be knowingly introduced. Our experience in Hudspeth County has yielded the realization that despite these international agreements —including the more recent but equally inadequate NAFTA regulations—protecting the border environment depends on the nearly nonexistent resources of border communities. The danger is that border environmental policy occurs then by default, or even accident, without comprehensive vision or the ability to affect unified permanent change.

*You mention that the nuclear waste dumping was reborn three different times in Hudspeth County? What is the history of ACES through that?*

Well, basically what happened was that it took about a year to defeat the plan in Dell City. Then it moved to Fort Hancock and then to Sierra Blanca. When the Texas Low Level Radioactive Waste Disposal Authority targeted each town for the dump, that town became the central activist mechanism. In other words, when it was near Dell City, it was Dell City that was really fighting it. And when it was near Fort Hancock, it was Fort Hancock and later El Paso that fought it. And finally now that it is in Sierra Blanca, it is largely Sierra Blanca, with the help of Austin activists, that is fighting it. Local store owner Billy Addington with his group "Save Sierra Blanca" has worked tirelessly to keep the dump out of Sierra Blanca.

The first time near Dell City, ACES was the fundamental organization that protested. We applied pressure in as many ways as we could think of to stop it. We met with the Board of Regents at the University of Texas because the land that the state wanted was UT land. Then, after about a year and without explanation, we got a call that the Texas Low Level Radioactive

Waste Disposal Authority was dropping Dell City as a site for the nuclear waste dump. It happened overnight.

*So you thought that you had won?*
So we thought we had won. In fact I was just finishing painting a mural at the Catholic Church in Dell City. I accepted a job with the Metropolitan Museum in New York City and I left. I thought, Well, that was good. I can now go back to my work.

*What year was that?*
That was 1984. And much to our horror, a few months later the officials showed up in Fort Hancock saying, Well, we are moving over to Fort Hancock and starting all over again. ACES became a supporting group to the efforts of the Fort Hancock citizens who were concerned about this dump. We gave them all of our information.

In Fort Hancock, the state was so confident of success that they even built a highway ramp that was going to lead to the dump. Now that ramp goes nowhere. It just ends in the middle of the desert. But this time, the city of El Paso became concerned—Fort Hancock is much closer to El Paso than Dell City. They hired a legal team and filed suit against the Texas Low Level Radioactive Waste Disposal Authority. And they won. Judge Bill Moody ordered the Authority to leave Fort Hancock.

Unfortunately for Hudspeth County, before they left, the Authority made a deal with the El Paso legal team: they would leave Fort Hancock if the legal team would agree not to interfere with them anywhere else in Hudspeth County. To our dismay, the legal team agreed. The Authority then went to the Texas Legislature where it drew a 300-square mile box in Hudspeth County on a map. The Authority asked the Legislature to mandate that the nuclear waste dump be placed in that box, regardless of geology, hydrology or ecology. The Legislature declared the mandate and the Authority moved the dump to Sierra Blanca.

The people of Sierra Blanca had no voice in that agreement.

ACES was told that the El Paso legal team assisted the Authority in drawing the box, and I was told directly by El Paso's leading rights group, EPISO, that we would have to face the inevitable. The nuclear waste dump was coming to Hudspeth County. We were screwed.

*So you felt like you had been sold out?*

Very much so because we gave the legal team all of our files and we were very supportive. They knew the deal with the state was something that we found totally unacceptable. Imagine how the people in Sierra Blanca felt. Suddenly, they were the next sitting duck. The whole experience was just a nightmare.

IN ITS CURRENT VERSION, the state is closer than it has previously been to realizing its dump. The dump will receive over 90% of its radioactive wastes from nuclear power plants. Texas is also seeking Congressional approval to open the dump to receive wastes from sources nationwide. Initially planned to service only the state of Texas and its two nuclear power plants, it now plans to accept wastes from the states of Maine and Vermont, both of which are seeking dumping sites for two aging nuclear power plants. Connecticut has offered the state $100 million to be included in the plan.

*There must be huge pressure to open these dumps.*

Actually what it all boils down to is an issue of liability. As long as the waste that has been generated sits on-site at the nuclear power plant, the companies themselves are liable for it and for any damages that it creates. But the minute it is moved with a truck and taken to South Carolina or Nevada or West Texas, the companies are no longer liable. There is tremendous lobbying pressure by nuclear power companies to get the government to support opening new dumps so that they can escape long-term liability for this stuff that is poisonous for thousands and thousands of years. The University of Texas system is one of the biggest promoters of the Texas dump because it generates a lot of radioactive waste. And so you've got state and federal governments accommodating industry and others by essentially saying that once the waste arrives in Sierra Blanca, it belongs to you and me and to whoever is paying taxes in Texas. So you can't go back to Houston Lighting & Power or Texas Utilities and say, you've polluted our groundwater. Now you have to pay for it. Because once we take it, it is ours.

CURRENT LEGISLATION pending approval in the U.S. Congress will allow Texas to contract for radioactive waste importation not only with Maine and Vermont, but with any state or entity—public or private, national or international. The contracts will be decided by an eight-member commission. The commission will not be required to give notification, veto privilege or accountability to the citizens along the U.S./Mexico border.

*Who are the folks who are supporting dumping along the border?*
Ann Richards is one of them—our lovely darling Ann Richards. It has been reported that Ann Richards, since her retirement as Governor of Texas, has now been lobbying for the nuclear power companies in Texas. Ann Richards' friend, Sarah Weddington, whom you may know as the attorney who won Roe Vs. Wade, is a primary lobbyist for Maine Yankee Nuclear Power. In Austin nearly all the Democrats and Republicans are in favor of dumping along the Texas/Mexico Border. We have asked for referendums, for voting privilege. We think the people in the Trans-Pecos should be asked whether they want to establish this dump in their region. We can't get anywhere with the Democrats or the Republicans. I think Ann Richards did a lot of damage by talking all of her colleagues, both on federal and state levels, into supporting this.

*What has been the response from the local government of Sierra Blanca?*
This is an important element to consider. The county commissioners and the county judges for two or three

administrations have been completely seduced by the government and the industry. They are in love with radioactive waste. Some of the other counties on the border have terrific local government and it has made all the difference in the world.

*This region has attracted other people interested in dumping wastes. Let's talk about the Merco sludge dump. When did Merco Joint Venture start wanting to get into Hudspeth County?*

Well, we learned about it in early 1992. They may have been poking around in '91. I'm not sure when exactly they learned about Hudspeth County.

IN 1992 Merco Joint Venture, Inc., a private sewage company based in Oklahoma and New York, quietly purchased a 128,000-acre ranch north of the nuclear waste site. Unknown to the citizens in Hudspeth County, Merco had a six-year contract with the City of New York to dispose of the sludge produced by its urban industrial sewage plant. This sludge is the same material which the U.S. Congress banned New York City from dumping in the Atlantic Ocean. Before it came to the Texas/Mexico border, Merco had tried in vain for one year to establish its operation on farmland in Oklahoma. In Texas, within a record 23 days, the company managed to secure the necessary registration papers it needed to start dumping. Their application to the Texas Water Commission was pushed ahead of at least 60 other pending applications and immediately approved. The company has now been dumping the sludge from New York City on the border since July 1992, under the guise of providing fertilizer for overgrazed rangeland.

Merco now spreads one-fifth of New York City's sludge, about 225 tons a day, on the ranch.

*Why was Merco thrown out of Oklahoma?*

Because of the controversy over the toxicity of the material and the fact that what they wanted to do with it is still very unproven. There is a big movement across the country to put sewage sludge on farmland, but there is a lot of argument as to whether it is really safe because some of the materials won't biodegrade. Also, some of the materials are not eliminated in the sewage treatment process. The EPA is endorsing it right now simply because it helps them keep it out of landfills. I think their endorsement is premature. The State of Oklahoma certainly thought so.

> IN A MANNER devastating to local habitats, native vegetation is first mulched and leveled to within inches of the ground, the sewage is then slung out over the desert surface where it lies in the hot sun, unincorporated into the soil. High in lead and heavy metals, organic chemicals and pathogens, the material was deemed too toxic to put on land in New York state. However, the Texas Natural Resource Conservation Commission declared that it was satisfied with the operation on the border. Now Merco, nearing contract renewal negotiations with the city of New York, indicated that it will seek a 20-year extension.

*In Oklahoma, was Merco pushed out by citizen reaction or by legislative process?*
They were pushed out by citizen reaction. Also, the state of Oklahoma had decided that Merco would have to go through a public hearing before they got their license. Merco apparently did not want to go through a public hearing so they left.

*So, in Oklahoma they got the sort of democratic process that you were denied in Texas?*
Yes. When we asked for a public hearing, the Texas Water Commission would agree to it only after the company was given their registration papers. By then it would be meaningless because you had no impact on whether Merco gets its permission.

*How long does the process usually take for somebody to get their registration papers for dumping?*
Well, that is a very interesting question. I was told a year to a year-and-a-half minimum. When Merco left Oklahoma they were running out of time to fulfill their contract with New York City. They had been dilly-dallying around in Oklahoma for at

least a year. By the time they came to Texas, they were in a real pinch to get something going. They made that very clear to the Texas Water Commission. They also greased the skids by offering Texas Tech a $1.5 million grant to "study" the effects of sewage on rangeland. Texas Tech immediately wrote the Texas Water Commission to lobby for Merco's project. Now every year Texas Tech produces a paper glorifying Merco's project and then they get more money.

Who knows what else? We know of at least one $10,000 contribution to Ann Richards' campaign from one of the principals of Merco. You can figure out the rest for yourself. Basically the thing was slammed through in 23 days. There has never been a case like that before. And this is the biggest sludge dumping project in the world!

*What has been the community's response to the sludge dumping?*
I think between the county government pressuring the people of Sierra Blanca and the companies like Merco intimidating the people personally, the people are scared. Merco recently won $5 million in a libel lawsuit in West Texas which has effectively gagged the media from future criticism of its project, even though it was being investigated by a grand jury for criminal activities. Significant evidence was withheld from the jury by the federal judge. Many of us believe the trial violated the free speech rights of the media and citizens, as well as right-to-know efforts of activists. Now everyone is terrified to openly criticize Merco for fear of being sued.

*What about the local government's response? Was it the same as in the situation with the nuclear waste dump?*
Yes, they all think it is just fine. Meanwhile Sierra Blanca is getting lots of money. They just received new stadium lights for their football field. Together the state officials promoting the nuclear dump and Merco created an entity in Sierra Blanca called the Community Development Corporation. This is a non-profit

corporation which receives big checks from both Merco and the states of Texas, Maine and Vermont for the impact of their dumping on the community. However, the money can only be spent within 10 miles of Sierra Blanca so none of the overall regional impact of the dumping is taken into account.

They are keeping the people of Sierra Blanca intimidated and obligated. They've done everything from A to Z. They've even tried to start a newspaper because they were so angry with my mother's coverage of the dumping in her newspaper. She was reprinting stories and information about sewage sludge and nuclear waste. Their newspaper was full color. It has opened and closed about four times. Right now it's closed again. It was called the *Southwestern Sun News* and it was completely pro-dumping. All the ads were from pro-dumping people. It is sort of like they are taking over the community, and I think increasingly the people in town are quite frightened.

You know, a couple of our commissioners work for Merco.

*They actually work for Merco? You mean the county commissioners? They have jobs? Out of how many?*

Well there are only four county commissioners and two of them work for Merco. The previous county judge owns the only title company in the county and he has admitted to earning thousands of dollars from doing the land sale for Merco and the Texas Low Level Waste Disposal Authority.

*What's that judge's name?*

Billy Love. Our current judge is James Peace. We've gone from Love to Peace and we still have this stuff.

# Benjamin Alire Sáenz

# Exile
## *El Paso, Texas*

*Do you know what exile is?*
*I'll tell you,*
            *exile*
*is a long avenue*
*where only sadness walks.*

—ROQUE DALTON

THAT MORNING—when the day was new, when the sun slowly touched the sky almost afraid to break it—that morning I looked out my window and stared at the Juárez Mountains. Mexican purples—burning. I had always thought of them as sacraments of belonging. That was the first time it happened. It had happened to others, but it had never happened to me. And when it happened it started a fire, a fire that will burn for a long time.

As I walked to school, I remember thinking what a perfect place Sunset Heights was: turn of the century houses intact; remodeled houses painted pink or turquoise; old homes tastefully gentrified by the aspiring young; the rundown Sunset

Grocery store decorated with the protest art of graffiti on one end and a plastic-signed "Circle K" on the other. This was the edge of the piece of paper that was America, the border that bordered the University—its buildings, its libraries; the border that bordered the freeway—its cars coming and going, coming and going endlessly; the border that bordered downtown—its banks and businesses and bars; the border that bordered the border between two countries. The unemployed poor from Juárez knocking on doors and asking for jobs—or money —or food. Small parks filled with people whose English did not exist. The upwardly mobile living next to families whose only concern was getting enough money to pay next month's rent. Some had lived here for generations, would continue living here into the next century; others would live here a few days. All this color, all this color, all this color beneath the shadow of the Juárez Mountains. Sunset Heights: a perfect place with a perfect name, and a perfect view of the river.

After class, I went by my office and drank a cup of coffee, sat and read, and did some writing. It was a quiet day on campus, nothing but me and my work—the kind of day the mind needs to catch up with itself—the kind of uneventful day so necessary for living. At about three o'clock I put my things together in my torn backpack and started walking home. I made a mental note to sew the damn thing. *One day everything's gonna come tumbling out—better sew it.* I'd made that mental note before.

Walking down Prospect, I thought maybe I'd go for a jog. I hoped the spring would not bring too much wind this year. The wind, common desert rain; the wind blew too hard and harsh sometimes; the wind unsettled the desert—upset things —ruined the calmness of the spring. My mind wandered, searched the black asphalt littered with torn papers; the chained dogs in the yards who couldn't hurt me; the even bricks of all the houses I passed. I belonged here, yes. I belonged. Thoughts entered like children running through a park. This year, maybe the winds would not come.

I didn't notice the green car drive up and stop right next to me as I walked. The border patrol interrupted my daydreaming: "Where are you from?"

I didn't answer. I wasn't sure who the agent, a woman, was addressing.

She repeated the question in Spanish, "¿De dónde eres?"

Without thinking, I almost answered her question—in Spanish. A reflex. I caught myself in midsentence, and stuttered in a non-language.

"¿Dónde naciste?" she asked again.

By then my mind had cleared, and quietly I said: "I'm a U.S. citizen."

"Were you born in the United States?'

She was browner than I was. I might have asked her the same question. I looked at her for a while—searching for something I recognized.

"Yes," I answered.

"Where in the United States were you born?"

"In New Mexico."

"Where in New Mexico?"

"Las Cruces."

"What do you do?'

"I'm a student."

"And are you employed?"

"Sort of."

"Sort of?" She didn't like my answer. Her tone bordered on anger. I looked at her expression and decided it wasn't hurting anyone to answer her questions. It was all very innocent, just a game we were playing.

"I work at U.T.E.P. as a teaching assistant."

She didn't respond one way or another. She looked at me as if I were a blank. Her eyes were filling in the empty spaces as she looked at my face. I looked at her for a second and decided she was finished with me. I started walking away. "Are you sure you were born in Las Cruces?" she asked again.

I turned around and smiled, "Yes, I'm sure." She didn't smile back. She and the driver sat there for a while and watched me as I continued walking. They drove past me slowly, and then proceeded down the street.

I didn't much care for the color of their cars.

"Sons of bitches," I whispered, "pretty soon I'll have to carry a passport in my own neighborhood." I said it to be flippant; something in me rebelled against people dressed in uniforms. I wasn't angry—not then—not at first, not really angry. In less than ten minutes I was back in my apartment playing the scene again and again in my mind. It was like a video I played over and over—memorizing the images. Something was wrong. I was embarrassed, ashamed because I'd been so damned compliant like a piece of tin foil in the uniformed woman's hand. Just like a child in the principal's office in trouble for speaking Spanish. "I should have told that witch exactly what I thought of her and her green car and her green uniform." I lit a cigarette and told myself I was overreacting. "Breathe in—breathe out—breathe in—breathe out—no big deal—you live on a border. These things happen—just one of those things. Just a game...." I changed into my jogging clothes and went for a run. At the top of the hill on Sun Bowl Drive, I stopped to stare at the Juárez Mountains. I felt the sweat run down my face. I kept running until I could no longer hear *Are you sure you were born in Las Cruces?* ringing in my ears.

$\int$CHOOL LET OUT in early May. I spent the last two weeks of that month relaxing and working on some paintings. In June I got back to working on my stories. I had a working title which I hated, but I hated it less that the actual stories I was writing. It would come to nothing; I knew it would come to nothing.

From my window I could see the freeway. It was then I realized not a day went by that I didn't see someone running across the freeway or walking down the street looking out for someone. They were people who looked not so different from me—except they lived their lives looking over their shoulders.

One Thursday, I saw the border patrol throw some men into their van—throw them—throw them as if they were born to be thrown like baseballs, like rings in a ringtoss at a carnival—easy inanimate objects, dead bucks after a deer hunt. The illegals didn't even put up a fight. They were aliens, from somewhere else, somewhere foreign, and it did not matter that the "somewhere else" was as close as an eyelash to an eye. What mattered was that someone had once drawn a line, and once drawn that line became indelible and hard and could not be crossed.

The men hung their heads so low that they almost scraped the littered asphalt. Whatever they felt they did not show; whatever burned did not burn for an audience. I sat at my typewriter and tried to pretend I saw nothing. What do you think happens when you peer out windows? Buy curtains.

I didn't write the rest of the day. I kept seeing the border patrol woman against a blue sky turning green. I thought of rearranging my desk so I wouldn't have to be next to the window, but I thought of the mountains. No, I would keep my desk near the window, but I would look only at the mountains.


TWO WEEKS LATER I went for a walk. The stories weren't going well that day; my writing was getting worse instead of better; my characters were getting on my nerves—I didn't like them—no one else would like them either. They did not burn with anything. I hadn't taken a shower, hadn't shaved, hadn't combed my hair. I threw some water on my face and walked out the door. It was summer; it was hot; it was afternoon, the time of day when everything felt as if it were on fire. The worst time of the day to take a walk. I wiped the sweat from my eyelids, and instantly it reappeared. I wiped it off again, but the sweat came pouring out—a leak in the dam. Let it leak. I laughed. A hundred degrees in the middle of a desert afternoon. Laughter poured out of me as fast as my sweat. I turned the corner and headed back home. I saw the green van. It was parked right ahead of me.

A man about my height got out of the van and approached me. Another man, taller, followed him. "¿Tienes tus papeles?" he asked. His gringo accent was as thick as the sweat on my skin.

"I can speak English," I said. I started to add: I can *probably speak it better than you,* but I stopped myself. No need to be aggressive, no need to get any hotter.

"Do you live in this neighborhood?"

"Yes."

"Where?"

"Down the street."

"Where down the street?"

"Are you planning on making a social visit?"

He gave me a hard look—cold and blue—then looked at his partner. He didn't like me. I didn't care. I liked that he hated me. It made it easier.

I watched them drive away and felt as hot as the air, felt as hot as the heat that was burning away the blue in the sky.

There were other times when I felt watched. Sometimes, when I jogged, the green vans would slow down—eye me—I felt like prey, like a rabbit who smelled the hunter. I pretended not to notice them. I stopped pretending. I started noting their presence in our neighborhood more and more. I started growing suspicious of my own observations. Of course, they weren't everywhere. But they were everywhere. I had just been oblivious to their presence, had been oblivious because they had nothing to do with me; their presence had something to do with someone else. I was not a part of this. I wanted no part of it. The green cars and the green vans clashed with the purples of the Juárez Mountains. Nothing looked the same. I never talked about their presence to other people. Sometimes, the topic of the la migra would come up in conversations; I felt the burning; I felt the anger, would control it. I casually referred to them as the Gestapo, the traces of rage carefully hidden from the expression on my face—and everyone would laugh. I hated them.

When school started in the fall, I was stopped again. Again I had been walking home from the University. I heard the familiar question: "Where are you from?"

"Leave me alone." I stared.

"Are you a citizen of the United States?"

"Yes."

"Can you prove it?"

"No. No, I can't."

He looked at my clothes: jeans, tennis shoes, and a casual California shirt. He noticed my backpack full of books.

"You a student?"

I nodded and stared at him.

"There isn't any need to be unfriendly—"

"I'd like you to leave me alone."

"Just trying to do my job," he laughed. I didn't smile back. Terrorists. Nazis did their jobs. Death squads in El Salvador and Guatemala did their jobs, too. An unfair analogy. An unfair analogy? Yes, unfair. I thought it; I felt it; it was no longer my job to excuse—someone else would have to do that—someone else. The Juárez Mountains did not seem purple that fall. They no longer burned with that color.

In early January I went with Michael to Juárez. Michael was from New York and had come to work in a home for the homeless in South El Paso. We weren't in Juárez for very long—just looking around and getting gas. Gas was cheap in Juárez. On the way back, the customs officer asked us to declare our citizenship. "U.S. citizen," I said. "U.S. citizen," Michael followed. The customs officer lowered his head and poked it in the car. "What are you bringing over?"

"Nothing."

He looked at me. "Where in the United States were you born?"
"In Las Cruces, New Mexico."
He looked at me a while longer. "Go ahead," he signaled.

I noticed he didn't ask Michael where he was from. But Michael had blue eyes; Michael had white skin; Michael didn't have to tell the man in the uniform where he was from.

THAT WINTER, Sunset Heights seemed deserted to me. The streets were empty like the river. One morning, I was driving down Upson Street toward the University, the wind shaking the limbs of the bare trees. Nothing to shield them—unprotected by green leaves. The sun burned a dull yellow. In front of me I noticed two border patrol officers were chasing someone, though that someone was not visible. One of them put his hand out, signaling me to slow down as they ran across the street in front of my car. They were running with their billy clubs in hand. The wind blew at their backs as if to urge them on, as if to carry them.

In late January Michael and I went to Juárez again. A friend of his was in town, and he wanted to see Juárez. We walked across the bridge, across the river, across the line into another country. It was easy. No one was there to stop us. We walked through the streets of Juárez, streets that had seen better years, that were tired now from the tired feet that walked them. Michael's friend wanted to know how it was that there were so many beggars. "Were there always so many? Has it always been this way?" I didn't know how it had always been. We sat in the Cathedral and the old chapel next to it, and watched people rubbing the feet of statues. When I touched the feet of one of them, it was warmer than my own hand. We walked to the marketplace, and inhaled the smells. Grocery stores in the country we knew did not have such smells. On the way back we stopped in a small bar and had a beer. The beer was cold and cheap.

Walking back over the bridge, we stopped at the top and looked out at the city of El Paso. "It actually looks pretty from here, doesn't it?" I said. Michael nodded. It did look pretty. We looked off to the side—down the river—and watched the wetbacks trying to get across for a long time. Michael's friend said it was like watching the *CBS Evening News*.

As we reached the customs building, we noticed that a border patrol van pulled up behind the building where the other green cars were parked. The officers jumped out of the van and threw a handcuffed man against one of the parked cars. It looked like they were going to beat him. Two more border patrol officers pulled up in a car and jumped out to join them. One of the officers noticed we were watching. They straightened him out, and walked him inside—like gentlemen. They would have beat him. They would have beat him. But we were watching.

My fingers wanted to reach through the wire fence, not to touch it, not to feel it, but to break it down, to melt it down with what I did not understand. The burning was not there to be understood. Something was burning, the side of me that knew I was treated different, would always be treated different because I was born on a particular side of a fence, a fence that separated me from others, that separated me from a past, that separated me from a country of my genesis and glued me to a country I did not love because it demanded something of me I could not give. Something was burning now, and if I could have grasped the source of that rage and held it in my fist, I would have melted that fence. Someone built that fence; someone could tear it down. Maybe I could tear it down; maybe I was the one; maybe then I would no longer be separated.

THE FIRST DAY in February I was walking to a downtown Chevron station to pick up my car. On the corner of Prospect and Upson a green car was parked—just sitting there. A part of my landscape. I was walking on the opposite side of the street. For some reason I knew they were going to stop me. My heart clenched like a fist; the muscles in my back tied themselves into knots. *Maybe they'll leave me alone. I should have taken a shower this morning. I should have worn a nicer sweater. I should have put on a pair of socks, worn a nicer pair of shoes. I should have cut my hair; I should have shaved....*

The driver of the car rolled down his window. I saw him from the corner of my eye. He called me over to him— *whistled me over*—much like he'd call a dog. I kept walking. He whistled me over again. *Here, boy.* I stopped for a second. Only a second. I kept walking. The border patrol officer and a policeman rushed out of the car and ran toward me. I was sure they were going to tackle me, drag me to the ground, handcuff me— they stopped in front of me.

"Could I see your driver's license?" the policeman asked.

"Since when do you need a driver's license to walk down the street?" Our eyes met. "Did I do something that was against the law?"

The policeman was annoyed. He wanted me to be passive, to say: "Yes, sir,"—to approve of his job.

"Don't you know what we do?"

"Yes. I know what you do."

"Don't give me a hard time. I don't want trouble; I just want to see some identification."

I looked at him, looked, and saw what would not go away: neither him nor his car nor his job nor what I knew nor what I felt. He stared back. He hated me as much as I hated him. He saw the bulge of my cigarettes under my sweater and crumpled them.

I backed up a step. "I smoke. It's not good for me, but it's not against the law. Not yet, anyway—and don't touch me. I don't like that. Read me my rights, throw me in the can, or leave me alone." I smiled.

"No one's charging you with anything."

My eyes followed them as they walked back to their car.
Now it was war and *I had won this battle.* Had I won this battle?
Had I won?

THIS SPRING MORNING, I wake. I sit at my desk, wait for
the coffee to brew, and look out my window. This day, like
everyday, I look out my window. Across the street a border patrol van stops and an officer gets out. So close I could touch him.
On the freeway—this side of the river—a man is running. I put
on my glasses. I am afraid he will be run over by the cars. I
cheer for him. *Don't get run over. Be careful.* So close to the other
side he can touch it. The border patrol officer gets out his walkie-
talkie and runs toward the man who has disappeared from my
view. I go and get my cup of coffee. I take a drink—slowly it
mixes with yesterday's tastes in my mouth. The officer in the
green uniform comes back into view. He has the man with him.
He puts him in the van. I can't see the color in their eyes. I see
only the green. They drive away. There is no trace that says
they've been there. The mountains watch the scene and say nothing. The mountains, ablaze in the spring light, have been watching—and guarding—and keeping silent longer than I have been
alive. They will continue their vigil long after I am dead.

The green vans. They are taking someone away. They are taking. Green vans. This is my home, I tell myself. But I am not
sure if I want this to be my home anymore. The thought crosses
my mind to walk out of my apartment without my wallet. The
thought crosses my mind that maybe la migra will stop me again.
I will let them arrest me. I will let them warehouse me.
I will let them push me in front of a judge who will look at me
like he has looked at the millions before me. I will be sent back
to Mexico. I will let them treat me like I am illegal. But the
thoughts pass. I am not brave enough to let them do that to
me—and never will be.

Today, the spring winds blow outside my window. The reflections I see on the pane have words written on them— graffiti burning questions into the glass: *Sure you were born...Identification...Do you live?...* The winds will unsettle the desert—cover Sunset Heights with green dust. The vans will stay in my mind forever. I cannot banish them. I cannot banish their question: *Where are you from?*

# Richard Rodriguez

# Pocho Pioneer

*EDITOR'S NOTE: Richard Rodriguez delivered this speech in November 1994 at a White House Conference, "A New Moment in the Americas." Pocho is a slang term referring to a Mexican who has been Americanized.*

IT IS APPROPRIATE that I come to this distinguished encuentro as something of a naysayer. It is appropriate, though ironic, that I sound a sour note in the midst of all your talk about "a new moment in the Americas." As a child I grew up in blond California where everyone was optimistic about losing weight and changing the color of her hair and becoming someone new. Only my Mexican father was dour and sour in California—always reminding me how tragic life was, how nothing changes, reminding me that everything would come to nothing under a cloudless sky.

Mexicans speak of "el fatalismo del Indio"—the sadness at the heart of Latin America. As a child, when I looked South, I shuddered at the Latin sensibility. I turned away from it, spent my childhood running toward Doris Day and Walt Disney.

You cannot imagine the irony with which I regard this meeting. My Latin American colleagues have travelled several thousand miles north to speak about the new democratic spirit in their countries, the new spirit of individualism. We of the north, by contrast, have become a dark people. We do not vote. We have lost our optimism. We are besotted with individualism and we have grown lonely. We, in California, now sound very much like my Mexican father.

I end up a "pocho" in the United States, reflecting on the tragic nature of life.

Clearly, I am a freak of history. I carry this Indian face; I have a Spanish surname; my first name is Richard (*Ree-cherd*, Mexico calls me). The great Octavio Paz, in *The Labyrinth of Solitude*, has a chapter concerned with the "pachuco"—the teenaged gangster in Los Angeles. For Paz the gang kids of California represent the confusion within the Mexican-American— caught between two cultures. The child does not know where he belongs. The child has lost his address. The child no longer belongs to Mexico, neither does he fit into the United States. The Mexican-American is a tragic figure, a pathetic one. Señor Paz is right about Mexican-Americans, but he is also arrogant and wrong about us.

Consider these the reflections of a pocho....

You know, we sit here in this elegant room, talking about the new moment in the Americas as though the moment has just happened, today—November 12, 1994. We act as though we are the witnesses of its happening. In fact, the so-called moment, the discovery of the Americas by Americans, has been going on for nearly a century. But the discovery has been mainly by peasants. They were the first Americans who trespassed American borders.

I speak of the hundreds of thousands of migrant workers who have been coming to the United States since the turn of the century. The two largest groups: Puerto Ricans and Mexicans. Back and forth they went, across borders, time zones, languages, faiths. Between Puerto Rico and New York, between Los Angeles and Mexico.

The Puerto Ricans found themselves, at the end of the nineteenth century, suddenly part of the United States. The Mexicans found themselves in places like Arizona and California, which used to be part of Mexico. The Mexicans and Puerto Ricans were like no other immigrant group the United States had ever seen. There was something wrong with us.

And yet I would like to argue that we were the first Americans—Americans, that is, in the sense we are talking today. The peasants of Puerto Rico and Mexico were the first people who saw the hemisphere whole.

Oh, there is President Salinas de Gortari today with his Harvard degrees, as there are the new "technocrats" of Latin America with their Ivy League degrees. Business executives and government officials in the United States sigh with relief at meeting this new class of Latin Americans.

"At last, Señor Salinas, we understand you. You speak our language. You are our kind of Mexican. Let's talk business."

Do not listen to the flattery of the United States, Señor Salinas. I am sorry to have to tell you that you have been preceded North to the United States by several decades, by millions of peasants.

Mexican-Americans, Puerto Ricans—we were a puzzle to the United States. We were people from the South in an east-west country. (The United States has written its history across the page, east to west. The United States saw its manifest destiny unfolding in the western migration.) Land was the crucial metaphor for possibility in the United States' scheme of things. As long as there was land, there was possibility. As long as you could move West, you had a future. As long as you could leave Maryland for Nebraska, then you could change the color of your hair, change your religion. As long as you could leave Kansas for Nevada, you could drop your father's name or shorten it. You could drop the embarrassing "ini" or "izzi" or "stein." You could become someone other than your father.

I am going to California to become Tab Hunter. Yes, I like that name. Me llamo Tab Hunter.

The crisis in California today is due to the fact that the United States has run out of land. The metaphor of the west has been exhausted. The end had been decades in coming. As early as the 1860s, there were premonitions of finitude in California. In the 1860s, when California was newly U.S. territory, environmentalists reached the coast with a sense of dread. John Muir stood at the beach in the 1860s and announced to the United States that he had come to the edge of possibility: America is a finite idea. We have to start saving America. We have to start saving the land. Conserving America. The message went back—west to east—back to the crowded brick cities of the East Coast.

I grew up in the 1950s when California was filling with people from Nebraska and Minnesota. People arrived from Brooklyn, or they came from Chicago. They came for a softer winter. They came to recreate themselves.

But shortly we ran out of land. Los Angeles got too crowded and needed to reinvent itself as Orange County. Then Orange County got too crowded and had to reinvent itself as north county San Diego. Then north county San Diego got too crowded. Now Californians are moving into the desert. We don't have enough room any more, we say.

Suddenly foreigns immigrants are coming. They are pouring into California from the South. ("We are sorry to intrude, señor, we are looking for work.") They come from Latin America, talking of California as "el Norte," not the West Coast. El Norte is wide open. The West Coast is a finite idea. *Whose map is correct?*

There are planes landing in Los Angeles today, planes from Thailand, from Hong Kong, planes from Seoul and from Taiwan. People getting off the planes say about California, "This is where the United States begins." Those of us in the United States who believe in the western route to California say, "No, no. California is where the United States comes to an end." *Whose myth is true?*

People in the United States used to say, "Go West, young man." We meant, go West toward possibility. Now that we have hit against the wall of the coastline, we start talking about going East. "Go East, young man!"

"I'm leaving California; I'm going to Nebraska."

"I'm leaving California; I'm going to Colorado."

And, for the first time, today Californians speak of the North and the South. Not because we want to. Not because we are accustomed to looking North and South. It's only because the West is a finite idea.

"I'm going to get a condominium in Baja California. You know, there are condos throughout Baja where everyone speaks English. We're going to make Baja our national park."

Or, "I'm leaving California for Canada. I'm going to Vancouver. There are too many ethnics in California. I'm going to Canada where the air is cleaner."

Go North, young man.

Puerto Ricans, Mexicans—early in this century we were a people from the South in an east-west country. We were people of mixed blood in a black and white country. America's great scar, its deep tear, has always been the black and white division. Puerto Ricans and Mexicans tended to be of mixed race. Hard, therefore, for the United States to classify or even see.

For the last thirty years in the United States, Hispanics have impersonated a race. We have convinced bureaucrats in Washington—bureaucrats who knew nothing about us and cared less—that we constituted a racial group. It was essential, if the United States were ever to recognize us, that we be a racial group, people subject to "racial discrimination."

The only trouble is, Hispanics do not constitute a racial group. But what does the United States care? There we are in the ponderous morning pages of *The New York Times,* listed on a survey alongside black, white, Asian.

Puerto Ricans, Mexicans—we were Catholics in a Protestant

country. And millions of us were Indians in a country that imagined the Indian to be dead. Today, Los Angeles is the largest Indian city in the United States. All around the city, you can see Toltecs and Aztecs and Mayans. But the filmmakers of Hollywood persist in making movies about the dead Indian. For seven dollars, you can see cowboys kill the Indians. We are sorry about it. We feel the luxury of regret from our swivel seats.

On the other hand, I remember a chic dinner party in Mexico City. (You know, rich Mexicans can be very polite when they say cruel things. It is their charm.) One Mexican, a drink in his hand, said to me, "You are a writer? Very interesting. Your work has been translated in Mexico?"

I replied, "Well, not much."

He said, "Well, we Mexicans are not going to know what to make of you as a writer." He said, "We're not accustomed to writers who look like you."

Seriously, let me apologize. I must *apologize* for not being able to speak to many of you in your own language. I suffer from this strange disability. I can understand spoken Spanish, can read it. But I can't speak Spanish with ease. I walk through Latin American cities like a sleepwalker, comprehending everything but unable to join the conversation.

How shall I explain my disability? Elena Castedo, in her wonderful essay on the United States, suggested that we in the United States are afraid of foreign languages. That is true, but not quite right. Better to say that we are obsessed with foreign languages. Most of us in this country are one or two generations from a grandparent who scolded us for losing her language. There is an enormous guilt in the American soul.

I want you to know that I have been haunted by Spanish for most of my life. I understand your jokes and your asides. I hear your whisperings. I smile feebly in response. I feel so guilty about not being able to join you. It is because I have taken this new lover, American English, this blond lover of mine has taken my breath away.

Hispanics in the United States turn into fools. We argue among ourselves, criticize one another, mock one another for becoming too much the gringo. We criticize each other for speaking too much Spanish or not enough Spanish. We demand that our politicians provide us with bilingual voting ballots, but we do not bother to vote. We are, as Señor Paz observed decades ago, freaks of history.

I have heard Mexicans of the middle class say to their children when their children head for the United States to go to college, "Stay away from those Chicanos, whatever you do. Stay away from them because they're crazy. They think of themselves as 'minorities.'"

We are Mexico's Mexicans. Everything Mexico loathes about herself, she hates in us. We lost our culture to a larger power. Mexico lost her tongue to Cortés. For us Cortés is Uncle Sam. If I go back to Mexico, Mexico comes closer to me, breathes in my ear. "Hijito, háblame en español," Mexico says.

I say, "Ay, Madre, no puedo. No más un poquito."

"Un poquito. Un poquito. ¡Tu propio idioma...!"

Then, POCHO.

Michael Novak was speaking last night about what unites the hemisphere. What unites us as Americans, he said, is our willingness to say goodbye to the motherland. We say to Europe, farewell. And there is bravery in that cry of goodbye.

The only trouble is that adiós was never part of the Mexican-American or the Puerto Rican vocabulary. We didn't turn our backs on the past. We kept going back and forth, between past and future. After a few months of work in New York or Los Angeles, we would cross the border. We were commuters between centuries, between rivals. And neither country understood us.

Abuelita didn't understand us because our Spanish was so bad. On the other hand, people in the United States would wonder what was wrong with us. Why do you people need to keep going back home? (In a country that believes so much in the future our journey home was almost a subversion.) The United States said to us, "When my parents left Sweden, they didn't keep going back to Sweden. But you—you keep turning back. What's the matter with you? Are you a mama's boy?"

Pocho.

Someone said last night that the gringo had hijacked the word "American" and given it to himself with typical arrogance. I remember my aunt in Mexico City scolding me when I told her I was from America. Didn't I realize the entire hemisphere is America? Listen, my Mexican aunt told me, "People who live in the United States are norteamericanos."

Well, I think to myself—my aunt is now dead. God rest her soul—but I think to myself, I wonder what she would have thought when the great leaders—the president of Mexico, the president of the United States, the Canadian prime minister— signed the North American Free Trade Agreement. Mexico woke up one morning to realize that she's a norteamericana.

I predict that Mexico will have a nervous breakdown in ten years. She will have to check into a clinic for a long rest. She will need to determine just what exactly it means that she is, with the dread gringo, a North American.

Meanwhile, peasants keep crossing the border. The diplomats keep signing the documents. But has anyone ever met a North American? Oh, I know. You know Mexicans. And you know Canadians. But has anyone met a North American?

I have.

Let me tell you about him, this North American. He's a Mixteco Indian who lives in the Mexican state of Oaxaca. He is trilingual. His primary language is the language of the tribe. He speaks Spanish, the language of Cortés, as a second language. Also, he has a working knowledge of U.S. English.

He knows thousands of miles of dirt roads and freeways. He commutes between two civilizations. He is preyed upon by corrupt Mexican police who want to "shake him down" because he has hidden U.S. dollars in his shoes. He is pursued as "illegal" by the U.S. border patrol. He lives in a sixteenth century village where his wife watches blond Venezuelan soap operas. There is a picture of La Virgen de Guadalupe over his bed. He works near Stockton, California, where there is no Virgin Mary but the other Madonna—the rock star.

This Mexican peasant knows two currencies. But he is as illegal on one side of the border as he is an embarrassment to his government on the other side of the line. *He* is the first North American.

People in the United States have always been wary of Mexican water. We love your beaches and your pre-Columbian ruins. But we are afraid to sing in the shower at the hotel. On the other hand, we have always trusted Canadian water. We drink gallons of it. We also assumed that Canadian water was clean.

But there is a virus in Canadian water called "multiculturalism" which is making its way into the United States' blood stream. The most interesting thing we think to say about one another now in the United States is that we are multicultural. But, of course, when people in the United States talk about multiculturalism, they mean, like the Canadians, culture to signify only race or ethnicity. In fact, culture means many other things, too.

Culture means region. What part of the world, what sky governs your life? I come from California.

Culture means age. The old man looks at the young boy with incomprehension.

Sex is culture—that great divide between the male and female, their delight and their frustration.

Religion. The United States is a Protestant country though we do not like to describe ourselves in that way.

We are a Puritan country.

A friend of mine, Pico Iyer, who writes of the confusion of cultures in the U.S. metropolis, speculates about the inevitable confusion that results when so many races, so many languages, altars, meet in modern Los Angeles. I think the more interesting dilemma for the post-modern citizen of the city is that she feels herself multicultural within herself: *How shall I reconcile the world within my own soul?*

My father remembers a Mexico that no longer exists. My father remembers a village. "Where is it, Papa? Show me where, in the state of Colima, you were a boy. Where?"

He explores the map with his finger. The city of Colima has swallowed up the village. The city has grown bloated, has larded itself over the countryside, obliterating the village.

"It is not there," he says.

We Mexican-Americans end up like the British Columbians. If you go to British Columbia, you can visit houses and see the Queen of England on the wall. People use tea cozies in British Columbia. They remember an England that is nothing like the Britain of blue-haired soccer punks who beat up Pakistanis on Saturday nights. The British Columbians remember an England that exists nowhere on earth but on a faded post card.

My father remembers a Mexico that used to be a village.

A friend of mine, a European, was a hippie in northern Mexico during the 1960s. Recently my friend took his son back to Mexico to look for the villages where he was a bohemian.

My friend phoned me the other night with chagrin. He said, "Everything has changed. The little towns—no one hangs out anymore. All the Mexicans are working at the local maquiladora." And he says, "Thirty years ago, Mexicans used to walk around these small towns wearing guns. Now nobody wears guns."

I say to my friend, "If you want to see Mexicans wearing guns, go to East Lost Angeles." My relatives in Mexico City, they watch ESPN. My niece in Mexico City is inordinately proud of her tee-shirt which proclaims HARD ROCK CAFE. My relatives in Mexico City have wandered away from Roman Catholicism in favor of Buddhism. My relatives in Mexico City are divorced.

At this moment, about this time in the afternoon, there are minibuses going South—Jehovah's Witnesses, Mormons. This is the great moment of conversion in the Mormon world. By the end of the century, half of the world's Mormon population will be Spanish-speaking, at which time what will we think of Salt Lake City? And of course, here come the evangelical Christians. They are converting Latin America. The great soul of Latin America is turning toward the Easter promise of Protestantism. "You are redeemed! You can change! You can become a new man! You can put away the old ways, become something new, praise the Lord! Hallelujah!"

A Lutheran pastor I know in San Francisco works with immigrants from Central America. He often notices that, without even asking, without even thinking too much about it, the immigrants convert to Protestantism as they settle in the United States. The conversion becomes part of their Americanization. They seem to sense that in becoming Americans, they should also become Protestant.

On the other hand, the other day in Tijuana, Mexico, I met three boys from an evangelical church called Victory Outreach. (Victory Outreach works with kids who suffer from serious drug problems.) The kids said they are coming to the United States this year—502 years after Columbus—to convert us back to our Protestant roots. The youngest one said, "Those Americans are so sad."

Someone once asked Chou En-lai, the Chinese prime minister, what he thought of the French Revolution. Chou En-lai gave a wonderful Chinese response. He said, "It's too early to tell."

I think it may be too early to tell what the story of Columbus means. The latest chapter of the Columbus story might be taking place right now, as the Hispanic evangelicals head north.

The kids on the line tonight in Tijuana, if you ask them why they are coming to the United States of America, will not say anything about Thomas Jefferson or notions of democracy. They have not heard about Thomas Paine or the *Federalist Papers*. They have only heard that there is a job in Glendale, California, at a dry cleaners.

222 ■ THE LATE GREAT MEXICAN BORDER

They are going back to Mexico in a few months, they insist. They are only going to the United States for the dollars. They don't want to be gringos. They don't want anything to do with the United States, except the dollars.

But then a few months will pass, and they will not go back to Latin America. What will happen, of course, to their surprise, is that the job in Glendale will make them part of the United States. (Work in the United States is our primary source of identity.)

People in this country, when they meet one another, do not ask about family or where the other comes from. The first thing people in the U.S. ask each other at cocktail parties is what the other does for a living.

The hemisphere, the story of the hemisphere, began with a little joke about maps and the fact that Columbus, our papasito, our father, got it all wrong. He imagined he was in some part of the world where there were Indians. He thought he had come to India.

We laugh today because papi didn't know where he was. But I'm not sure we know where we are, either. We are only beginning to look at the map. We are only beginning to wonder what the map of the hemisphere means.

The story of the Americas began with a cartographer's whimsy in the Renaissance: *Is the world flat?* And to the delight of the mapmaker, the explorer set out on the sea to discover the great human possibility of roundness.

Mexican-Americans, Puerto Ricans—we ended up in the United States city. We are people from the village. We ended up in the city. We ended up with a bad knowledge of English, a failing knowledge of Spanish. Yet we were remarkable people. We travelled many thousands of miles, some of us on foot. We ended up cooking for the United States or making beds or gardening. We have become the nannies of North America. We take care of the blond children of Beverly Hills and Park Avenue —these children will become the next generation of Hispanics. We have subverted, invaded, the wealthiest homes in America.

The kids in East LA, the kids that Octavio Paz was talking about forty years ago, the pachucos have turned murderous against one another. Several months ago I was talking to some gang kids in Los Angeles about New York. The photographer working with me was from New York. I asked one of the gang kids, "Would you like to see New York some day?"

The littlest one piped in response, "Not me, man."

I said, "Why not? Don't you want to see where Joe, the photographer, comes from?"

"Not me, man! I'm Mexican. I belong here."

Here? This boy lives within four blocks. If he goes a fifth block he's going to get his head blown off because he doesn't use the right sign language or he is wearing the wrong color today. This Mexican kid couldn't even find his way to the beaches of Los Angeles.

The odd thing, the tragic irony, is that many times our fathers and grandfathers who were so brave, who travelled so many thousands of miles, trespassed borders, end up with grandchildren who become Chicanos, timid children who believe that culture is some little thing put in a box, held within four blocks.

One of the things that Mexico has never acknowledged about my father, I insist that you today at least entertain—the possibility that my father and others like him were the great revolutionaries of Mexico. They, not Pancho Villa, not Zapata, were heralds of the modern age. They went back to Mexico and changed Mexico forever. The man who worked in Chicago in the 1920s returned one night to his village in Michoacán. The village gathered around him—this is a true story—and the village asked, "What is it like up there in Chicago?"

The man said, "It's okay."

That rumor of "okay" spread across Michoacán, down to Jalisco, across Jalisco into Oaxaca, from village to village to village.

There are now remote villages in Latin America that have become the most international places in the world. Tiny Peruvian villages know when farmers are picking pears in the

Yakima Valley in the state of Washington.

We talk about the new moment in the Americas. The moment has been going on for decades. People have been travelling back and forth.

I am the son of a prophet. I am a fool. I am a victim of history. I am confused. I do not know whether I am coming or going. I speak bad Spanish. And yet, I will tell you this: to grow up Hispanic in the United States is to know more Guatemalans than if I grew up in Mexico. Because I live in California, I know more Brazilians than I would know if I lived in Peru. Because I live in California, it is routine for me to know Nicaraguans and Salvadorans and Cubans—as routine as meeting Chinese or Greeks.

People in California talk about the "illegals." But there was always an illegality to immigration. It was a rude act, the leaving of home. It was a violation of custom, an insult to the village. A youthful act of defiance. I know a man from El Salvador who has not talked to his father since the day he left his father's village. (It is a sin against family to leave home.) Immigrants must always be illegal. Immigrants are always criminals. They trespass borders and horrify their grandmothers.

But they are also our civilization's prophets. They, long before the rest of us, long before this room, long before this conference was ever imagined, they saw the hemisphere whole.

# Notes on Contributors

MAX AGUILERA-HELLWEG is a photojournalist who has experienced the world as few are able; crawling through tunnels with "illegal aliens," driving cattle in Wyoming, playing war at Camp Pendleton, photographing the TB ward at Bellevue, girl gangs in East LA, and brothels in Bangkok where twelve year old girls had been sold off by their parents. Some of his clients are *Esquire, Life, The New York Times* and *GQ*. He is now studying at Columbia University to become a doctor.

CHARLES BOWDEN gets his mail in Tucson, Arizona, and lives wherever he can. *Blood Orchid* (Random House) is his eleventh book.

BARBARA FERRY is a freelance journalist with an on-again, off-again relationship with the Border, having lived at various times in Harlingen and El Paso, Texas, and Bisbee, Arizona. She has produced programming for National Public Radio in Spanish and English. An activist for the rights of refugees, she has served for organizations in Harlingen and in El Salvador during that country's civil war. She now works in Washington, DC.

GUILLERMO GÓMEZ-PEÑA was born and raised in Mexico City. He is an interdisciplinary artist/writer who came to the United States in 1978. Since then he has been exploring cross-cultural issues and North-South relations through performance, bilingual poetry, journalism, video, radio and installation art. He has contributed to the national radio magazines *Crossroads* and *Latino USA*, and is a contributing editor to *High Performance* magazine and *The Drama Review*. He is a 1991 recipient of the MacArthur Fellowship. *Warrior for Gringostroika* was recently published by Graywolf Press and his second book, *The New World Border*, is coming out from City Lights.

TERESA LEAL lives and works on both sides of the U.S./Mexico Border in Nogales, Arizona, and Nogales, Sonora. Always an activist, she is currently organizing for Comadres which works to enable and empower women living in squatter communities in Mexico. When the piece in the anthology—"Recipe for a Radical"—was written, she was running for mayor of Nogales, Sonora, in an effort to bring attention to the poor in the city.

LINDA LYNCH is a painter who has spent the last 13 years fighting radioactive dumping in her community of Hudsbeth County. She now lives in Chicago where she is trying once again to work full-time as an artist.

RUBÉN MARTÍNEZ is a poet, performer and Emmy-Award winning journalist. He is the Los Angeles Bureau Chief for Pacific News Service and is a co-host of PBS-affiliate KCET-TV's public affairs program, "Life and Times." Martínez's *The Other Side: Notes from the New L.A., Mexico City and Beyond* (Vintage), a collection of essays and poetry, has won widespread critical acclaim. He is also a contributor to National Public Radio's "All Things Considered."

TOM MILLER has written about the American Southwest and Latin America for more than twenty-five years. His six books include *The Panama Hat Trail* (Morrow; Vintage), *Trading with the Enemy: A Yankee Travels through Castro's Cuba* (Atheneum; Basic Books), and *On the Border* (Harper & Row, University of Arizona Press), which has been translated into Spanish, French and Japanese. Miller, a veteran of the underground press of the 1960s, has appeared in *The New York Times, Esquire, LIFE,* and *Rolling Stone,* among other publications, and has worked as a consultant for public radio and network television.

GARY PAUL NABHAN, Ph.D., is an ethnobotanist who serves as Director of the Sonora Desert Museum. A MacArthur Fellow, Nabhan's work conserves and celebrates the vital links among indigenous cultures, plants and animals. Among his seven books is *Gathering the Desert,* winner of a John Burroughs Medal for Nature Writing.

DEBBIE NATHAN lives in El Paso and has been doing journalism, essays and short fiction about the border since the late 1970s. Her work has appeared in such publications as *The Texas Observer, The Village Voice, The Nation, MS. Magazine* and Pacific News Service. She is the author of *Women and Other Aliens: Essays from the U.S./Mexico Border* (Cinco Puntos Press) and *Satan's Silence: Ritual Abuse and the Making of a Modern American Witch Hunt* (Basic).

DICK J. REAVIS is a dedicated journalist who has served as a staff writer for *The Dallas Observer* and a Senior Editor for *Texas Monthly.* Articles of his have been included in such publications as *Mother Jones, The New York Times, The Wall Street Journal* and *Soldier of Fortune.* His books include *The Ashes of Waco* (Simon & Schuster), *Texas* (Fodors/Random House/Compass), *Conversations with Moctezuma* (William Morrow & Co) and *Without Documents* (Condor Publishers). He also translated and edited *Diary of an Undocumented Immigrant* (Arte Público Press).

LUIS J. RODRÍGUEZ is an award winning poet, journalist and critic whose works have appeared in *The Los Angeles Times, The Nation, U.S. News & World Report, Utne Reader* and others. His piece in this anthology is excerpted from his book about growing up in Watts and the East Los Angeles area,

*Always Running: La Vida Loca, Gang Days in L.A.* (Curbstone Press). His book of poems, *Poems Across the Pavement,* is from Tia Chucha Press.

RICHARD RODRIGUEZ is the son of Mexican immigrant parents. He is the author of *Days of Obligation* (Penguin), a book about Mexico and the United States. The piece that he contributed, "Pocho Pioneer" was originally a speech which he delivered in November 1994 at a White House conference, "A New Moment in the Americas." He is an associate editor of Pacific News Service.

BENJAMIN ALIRE SÁENZ is a poet, essayist and novelist who was born in Old Picacho, a small farming village outside of Las Cruces, NM, forty-two miles north of the U.S./Mexico Border. His novel *Carry Me Like Water* was published by Hyperion, and his second novel *An Old God Never Dies* will be published by Harper-Collins. His books of poems are *Dark and Perfect Angels* (Cinco Puntos Press), which won the Southwest Book Award, and *Calendar of Dust* (Broken Moon), winner of the American Book Award.

LUIS ALBERTO URREA was born in Tijuana. He worked there among the garbage pickers, missionaries, whores and orphans through the 1980s. His first book, *Across the Wire,* won the Christopher Award. He wrote the novel *In Search of Snow* and a book of poems *The Fever of Being,* which won the Western States Book Award and the Colorado Book Award. His newest book, in which the anthologized piece appears, is *By the Lake of Sleeping Children: The Secret Life of the Mexican Border.* It will be published this year by Anchor Press.

ALAN WEISMAN is the author of *La Frontera: The United States Border With Mexico* (Harcourt Brace Jovanovich) and *We, Immortals* (Pocket Books). His reports from all over the world have appeared in *The Atlantic, Harper's, The New York Times Magazine, The Los Angeles Times Magazine, Audubon* and others. He is a frequent contributor to National Public Radio, American Public Radio and Public Radio International. Weisman is currently a contributing editor of *The Los Angeles Times Magazine* and an associate producer for Homelands Productions. He lives in Sonoita, Arizona.

*About the editors:*
BOBBY BYRD and SUSANNAH MISSISSIPPI BYRD (father and daughter) have lived in El Paso on the U.S./Mexico Border for the last 19 years. Bobby Byrd is a poet, novelist, essayist and co-publisher of Cinco Puntos Press. His most recent book of poems is *On the Transmigration of Souls in El Paso.* Susannah Mississippi Byrd has returned home after graduating from Emory University and hiking the Appalachian Trail. She has joined Cinco Puntos Press as the Marketing Director. This is her first book.